HERE IS WHAT PEOPLE ARE SAYING ABOUT OUR CULINARY SPANISH CHATBOOK:

"Culinary Spanish Chatbook is an Exciting New Book! It is a sortie into the contextualized-curriculum environment that will deeply strengthen the power of our Culinary and Hospitality Management Degrees. Maestra Julia is an engaged and dynamic instructor in the classroom whose passion para el Español y la cocina has also permeated this project."

—Chef Brian O'Malley Academic Director
Institute for the Culinary Arts
Metropolitan Community College

"Culinary Spanish Chatbook is a 'must have' for everyone working in the food industry. There is nothing more frustrating than not being able to communicate with a co-worker. This book is a great tool to help break down those barriers, and it's realistic, upbeat approach makes learning Spanish fun."

—Karen Popp, Operations Manager
WheatFields Eatery and Bakery

"Julie has taught Spanish for the Institute for the Culinary Arts for many years, and always to rave reviews from her students."

—James E. (Jim) Trebbien, Executive Director / Dean
Institute for the Culinary Arts

"Welcome to the way you will learn Spanish. This is the perspective that should be taken with all languages. Gracias Maestra!"

—Phil Nicols, Culinary student

"Using this book to learn Spanish is a great way to show respect to people that you work with."

—Brian Isaacs, Executive Chef

"I would say: Spanish Chat with Julie is an experience of enthusiasm for the topic. She is pragmatic, able to teach at the appropriate level and yet challenging in a polite way."

—Dr. Charles Filipi, Professor of Surgery
Creighton University

PRAISE FOR ANOTHER GREAT BOOK, BUSINESS SPANISH CHATBOOK:

"The practical and enjoyable lessons were designed to teach our employees to communicate with our Spanish-speaking customers. We learned the language, plus important cultural facts about Spanish-speaking countries."

—Pat Tooles, Corporate Performance
Omaha Public Power District

"The lessons are easy to follow and understand, and the phrases we learned were exactly what we needed to better serve our customers. Julie has that rare gift of making learning fun. She brings such exuberance to her classes, the students learn very easily."

—Terry Wingate, Volunteer Coordinator
Omaha Public Library

"I have really enjoyed the Business Spanish Chatbook. The pronunciation guides and phrases are valuable tools that I use often in my day-to-day work."

—Jill Regester, Communications Manager
Woodmen of the World Insurance Agency

HERE IS WHAT PEOPLE ARE SAYING ABOUT OUR SPANISH CHATBOOK:

"As a Training Manager for a regional casino, having our Leaders understand basic conversational Spanish is critical to their success in interacting with their teams. Julie does a phenomenal job making the classes she teaches fun and interactive. I would highly recommend Julie as a competent, passionate, and enthusiastic trainer."

—Jackie Hansen, Casino Training Manager

"As a tenured educator and facilitator I truly appreciated Julie's ability to flexibly adapt to multiple learning styles in her training/classroom. She infuses many aspects into her curriculum, hence maximizing student results. Two years of studying Spanish was nothing compared to what I learned in two weeks time with Julie. Her philosophy works!"

—Spencer K. Terry, Private Consultant

CULINARY SPANISH CHATBOOK

chat•book (*chat-bŭk*) —*noun* **1 :** A conversational workbook with culinary Spanish lessons

BY
JULIE JAHDE POSPISHIL

WITH CONTRIBUTIONS FROM
BRADLEY POSPISHIL

www.SpanishChatCompany.com
Omaha, Nebraska

Copyright @ 2011 by Spanish Chat Company, LLC

All rights reserved. No part of this book may be reproduced or transmitted in any form or by any means, electronic or mechanical, including photocopying, recording, or by any information storage and retrieval system, without permission in writing from the publisher. The author acknowledges that there are many differences in language translation and have attempted to select a form of Spanish that will be understood in the vast majority of Spanish-speaking situations. For more information and to contact the authors: www.SpanishChatCompany.com.

ISBN 13: 978-0-9824625-2-2

ISBN 10: 0-9824625-2-2

LCCN: 2010914913

Library of Congress Cataloging-in Publication Data on file with publisher.

Published by: Spanish Chat Company, LLC
www.SpanishChatCompany.com

Printed in the United States of America
10 9 8 7 6 5 4 3 2 1

Acknowledgments

Culinary Spanish Chatbook is dedicated to the many Hispanic employees that are working very hard to support their families. I hope we build bridges through communication because we have amazing people employed in the front of our restaurants and "behind the scenes" in the back of the house. Now you can speak their language and get to know a new "amigo" or "amiga."

The biggest thank you to my husband, Brad Pospishil, who co-authored our first book, *Business Spanish Chatbook*. The Extra Grammar section and Country Facts are examples of his expertise and historical knowledge. I appreciate all of his love and support on my many projects and our marvelous adventures together. Gracias y saludos to my family and friends, son Jaden, daughter Elena, my students and future travelers everywhere. Thanks to Indira Engel, Jodi Hansen, Andrew Jahde, Gonzalo Baron, editor Dana Campbell, graphic designer Wendy Iske and phone friend Laura Mattuch. I am grateful to Executive Chef Brian Isaacs and his wife Jessica, and restaurant staff, especially Ciro Sanchez and Felix Sangado. A huge thank you to Karen and Andrew Popp and the Wheatfields staff. Special thanks to Metropolitan Community College-Institute for Culinary Arts, Executive Director/Dean Jim Trebbien, Academic Director Chef Brian O'Malley, Chef Vieva McClure, Chef Oystein Solberg, JoEllyn Zuk, and, Chef Brian Young, along with Jamal Malone, Luis Mujica and Jesus Garibay. Also, a general gracias to the many restaurant workers that helped me with useful culinary lingo and book editing. An extra thanks to my parents and grandparents who have been amazing role models for me and have taken care of my children while I worked on the book. Thank you to my friends and family for helping me make my dreams become realities. Keep smiling!

ABOUT THE AUTHOR

Julie Jahde Pospishil studied for a semester at the University in San Sebastian, Spain, and has an M.A. in Education-Language Acquisition from the University of Nebraska–Omaha. She has taught Spanish for 16 years customizing Adult Spanish Classes for Boystown Pediatrics–Bergan Mercy Hospital, Omaha Public Power Development (OPPD), Omaha Public Libraries, Dana College, Woodmen of the World, Casinos, Communications Companies, Banks and Metropolitan Community College. She has taught Spanish for Culinary Professionals for the past five years. She loves traveling with her husband, Brad, and has spent summers in 15 different Latin American countries, meeting many amigos. Julie currently teaches *Spanish Chatbook, Business Spanish Chatbook* and *Culinary Spanish Chatbook* classes, directs a summer Spanish camp and cooks Latin American dishes with her children, Jaden and Elena. She believes "everyone smiles in the same language" and "donde existe voluntad, siempre hay un camino." = "Where there's a will, there's a way."

Contributor Brad Pospishil has been a Spanish teacher for the past 12 years at Omaha North Magnet High School. He has a B.A. from Rockhurst University and an M.S. from the University of Wisconsin–Madison in Industrial Relations. He studied Spanish at the University of Nebraska–Lincoln and at ITESM-Querétaro, México. He received his teaching certificate from UNL with endorsements in Spanish, history and government. Brad has traveled extensively in Latin America with his wife, Julie, on "Aventuras con Julia."

CONTENTS

INTRODUCTION: A TOUR OF THE BOOK 1
    Survey of goals and needs... 3

LESSON 1: READ AND CHAT IN SPANISH IN JUST FIVE MINUTES 5
    Pronunciation of vowels and consonants.. 6
    Greetings and goodbye phrases... 8
    Choosing a Spanish name... 9
    Using two last names... 10
    Tú versus usted... 12
    Accent marks 12
    Helpful introductory phrases.. 13
    Categorizing Hispanics and Latinos 17
    Famous Hispanic-Americans... 18
    "Tic-Tac-Toe" game board... 20
    Desktop Phrase guide.. 23
    Map of Spanish Speaking Countries 24

LESSON 2: FRONT OF THE HOUSE CHATS WITH THE BACK 25
    Useful restaurant lingo.. 26
    Connecting the front of the house to the back of the house...................... 27
    Numbers 1–9,000.. 30
    "Más o Menos" game 31
    Servers in the front talking to expo in the back 31
    Question words.. 34
    Spain 36
    Variations in the Spanish language 38
    The four ways of saying "the" 40
    "Toma Todo" game 42

LESSON 3: CHAT WITH THE BUSERS 45
    Server communicates with buser 48
    Gender differences / Machismo / Hispanic families................................... 49
    Supervising Latino employees 49
    Expressing likes and dislikes 49
    Describing your family / Your job / Your age 51
    México.. 54
    Historical perspectives.. 56
    Set the table in the dining room area.. 57
    Alphabet.. 58
    Server requests help from a buser 60
    "Bingo" game board and directions 63

Lesson 4: Chat with the Cleaning Crew 67

- Family presentation 68
- Legends and myths 68
- Communicating with the cleaning staff 69
- The Mayan number system 71
- Cleaning the bathroom and/or kitchen areas 72
- Three very useful verbs: to have = tener, to want = querer and to go = ir ... 74
- Cleaning the floors 78
- Locating Central American countries 80
- Guatemala / El Salvador / Honduras / Nicaragua 81
- "Which One Is The Lie?" A true/false game 84

Lesson 5: Time For A chat with the Manager 87

- Telling time 89
- Daily routine / Reflexive verbs 90
- Tomorrow = Mañana / Tardiness 91
- Holidays and fiestas 91
- Months of the year / Days of the week 92
- Weather 94
- Scheduling phrases / Time 95
- Paychecks and Direct Deposit 96
- Manager phrases to communicate with employees 97
- Aztec Calendar 100
- Costa Rica / Panamá 101
- The verbs to be = ser versus estar 104
- "Around the World" and "Tic-Tac-Toe" games 108

Lesson 6: Chat with the Line Cooks 111

- Conquistadors / Why Spanish is spoken throughout the Americas ... 112
- Kitchen and back of the house phrases 114
- Communication styles 116
- Colombia / Ecuador / Venezuela 117
- Locating South American countries 118
- Phrases for cooking on the line 119
- Pots / Pans / Cookware / Kitchen equipment 120
- Regular present tense –ar verb conjugation 121
- Number practice / "Bingo" game 126

Lesson 7: Prep, Bake and Chat 129

- Prep area phrases 131
- Exclamations 132
- Adjectives / Colors 133
- Inca Empire 135
- Baking phrases 136
- Bolivia / Perú / Chile 141
- Regular present tense –er/–ir verb conjugation 143
- "Tic-Tac-Toe" game 147

Lesson 8: Chat About Dishwashing And First Aid 151

- First Aid / Safety / Personal Hygiene phrases 152
- Giving and receiving directions 154
- Back of the House- Dishwasher phrases 155
- Bilingual employees 156
- This / That / These / Those 159
- Language acquisition—English versus Spanish 160
- Preterite past tense 160
- Argentina / Uruguay / Paraguay 163
- Final project ideas 165
- "Toma Todo" game 168

Lesson 9: Travel Tips And Chat with Hispanic Customers 171

- Menus 173
- Latin American schedules 173
- Phrases for serving Hispanic customers 174
- Travel and completing restaurant service 176
- Puerto Rico / Dominican Republic / Cuba / Equatorial Guinea ... 179
- Travel advice 181
- Table settings 181
- Recipes 182
- Conversation starters and "Bingo" game 188

Lesson 10: Future Chatting Prospects 191

- Final project presentations and fiesta 192
- Proverbs 192
- Tongue twisters 194
- 10 ideas to continue learning in the future 195
- Grocery store scavenger hunt and field trip 197
- Feedback form 201

Summary 203

Extra Vocabulary 205
Additional vocabulary and cultural considerations relating to Lessons 1-9

- Lesson 1-List of Female / Male names in Spanish 206
- Lesson 2-Number chart 1–100 207
  - Number song / Meat / Seafood / From the ocean 208
  - Condiments / Side Dishes / Pastas / Appetizers 209
  - Beverages 210
- Lesson 3-Front of the house / Restaurant tour 210
  - Set the table / In the Dining Room / Family / Relatives 211
  - Human Resources / Professions / Workplaces 212
  - Things you like to do / Gustar 213
- Lesson 4-Cleaning and maintenance supplies 213
  - Parts of a uniform / Clothing 214
- Lesson 6-Utensils / Containers / Contents of the drawers 214
  - Kitchen equipment / Appliances 215
- Lesson 7-Basic adjectives / Opposites / Colors / Grains / Breads 216
  - Fruits / Vegetables 217
  - Spices / Baking Ingredients / Nuts 218
  - Desserts 219
- Lesson 8-First Aid / Health / Personal Hygiene / Body Parts 219
  - Medical phrases 220
  - Safety / Stores 221
- Lesson 9-Tourist needs / Hotel words / Metric system conversions / Temperature 222

Extra Grammar 223
Additional grammar explanations with practice exercises

- Lesson 1-Accent marks and when to use an accent 224
- Lesson 3-Gustar 226
  - Indirect and direct object pronouns 227
- Lesson 5-Reflexive verbs 228
  - Present progressive 228
- Lesson 7-Basic verb conjugation / Regular present tense 229
  - Stem changing verbs (boot verbs) / First person irregular verbs 232
- Lesson 8-This/that/these/those 235
  - Regular preterite 235
  - Irregular preterite 236
  - Skateboard verbs 240
  - Imperfect 241
  - Irregular imperfect 241
  - Preterite vs. imperfect 243

Answer Key
For all exercises in Lessons 1–10 and answers to Extra Grammar 245

GLOSSARY
Alphabetical word list of all the phrases in the book

    Spanish to English 271

    English to Spanish 281

SUBJECT INDEX 291

    Culinary Spanish Chatbook CD/Audio Track Listings 298

    Spanish Chatbooks Order Form 299

THE PYRAMID OF THE SUN, TEOTIHUACÁN, MÉXICO
IS ONE OF THE LARGEST IN THE WORLD.

Introduction: A Tour of the Book

Welcome = ¡Bienvenidos!

I am so glad you have joined this learning adventure, and I hope you will be able to use these phrases immediately. This book has useful, practical phrases designed to help busy professionals communicate with Latino employees and/or Hispanic customers. If you have forgotten your high school Spanish, and you really need to communicate, then this is the book for you.

Culinary Spanish Chatbook will help you speak in real-world Spanish right now. Each of the first nine lessons includes 12-15 culinary phrases. The first time a phrase is introduced, it will have the English phrase = the Spanish phrase followed by the pronunciation guide in italics. This guide is meant to help a native English speaker read the Spanish phrase out loud and pronounce the words correctly.

Each new word in the pronunciation guide is capitalized. For example, nice to meet you = mucho gusto *(Moo-cho Goose-toh)*. Two vowels are sometimes combined as indicated by a slash: Bien = *(Bee/ehn)*. An accent mark on a word shows that a particular syllable is stressed and should be emphasized when spoken. For example, telephone = teléfono *(Teh-LEH-foh-noh)* indicates to put the emphasis on the "*LEH*".

Lessons 1-8 are written in the informal Tú form that is most commonly spoken in the culinary environment. Lesson 9 uses the polite "usted" form that would be used with Hispanic customers. Usted is pronounced *Oos-tehd*—like the *oo* in the word moon. Our other books, *Spanish Chatbook* and *Business Spanish Chatbook* include over 100 phrases that use "usted" and will help travelers, supervisors and/or customer service representatives. These can be purchased on our website, www.SpanishChatCompany.com.

Each lesson in this book contains a review of the phrases from the previous lesson, 12-15 new phrases, spoken practice, multiple choice exercises, matching, a skit with a typical culinary conversation, grammar tidbits, translation practice, an exam, flashcards, games and puzzles. Awareness of the Hispanic culture is woven into each lesson with facts about each Spanish-speaking country, trivia questions, an explanation of cultural differences in culinary styles and overall cultural diversity considerations. For the activites, you will need dice, scissors and "Bingo" pieces made out of small scraps of paper.

A few partner exercises are included in each lesson. Find a friend, family member or native speaker to help you with these activities. A lunch study group that meets for an hour or two each week is ideal. Each lesson will take about 1-2 hours to complete. Many native speakers will have a variety of ways to say the same sentence, such as "How are you?", "How are you doing?", "How is it going?" and "What's up?" None of the ways are wrong. They are just, different styles. In *Culinary Spanish Chatbook*, I have chosen a phrase and will review that same phrase over and over. Feel free to change and customize it to fit the slang of your workplace. I tried to use correct Spanish without being too formal or too "Spanglish". Don't get discouraged. Keep trying to learn!

To improve your pronunciation, purchase the *Culinary Spanish Chatbook* CD/Audio tracks. Each time you see the Audio symbol on the left, follow along to improve your Spanish skills. On the audio tracks, native speakers pronounce the Spanish phrases, allow time for you to repeat them, and act out each of the phrases in conversational role plays. Listen to over 125 phrases and typical culinary conversations while driving, working, or exercising. Use the book and audio together to maximize your learning experience! Order the CD/Audio guide from our website, www.SpanishChatCompany.com.

Culinary Spanish Chatbook aims to help you apply knowledge of Spanish to your profession immediately by personalizing the activities and making learning enjoyable. Let's go! = ¡Vámonos! *(VAH-moh-nohs!)*

¡BIENVENIDOS! = WELCOME!

This survey will help you identify your goals and needs in order to create the best learning environment possible. Fill out this form and then discuss your answers with a partner or as a group.

Learning requires interest.

1. Why are you interested in learning Spanish? _____
   _____
   _____

Your background affects learning.

2. Have you ever taken a foreign language class? If so, where? How many years? _____
   _____
   _____

3. How would you rate your Spanish abilities? Mark the choice that best fits your current level.

🌎 **I understand Spanish.**
- ☐ Everything
- ☐ Most conversations
- ☐ Some
- ☐ A little
- ☐ Nada = Nothing

🌎 **I read in Spanish.**
- ☐ Easily without a dictionary to look up words
- ☐ Sporadically, with a dictionary to look up words
- ☐ Nunca = Never

🌎 **I speak in Spanish.**
- ☐ Fluently
- ☐ With some mistakes
- ☐ Lots of mistakes
- ☐ Nunca = Never

🌎 **I write in Spanish.**
- ☐ Well, with very few mistakes
- ☐ With some mistakes
- ☐ Lots of mistakes
- ☐ Nunca = Never

Please continue this survey on the next page.

You learn from your problems.

1. Describe a past experience where it would have been helpful to know Spanish. _____
   _____
   _____
   _____

"Practice makes perfect."

2. How do you plan to study Spanish outside of class? _____
   _____
   _____
   _____
   _____

3. How much time do you expect to practice Spanish each week? _____
   _____
   _____
   _____

You learn better in a positive and respectful environment.

4. What will you do to make learning Spanish a positive experience? ____
   _____
   _____
   _____

5. ¿¿¿Any other comments or questions??? _____
   _____
   _____
   _____

6. If you are in a group, this is the first page that you will tear out of your *Spanish Chatbook* conversational workbook. Please hand it to your teacher or group leader and add the following information:

Name = Nombre: _____

Email = Correo electrónico: _____

Phone number = Número de teléfono: _____

READ AND CHAT IN SPANISH IN JUST FIVE MINUTES

GOALS: In this lesson you will learn about these topics: pronunciation of vowels and consonants, how to learn to read and chat in Spanish in five minutes, common greetings and goodbye phrases, using two last names, tú versus usted, accent marks, helpful introductory phrases and categorizing Hispanics and Latinos and famous Hispanic-Americans.

1 = UNO

YOU CAN LEARN TO READ SPANISH IN FIVE MINUTES

This guide will help you pronounce and read every word in Spanish, although you will have to use detective skills to be able to understand anything. Read these words and phrases out loud, paying careful attention to the sounds of each letter.

THE VOWELS = LAS VOCALES:

The good news is, the vowels are always the same!

A *(ah)* la banana *(Lah Bah-nah-nah)* = the banana
la mamá *(Lah Mah-MAH)* = the mom

E *(eh)* las escaleras *(Lahs Ehs-cah-leh-rahs)* = the stairs
el empleado *(Ehl Ehm-pleh-ah-doh)* = the employee

I *(eee)* sí *(See)* = yes
qui-qui-ri-quí *(Kee-kee-ree-kee)* = cock-a-doodle-doo

O *(oh)* no *(No)* = no
¿Cómo? *(Koh-moh)* = How's that?

U *(oo)* as in moon Mucho gusto *(Moo-cho Goose-toh)* = Nice to meet you.

Note: When a strong vowel, (A, E, O) is combined with a weak vowel, (I, U) it makes a diphthong. When spoken, the two vowels are slurred together into the same syllable. In this book, you will see diphthongs with a slash mark, for example; ¿Entiendes? *(¿Ehn-tee/ehn-dehs?)* = Do you understand? Sometimes accent marks/tildes are used to break up the two syllables and override the diphthong rule. For example, el día *(dee-ah)* = the day. Listen to the native speakers on the *Culinary Spanish Chatbook* audio tracks to help you.

THE CONSONANTS = LAS CONSONANTES

B and V
sound similar   ¡Vámonos! *(VAH-moh-nohs)* = Let's go!

H is silent
(Cross it out)   Hola. *(Oh-lah)* = Hello
     Habla *(Ah-blah)* = talk

J and Ge and Gi
sound like H   Julia *(Who-lee/ah)* = Julie
     José *(Ho-seh)* = Joe
     gerente *(Heh-wren-teh)* = manager
     girasol *(Hee-rah-sohl)* = sunflower

QUE *(keh)*   ¿Por qué? *(Pohr Keh)* = Why?
     porque *(Pohr-keh)* = because

QUI *(kee)*   ¿Quién? *(Kee-ehn)* = Who?

LL *(yeah OR yah)*   Me llamo _____.
     (Meh Yah-moh) = My name is_____.

Ñ as in bunion   Señor/Sr. *(Sehn-your)* = Mr. or Sir
     Señora/Sra. *(Sehn-your-ah)* = Mrs. or Ma'am
     Señorita/Srta. *(Sehn-your-ree-tah)* = Miss (young, unwed)

RR is
trilled/rolled   Correcto *(Koh-rrehk-toh)* = correct
     Perro *(Peh-rroh)* = dog
     Without rolling the r it would be: Pero *(Peh-roh)* = but

Having trouble rolling your RR's? Your tongue muscle needs exercise. You should be able to roll your RR's if you spend a few months practicing this Spanish phrase:

     Un tigre, dos tigres, tres tigres = One tiger, two tigers, three tigers
     (Oon T-greh, Dohs T-grehs, Trehs T-grehs)

2 = DOS

There are some Spanish culinary words that resemble English words. English and Spanish are both Latin-based languages and some words are similar. Read these words out loud using your new pronunciation skills and then guess the meaning of each word. When you are finished, refer to page 246 in the Answer Key at the back of the book.

1. hamburguesas = _____
2. refrigerador = _____
3. café = _____
4. teléfono = _____
5. restaurante = _____
6. coliflor = _____

3 = TRES

Let's begin chatting with these common greetings and goodbyes. Read the phrase out loud using the italics to help with pronunciation.

1. Good morning. =
   Buenos días.
   (Bweh-nohs Dee-ahs.)

2. Good afternoon. Good evening. (12 p.m. – dark) =
   Buenas tardes.
   (Bweh-nahs Tahr-dehs.)

3. Good night. =
   Buenas noches.
   (Bweh-nahs Noh-chehs.)

4. See you later. =
   Hasta luego.
   (Ahs-tah Loo/eh-goh.)

4 = CUATRO

Circle the English choice that matches the Spanish phrase.

1. Buenos días
   a. Good afternoon.
   b. Good night.
   c. Good morning.
   d. Good job.

2. Hasta luego.
   a. Goodbye.
   b. See you later.
   c. Never again.
   d. See you soon.

3. Buenas noches.
   a. Good afternoon.
   b. Good night.
   c. Good morning.
   d. Good nachos.

4. Buenas tardes.
   a. Good afternoon.
   b. Good night.
   c. Good morning.
   d. Good tacos.

5 = CINCO

Choose a Spanish first name for yourself: (This is the one time in life where you get to choose your own name.) See Extra Vocabulary- Lesson 1 page 206 for a name list. Write your new name here:

Me llamo _____.
(Meh Yah-moh _____.) = My name is _____.

Next, find a Spanish-speaker and practice saying the appropriate greeting for the corresponding time of day, "buen _____."

For example use either; "buenos días, buenas tardes or buenas noches."
Then say, "me llamo _____". Finish with, "Hasta luego".

If you are working in a group, greet as many people as possible in the next three minutes. Note: "Me llamo..." literally means, "I am called..." Please do NOT mistakenly say, "Me llamo es..." which means "I am called is...". However you can say, "Mi nombre es..." which is a slightly more formal version of "My name is..."

6 = SEIS

In many Hispanic countries, people use two last names every day. You would use both last names when looking up someone in the phone book. There are even two blanks on most official government and school forms. This may cause confusion when dealing with human resources issues. Be aware that the father's last name, is always listed first, followed by the mother's last name. In other words, it is your paternal grandfather's last name followed by your maternal grandfather's last name. Confused? Look at the examples below.

Example: José Ramírez García marries María Cruz Vásquez. (See the following family tree.) Their son is named José Carlos Ramírez Cruz and their daughter is María Carmen Ramírez Cruz. A woman getting married may keep both her maiden names or add de _____ with her husband's last name. For example, if the daughter, María Carmen Ramírez Cruz, marries Luis Perez Morales, she may be María Carmen Ramírez Cruz de Perez or she may drop Cruz and be María Carmen Ramírez Perez.

In the United States, the son may shorten his name to Carlos Ramirez (dropping José and Cruz and also dropping the accent mark/tilde). He may choose to hyphenate his last name as Ramírez-Cruz. José Carlos may even be called Carlitos as a child. The daughter may be called Carmen Ramírez or even Carmen Perez. In many Latin American countries, children take pride in reciting not only their two last names, but adding on the names of more generations. Nicknames and using the endings of –ito and –ita is common throughout the Hispanic world. Instead of calling a co-worker "amigo", it would create better rapport if you would use the co-worker's name.

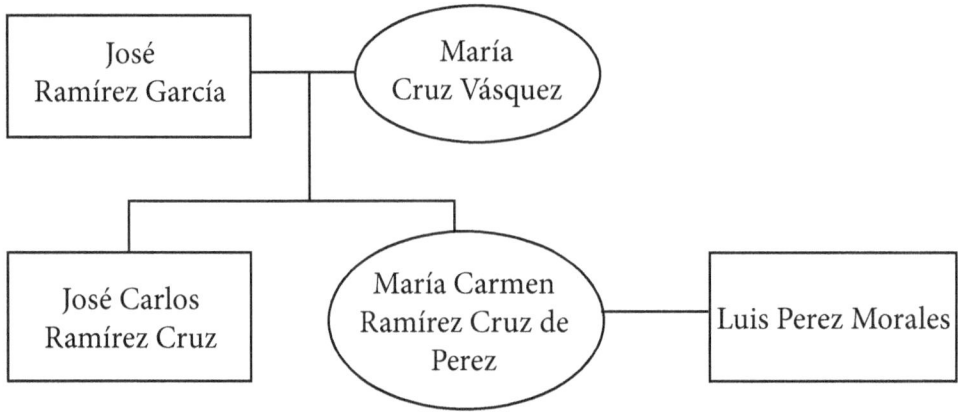

7 = SIETE

What would your Hispanic name look like? Try it out using the example below. Then ask a Hispanic friend if they ever use two last names.

For example, what was your father's last name? _____+

What was your mother's maiden name? _____ +

(For women only) de _____ (your husband's last name).

If you lived in a Spanish-speaking country, there would be space for these multiple names on most official forms and documents.

8 = OCHO

Practice this chant using rainsticks, maracas, drums, or some other instrument to provide rhythm: "A, E, I, O, U, ¿Cómo se llama usted? *(Ah, Eh, Eee, Oh, Ooh, Koh-moh Seh Yah-mah Oos-tehd?)* = A, E, I, O, U, What is your name?

At the end of the chant you say, "me llamo _____." *(Meh Yah-moh)* meaning, "my name is _____." Then say, "mucho gusto." *(Moo-cho Goose-toh.)* which means, "nice to meet you." If you have a group, play "hot potato" with a maraca. The person holding the maraca at the end of the chant says, "me llamo _____." The group then replies, "mucho gusto."

The authentic original rhyme in Latin America is, "A, E, I, O, U, un burro sabe más que tú," meaning "A, E, I, O, U, a donkey knows more than you." Remember back to when you or your child was learning to speak English. They started out with wha-wha for water and everyone cheered. We will work together as we take baby steps to learn this new language.

One funny example of a communication blunder happened in Spain, when the author pointed to some garlic cloves = ajo and accidentally said, "ojo" which means "eyeball." The shopkeeper thought it was so funny that he went over to the fish counter and got a fresh "ojo" and handed it to her with a big smile = sonrisa. Learn to laugh and cheer at your mistakes or mishaps because that means you are at least trying. In fact, many native speakers enjoy having fun with the language.

9 = NUEVE

When should you use Tú versus usted? (abbreviation Ud.) Both words mean YOU in Latin America. Tú *(Too)* is the casual and informal you versus usted *(oos-tehd* like the oo in moon), which is the polite and formal way of saying you. Usted is used as respect for customer service, courtesy, anyone older, or higher ranking. Use usted for an initial meeting. We will use the tú form because it is commonly used in the back of the house and kitchens. Tú is also used with close family members and friends in your same age group. When speaking with customers, use USTED! For more information on using the usted form, we recommend our book, *Business Spanish Chatbook*.

One company had complaints with a customer service representative who was always addressing clients in the informal tú form. Her evaluations were lower, due to this informality. If you are in doubt in a social situation, just ask, "Is it okay to use the tú form?" = "¿Me puede tutear?" *(Meh Pweh-deh Too-teh-ahr?)* For more than one person use ustedes *(Uds.)* = Y'all or all of you. In Spain, Vosotros is used instead of ustedes.

10 = DIEZ

Do you need an accent = tilde? Here are some computer keyboard shortcuts. For more Spanish marks and how and when to use an accent, see the Extra Grammar, page 225. Another method is to go to insert and select symbols. Note: check online help for more options if this doesn't work for your computer.

ON A PC: For á, é, í, ó, ú, Á, É, Í, Ó, Ú

Hold down these two keys at the same time; then the next letter you type will have an accent.

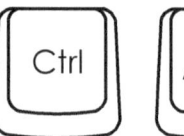

ON A MAC: For á, é, í, ó, ú, Á, É, Í, Ó, Ú

Hold down these two keys at the same time; then the next letter you type will have an accent.

11 = ONCE

Use these eight helpful introductory phrases to take control of the conversation and slow down the speaker. Working with a partner, have one person ask the question and the partner answer in Spanish.

1. Hello. How are you? =
   Hola. ¿Cómo estás?
   (Oh-lah, Koh-moh Ehs-tahs?)

2. I am fine. And you? =
   Estoy bien. ¿Y tú?
   (Ehs-toy Bee/ehn. Ee Too?)

3. Help me, please. =
   Ayúdame, por favor.
   (Ah-YOU-dah-meh, Pohr Fah-vohr.)

4. Slow down. Repeat that. =
   Más despacio. Repítelo.
   (Mahs Dehs-pah-see/oh.) (Reh-PEE-teh-loh.)

5. Do you understand? =
   ¿Entiendes?
   (¿Ehn-tee/ehn-dehs?)

6. What is your name? Your last name? =
   ¿Cómo te llamas? ¿Tu apellido?
   (Koh-moh Teh Yah-mahs?) (Too Ah-peh-yee-doh?)

7. My name is Julie. =
   Me llamo Julia.
   (Meh Yah-moh Who-lee/ah.)

8. Nice to meet you. Goodbye. =
   Mucho gusto. Adiós.
   (Moo-cho Goose-toh.) (Ah-dee/ohs.)

12 = DOCE

Now you have an opportunity to practice. Complete exercises 12 = doce and 13 = trece and then check your answers in the Answer Key. Find these Spanish words in the word search and then write the English on the line next to each word. The Spanish words are from the phrases in 11 = once. ¡Buena suerte! = Good luck!

A	O	D	E	S	P	A	C	I	O	L	M	S	I	P
V	D	S	M	R	T	S	A	Y	Ú	D	A	M	E	S
R	D	Í	A	S	M	X	T	O	Y	Z	B	S	Á	R
I	M	I	S	G	Á	C	D	G	Á	V	E	M	O	S
R	E	P	Í	T	E	L	O	H	I	S	S	J	K	E
T	P	D	M	L	B	R	A	D	T	M	T	Ñ	O	D
J	Í	S	U	P	Q	U	V	Á	W	Y	A	Z	E	N
T	N	V	C	Ó	M	O	S	N	O	R	R	J	L	E
E	E	C	H	T	L	A	B	R	O	M	D	N	E	I
L	I	O	O	L	M	F	O	V	R	A	E	N	N	T
L	B	J	H	U	L	P	A	Í	S	D	M	O	A	N
A	R	A	Í	G	W	F	L	N	M	U	S	C	P	E
M	B	D	D	E	R	U	A	N	I	T	O	H	X	V
A	E	E	N	O	T	S	U	G	L	P	M	E	C	R
S	A	N	P	U	W	T	Ú	Ñ	J	U	L	I	A	X

WORD SEARCH = BUSCAPALABRAS

CÓMO _____   TARDE _____
ESTÁS _____   MUCHO _____
DÍA _____   GUSTO _____
NOCHE _____   DESPACIO _____
AYÚDAME _____   REPÍTELO _____
ENTIENDES _____   POR FAVOR _____
BIEN _____   TÚ _____
MÁS _____   TE LLAMAS _____

13 = TRECE

Write the letter of the corresponding English phrase on the line next to the Spanish phrase.

1. _____ ¿Cómo te llamas?   A. *(ah)*   Do you understand?
2. _____ Repítelo.   B. *(beh)*   See you later.
3. _____ Hasta luego.   C. *(seh)*   Hello.
4. _____ Ayúdame, por favor.   D. *(deh)*   Slow down.
5. _____ Buenas noches.   E. *(eh)*   Repeat that.
6. _____ Estoy bien.   F. *(ehf-feh)*   And you?
7. _____ Hola.   G. *(heh)*   What is your name?
8. _____ Me llamo Julia.   H. *(ah-che)*   Goodbye!
9. _____ Más despacio.   I. *(eeee)*   Nice to meet you.
10. _____ ¡Adiós!   J. *(hoh-tah)*   Good morning.
11. _____ ¿Y tú?   K. *(kah)*   My name is Julie.
12. _____ Mucho gusto.   L. *(ehl-leh)*   Help me, please.
13. _____ Buenas tardes.   M. *(ehm-meh)*   I am fine.
14. _____ ¿Entiendes?   N. *(ehn-neh)*   Good night.
15. _____ Buenos días.   Ñ. *(enh-ñyeh)* How are you?
16. _____ ¿Cómo estás?   O. *(oh)*   Good afternoon.

14 = CATORCE

Have one person say the lines for María and the other person say the lines for José, replacing María and José with your new Spanish names. Then switch roles. If you have a group, have two people present this as a skit.

María: ¡Hola!
José: Buenas tardes.
María: Buenas tardes. ¿Cómo estás?
José: Estoy bien, gracias. ¿Y tú?
María: No estoy bien. Estoy muy mal. Ayúdame, por favor.
  (muy mal= very bad)
José: Con mucho gusto te ayudaré. ¿Cómo te llamas?
  (= With much pleasure, I will help you.)
María: Me llamo María. ¿Y tú?
José: Me llamo José. Mucho gusto. Hasta luego.
María: Hasta luego.

15 = QUINCE

Fill in the following blanks to write your own skit. Refer to 14 = catorce for help. If you have a group, present these to each other.

Estudiante #1 ¡Hola!
Estudiante #2 Buen _____.
  (Buenos días, Buenas tardes, Buenas noches)
Estudiante #1 Buen _____. ¿Cómo estás?
  (Buenos días, Buenas tardes, Buenas noches)
Estudiante #2 Estoy _____ gracias. ¿Y tú? (Bien, mal)
Estudiante #1 Estoy _____. ¿Cómo te llamas? (Bien, mal)
Estudiante #2 Me llamo _____. (Your Spanish name). ¿Y tú?
Estudiante #1 Me llamo _____. Mucho gusto.
Estudiante #2 Mucho gusto. Hasta luego.
Estudiante #1 Hasta luego.

16 = DIECISÉIS

Latina? Hispanic? Chicano? Mexican? Which one should you use? What is the correct term?

- Spanish is the language. Please don't call someone a "Spanish" person.

- Spanish speakers are any persons who speak Spanish regardless of race. ¡Felicidades! = Congratulations! You are now a Spanish speaker.

- Latinos are people from Latin America (Central and South America) not usually including Spain. Latino or Latina is used often in the media and for cultural events.

- Spaniards are people from Spain.

- Mexicans are people who were born in México.

- Chicanos and Mexican-Americans are U.S. citizens of Mexican descent.

- Guatemalans are people who were born in Guatemala or born to Guatemalan parents. This pattern would continue with every Spanish-speaking country represented.

- The United States of America in Spanish is "Los Estados Unidos de América," also abbreviated with E.E.U.U. Therefore, a United States citizen is known as "estadounidense." You would probably be understood if you said you were an "americano" or "norte americano," but the terms aren't entirely accurate. All the people in North, South and Central America are also Americans. North America includes the countries of Canada, México and the United States. The slang terms of güera or gringo or yanqui are sometimes used to refer to U.S. citizens. These may have negative connotations depending on context.

- Hispanics are people from the countries formerly ruled by Spain. The majority of Hispanics speak the Spanish language. The term Hispanic is used by the government to describe people from Spanish-speaking countries. Each of the following lessons will include cultural information about these Hispanic countries.

- Hispanic-Americans are U.S. citizens of Hispanic descent. Hispanic-Americans have made significant contributions to the United States history and culture and continue to influence many lives. In 2007, Hispanics comprised 15% of the U.S. population. A few influential people include César Chávez (labor leader), Gloria Estefan (singer), Alex Rodriguez (baseball player), Sonia Sotomayor and Elena Kagan (Supreme Court Justices), Rita Moreno (actress), Tito Puente (drummer) and many more.

- Hispanic Heritage Month: September 15–October 15 is the time to celebrate Hispanic culture and achievements of Hispanic Americans. México, Guatemala, El Salvador, Honduras, Nicaragua, Costa Rica and Chile all celebrate their independence days on either September 15, 16 or 18. During Hispanic Heritage Month you could post pictures of your Hispanic employees or make a display highlighting the contributions of famous Hispanics. Check for local events celebrating the Hispanic culture. Send the dates and times to staff members to encourage participation.

- Hispanics also are known for their slang. Some Spanish-speaking individuals may say the phrases differently from what you are learning in this book. Our best advice is to learn these phrases as a foundation and then expand and build your vocabulary. For example, you will hear some very casual phrases in many kitchens and among close friends. You may hear, "Hey, how are ya?" = "¿Oye, qué tál?" *(Oh-yeh, Keh Tahl?)* or "What's up?" = "¿Qué pasa?" *(Keh Pah-sah?)* You can respond by saying, "Nothing." = "Nada." *(Nah-dah.)* If you have worked in a kitchen before, you may have heard a few bad words in Spanish. Most people seem to be able to learn those very quickly and remember them on their own, so we will focus on "clean Spanish" in this book. If you really want to know, you will have to ask your acquaintances = compañeras.

17 = DIECISIETE

Translate these phrases. Write the English for the first eight phrases and write the Spanish for the last eight phrases. This may be done as an exam or as homework for the next lesson. When finished check your answers in the Answer Key.

1. Hola. _____
2. ¿Y tú? _____
3. Buenos días. _____
4. ¡Adiós! _____
5. Estoy bien. _____
6. ¿Entiendes? _____
7. Más despacio. _____
8. Buenas noches. _____
9. What is your name? _____
10. Repeat that. _____
11. Good afternoon. _____
12. See you later. _____
13. Help me, please. _____
14. Nice to meet you. _____
15. How are you? _____
16. My name is Julie. _____

18 = DIECIOCHO

To play this "Tic-Tac-Toe" game, you and your partner will share one board depicted here. Cut out the X and O pieces found on page 21. Put nine flashcards from page 21, Spanish-side up on the board. Player X will go first, choosing a square that will help to get three in a row. Player X will read the Spanish for that square and say what it means in English in order to cover it up with an X piece. Then it is Player O's turn. Player O will read the Spanish for the square and say what it means in English. Play until someone gets three in row, "Tres en Raya" or "Tic-Tac-Toe". To make it more difficult, put the English side up and say the answer in Spanish. ¡Buena suerte! = Good luck!

"Three In A Row" = "Tres en Raya" game board

CUT OUT THE GAME PIECES FROM PAGE 21

19 = DIECINUEVE

Cut these flashcards apart and save them in an envelope to use during the games in this book. Strive to review them every day.

Hello. How are you?	Good morning.	Good afternoon/ evening.
Good night.	See you later.	Nice to meet you. Goodbye!
My name is Julie.	I am fine. And you?	Help me, please.
What is your name?	Slow down. Repeat that.	Do you understand?

O O O O O O
X X X X X X

Buenas tardes. *(Bweh-nahs Tahr-dehs.)*	Buenos días. *(Bweh-nohs Dee-ahs.)*	Hola. *(Oh-lah.)* ¿Cómo estás? *(Koh-moh Ehs-tahs?)*
Mucho gusto. *(Moo-cho Goose-toh.)* ¡Adiós! *(Ah-dee/ohs!)*	Hasta luego. *(Ahs-tah Loo/eh-goh.)*	Buenas noches. *(Bweh-nahs Noh-chehs.)*
Ayúdame, por favor. *(Ah-YOU-dah-meh, Pohr Fah-vohr.)*	Estoy bien. *(Ehs-toy Bee/ehn.)* ¿Y tú? *(Ee Too?)*	Me llamo Julia. *(Meh Yah-moh Who-lee/ah.)*
¿Entiendes? *(Ehn-tee/ehn-dehs?)*	Más despacio. *(Mahs Dehs-pah-see/oh.)* Repítelo. *(Reh-PEE-teh-loh.)*	¿Cómo te llamas? *(Koh-moh Teh Yah-mahs?)*

AYÚDAME = HELP ME

Post this in your restaurant to help you in Spanish-speaking situations. Fill in the five blank rows with useful phrases from the other chapters.

GOOD MORNING. = BUENOS DÍAS.   *(Bweh-nohs Dee-ahs.)*
GOOD AFTERNOON. GOOD EVENING. = BUENAS TARDES.   *(Bweh-nahs Tahr-dehs.)*
MY NAME IS _____ =   ME LLAMO _____   *(Meh Yah-moh _____*
SLOW DOWN. = MÁS DESPACIO.   *(Mahs Dehs-pah-see/oh.)*
DO YOU UNDERSTAND? = ¿ENTIENDES?   *(Ehn-tee/ehn-dehs?)*
REPEAT THAT. = REPÍTELO.   *(Reh-PEE-teh-loh.)*
BEHIND.   SHARP. =   ATRÁS.   FILOSO.   *(Ah-trahs.)   (Fee-loh-soh.)*
HAVE A GREAT DAY. = QUE TENGA UN BUEN DÍA.   *(Keh Tehn-gah Oon Bwhen Dee-ah.)*
HOW DO YOU SAY ___ IN SPANISH? = ¿CÓMO SE DICE ___ EN ESPAÑOL?   *(Koh-moh Seh Dee-seh ___ Ehn Ehs-pah-ñyohl?)*

Map containing the Spanish-speaking countries

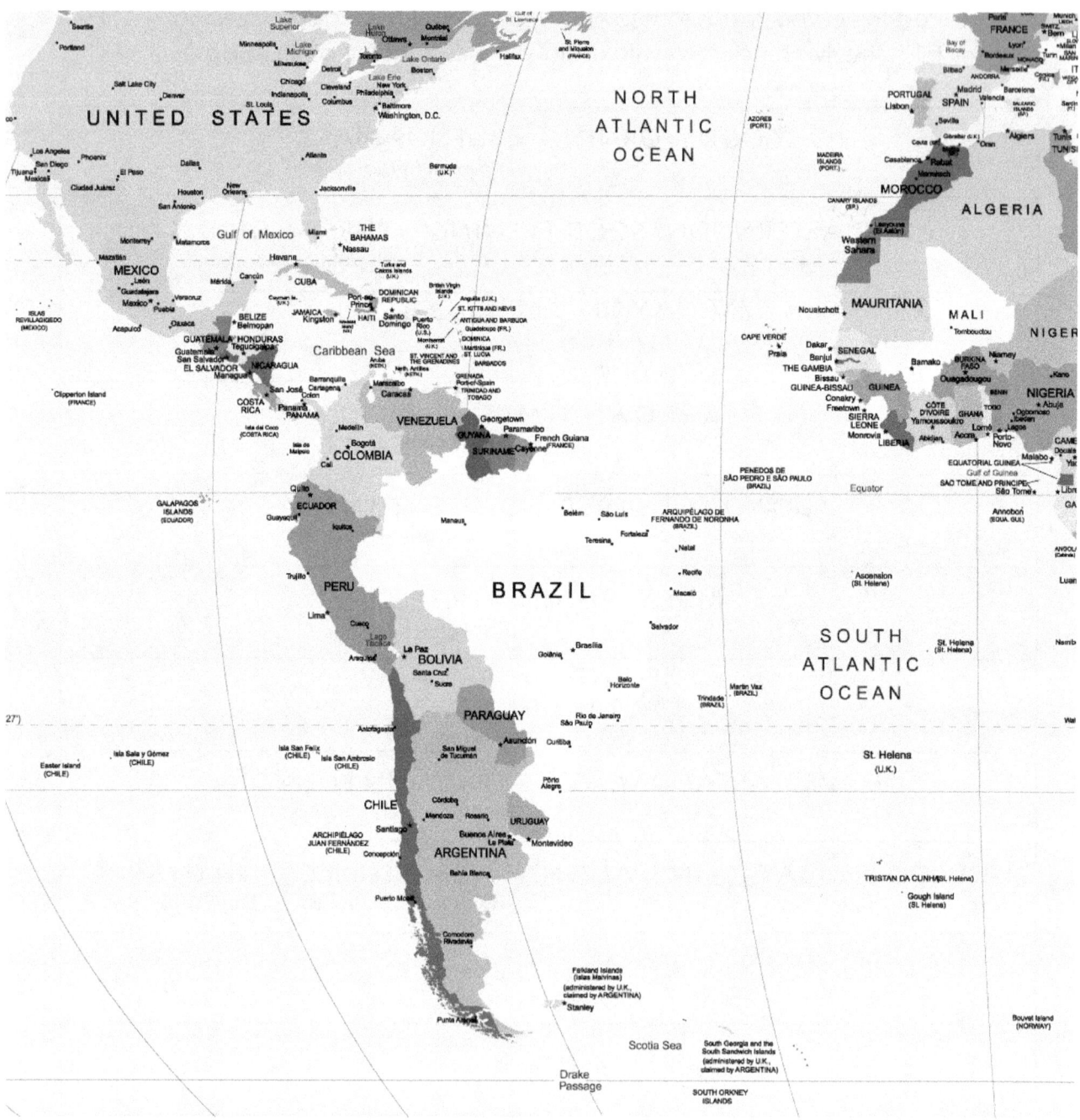

Circle all 21 Spanish-speaking countries on this map. Starting on the left of the front cover, here are the names corresponding to the flags of each country: Argentina, Bolivia, Chile, Nicaragua, Panama, Paraguay, Colombia, Uruguay, Venezuela, Mexico, Guatemala, Peru, Spain, El Salvador, Dominican Republic, Costa Rica, Cuba, Ecuador, Puerto Rico, Honduras, Equatorial Guinea.

FRONT OF THE HOUSE CHATS WITH THE BACK

GOALS: In this lesson you will learn about these topics: useful restaurant lingo, connecting the front and the back of the house, numbers 1–9,000, servers talking with expo in the back, question words, Spain, variations in the Spanish language and the four ways of saying "the."

20 = VEINTE

Begin by reviewing some of the phrases from Lesson 1. Fill in the missing Spanish word. Then take turns reading them aloud. Remember to use A, E, I, O, U to pronounce the phrases correctly.

1. Buenos _____
2. ¿Y _____?
3. ¿Cómo _____?
4. Estoy _____.
5. Mucho _____.
6. Ayúdame, _____.
7. Hasta _____.

21 = VEINTIUNO

Practice these three phrases that include useful restaurant lingo. Use the pronunciation in italics to guide you.

1. The plate is hot. =
   El plato está caliente.
   (Ehl Plah-toh Ehs-tah Kah-lee/ehn-teh.)

2. Hurry. Faster. =
   Apúrate. Más rápido.
   (Ah-POOH-rah-teh.) (Mahs RAH-pee-doh.)
   Note: To say, "get going", Mexicans use Ándale. *(AHN-dah-leh.)*

3. Excuse me. Behind. =
   Con permiso. Atrás.
   (Kohn Pehr-mees soh.) (Ah-trahs.)
   Note, depending on context: Excuse me. / I'm sorry. = Perdón. / Lo siento.
   (Pehr-DohN. / Loh See/ehn-toh.)

22 = VEINTIDÓS

Form groups of three people. Choose one person to be the server. The other two people will use phrases from Lesson 1 to introduce themselves to each other. Have the server walk by three different times saying each of the phrases from 21 = veintiuno. After practicing a few times, have each group of three people present these mini-skits to the larger group.

23 = VEINTITRÉS

Practice these five phrases that help the front of the house communicate and connect with the back of the house. Read the phrase out loud using the italics to help you with your pronunciation.

1. Put the mayonnaise on the side (apart). =
   Pon la mayonesa aparte.
   (PohN Lah Mah-yoh-neh-sah Ah-pahr-teh.)

2. Without nuts, there is an allergy. =
   Sin nueces, hay una alergia.
   (Seen Noo/eh-sehs, Eye Oon-ah Ah-lehr-hee/ah.)

3. The soup is cold, warm it up. =
   La sopa está fría, caliéntala.
   (Lah Soh-pah Ehs-tah FREE-ah, Kah-lee/EHN-tah-lah.)

4. I'm missing the fries. =
   Faltan las papas fritas.
   (Fahl-tahn Lahs Pah-pahs Free-tahs.)

5. This is wrong. Remake it without onions. =
   No está correcto. Hazlo de nuevo sin cebollas.
   (No Ehs-tah Coh-rrehk-toh.) (Ahs-loh Deh Noo/eh-voh Seen Seh-boh-yahs.)

24 = VEINTICUATRO

Complete the crossword puzzle by using words from each of the eight Spanish phrases from 21 = veintiuno and 23 = veintitrés. Find the opposite translation. If the clue is in Spanish, then write the English phrase. If the clue is in English, then write the Spanish phrase. There are no punctuation marks. Check your answers in the Answer Key when you are finished. ¡Buena suerte! Good luck!

HORIZONTAL
2   SOUP
4   SALAD
6   COLD
8   PLATE
10 CRAB
12 BEHIND

VERTICAL
1   MAYONESA
3   MÁS RÁPIDO
5   APERITIVO
7   CEBOLLAS
9   MESA
11 CALIENTE

25 = VEINTICINCO

Circle the English choice that matches the Spanish phrase.

1. La sopa está fría, caliéntala.
   a. The soup is frozen, call the boss.
   b. The soap is cold, warm it up.
   c. The soup is cold, warm it up.
   d. The soup is warm.

2. Hazlo de nuevo sin cebollas.
   a. We need a new one.
   b. Oz is a better place than here.
   c. Remake it without onions.
   d. Make it again without croutons.

3. Faltan las papas fritas.
   a. It's the fries fault.
   b. I'm missing the Dad's order.
   c. The baked potato is missing.
   d. I'm missing the fries.

4. Pon la mayonesa aparte.
   a. Put the mayonnaise on the side.
   b. May 5th is a part of our culture.
   c. Put on more mayonnaise.
   d. Only put mayonnaise on a part.

26 = VEINTISÉIS

Have you heard some of the numbers in Spanish from Dora or Sesame Street? Knowing the numbers in Spanish is important for traveling in Latin America and communicating with Hispanics. In Spanish, periods and commas are reversed from English. For example, periods are used in the thousands, instead of a comma. In Latin America, 3,000 would be written as 3.000. Commas are used in prices when we use periods. For example, in the U.S.A. we write: $5.84, versus $5,84 in Latin America. The exception is the countries that use the U.S. dollar as their currency. In Mexico, you may see a peso written with one line ($) and a dollar sign with two lines ($) to distinguish the difference.

Say los números = the numbers from 1–9,000 out loud using the number chart on the next page. Starting with the second row, notice any patterns and similarities as you read across the rows. Note: zero = cero.

THE NUMBERS = LOS NÚMEROS:

There is another number chart listing out all of the numbers from 0–100 in Extra Vocabulary: Lesson 2. Hang either chart in your office space for quick reference.

COUNTING BY 1'S	COUNTING BY 1'S	COUNTING BY 10'S	COUNTING BY 100'S	COUNTING BY 1,000'S
1 uno (Oo-noh)	11 once (Ohn-seh)	10 diez (Dee/ehs)	100 cien (See/ehn) 110 ciento diez (See/ehn-toh Dee-ehs)	1000 mil (Meel)
2 dos (Dohs)	12 doce (Doh-seh)	20 veinte (Veh/een-teh)	200 doscientos (Doh-see/ehn-tohs)	2011 dos mil once (Dohs-Meel Ohn-seh)
3 tres (Trehs)	13 trece (Treh-seh)	30 treinta (Treh/een-tah)	300 trescientos (Treh-see/ehn-tohs)	3.000 tres mil (Trehs Meel)
4 cuatro (Qwah-troh)	14 catorce (Kah-tohr-seh)	40 cuarenta (Qwah-rent-tah)	400 cuatrocientos (Qwah-troh-see/ehn-tohs)	4.000 cuatro mil (Qwah-troh Meel)
5 cinco (Seen-koh)	15 quince (Keen-seh)	50 cincuenta (Seen-qwehn-tah)	500 quinientos (Kee-nee/ehn-tohs)	5.000 cinco mil (Seen-koh Meel)
6 seis (Seh/ace)	16 dieciséis/ diez y seis (Dee/eh-see-seh/ace)	60 sesenta (Seh-sehn-tah)	600 seiscientos (Seh/ace-see/ehn-tohs)	6.000 seis mil (Seh/ace Meel)
7 siete (See/eh-teh)	17 diecisiete/ diez y siete (Dee/eh-see-see/eh-teh)	70 setenta (Seh-tent-tah)	700 setecientos (Seh-teh-see/ehn-tohs)	7.000 siete mil (See/eh-teh Meel)
8 ocho (Oh-cho)	18 dieciocho/ diez y ocho (Dee/eh-see/oh-cho)	80 ochenta (Oh-chen-tah)	800 ochocientos (Oh-cho-see/ehn-tohs)	8.000 ocho mil (Oh-cho Meel)
9 nueve (Noo/eh-veh) 10 diez (Dee/ehs)	19 diecinueve/ diez y nueve (Dee/eh-see-noo/eh-veh)	90 noventa (Noh-vehnt-tah)	900 novecientos (Noh-veh-see/ehn-tohs)	9.000 nueve mil (Noo/eh-veh Meel)

27 = VEINTISIETE

Play a game called, "Más o Menos" = "More or Less". When having a tough day, Hispanics will answer the question, "¿Cómo está? = How are you?" with the reply, "más o menos." For our "Más o Menos" game you will need partners. One partner will think of a number between 1 and 1,000. The other person will then try to guess the number in Spanish. If the guessed number is too low, the partner will say, "más." If the guessed number is too high, the partner will say, "menos." Of course, all numbers guessed must be done in Spanish. For example, 492 = cuatrocientos noventa y dos. For more practice with the numbers 1–100 use the song in Extra Vocabulary: Lesson 2.

28 = VEINTIOCHO

Practice these four phrases that the front of the house servers may use to communicate with expo or someone in the back of the house. Use the number chart from 26 = veintiséis to help you.

1. How much longer for the appetizer? =
   ¿Cuánto tiempo más para el aperitivo?
   (Qwahn-toh Tee/ehm-poh Mahs Pah-rah Ehl Ah-peh-ree-tee-voh?)

2. Did you get the ticket for table 18? =
   ¿Recibiste la orden para la mesa diez y ocho?
   (Reh-see-bees-teh Lah Ohr-dehn Pah-rah Lah Meh-sah Dee/eh-see/oh-cho?)
   Note: The "Spanglish" word "El ticket" is often used instead of la orden.

3. I need the salad for table 15. = Necesito la ensalada para la mesa quince.
   (Neh-seh-see-toh Lah Ehn-sah-lah-dah Pah-rah Lah Meh-sah Keen-seh.)

4. There is no crab. (86) =
   No hay cangrejo. (Ochenta y seis)
   (No Eye Kahn-greh-hoh. (Oh-chen-tah Ee Seh/ace)

29 = VEINTINUEVE

Now that you have seen all of the 12 phrases, it is time to put them together for an on-the-job conversation. Have one person say the lines for our server, Isabel de Castilla and another person say the lines for Hernán Cortés, who is in the back of the house. Then switch roles. If you have a group, have two people present this as a skit.

Isabel de Castilla:	Buenas tardes. ¿Cómo estás?
Hernán Cortés:	Bien. ¿Y tú?
Isabel de Castilla:	Estoy muy ocupada. Con permiso. Atrás, el plato está caliente. ¿Cómo te llamas?
Hernán Cortés:	Me llamo Hernán Cortés. ¿Y tú?
Isabel de Castilla:	Me llamo Isabel de Castilla. Mucho gusto. ¿Entiendes Inglés?
Hernán Cortés:	No, no entiendo mucho. Soy de Medellín, España.
Isabel de Castilla:	Ayúdame, por favor. Necesito la ensalada para la mesa quince. Sin nueces, hay una alergia. ¿Recibiste la orden?
Hernán Cortés:	No recibí la orden y el pollo no está listo para la ensalada.
Isabel de Castilla:	Apúrate. Más rápido. Hazla sin nueces, por favor. ¿Cuánto tiempo más para la ensalada? Ay, ay, ay. Falta pan.
Hernán Cortés:	Más despacio, repítelo.
Isabel de Castilla:	Necesito una ensalada sin nueces, rápido. Pon el pan aparte. Tengo otro problema. La sopa está fría, caliéntala.
Hernán Cortés:	Está bien. La sopa y la ensalada ya están listas.
Isabel de Castilla:	Gracias. Hasta luego.
Hernán Cortés:	De nada. Hasta luego.

New words = Palabras nuevas:

De nada = You're welcome.	Inglés = English
Recibiste = Did you receive	muy ocupada = very busy
No recibí = I didn't receive	Soy de ... = I'm from...
listo/listas = ready	Tengo otro problema. = I have another problem.

30 = TREINTA

Before doing this role play, find a partner and decide who will be Estudiante #1 and who will be Estudiante #2. Fill in the blanks using help from the Extra Vocabulary section starting on page 206. Then have each person read their part of the role play.

Estudiante #1	Buenas tardes. ¿Cómo estás?
Estudiante #2	_____.¿Y tú?
Estudiante #1	Estoy _____. Con permiso. Atrás. El plato está caliente. ¿Cómo te llamas?
Estudiante #2	Me llamo _____. ¿Y tú?
Estudiante #1	Me llamo _____. Mucho gusto. ¿Entiendes Inglés?
Estudiante #2	No, no mucho. Soy de_____.
Estudiante #1	Ayúdame, por favor. Necesito _____(entrée) para la mesa quince. Sin _____(ingredient), hay una alergia. ¿Recibiste la orden?
Estudiante #2	No recibí la orden y no hay _____(side dish) listo para la orden.
Estudiante #1	Apúrate. Más rápido. Hazlo sin _____(ingredient), por favor. ¿Cuánto tiempo más para la orden? Ay, ay, ay. Falta _____(side dish).
Estudiante #2	Más despacio, Repítelo.
Estudiante #1	Necesito _____(entrée), rápido. Pon _____(side dish) aparte. Tengo otro problema. La _____(another side dish) está fría, caliéntala.
Estudiante #2	Está bien. _____(entrée) y _____ (side dish) ya están listos.
Estudiante #1	Gracias. Hasta luego.
Estudiante #2	De nada. Hasta luego.

31 = TREINTA Y UNO

You probably have a few preguntas = questions. Read these question words and make a list of five questions you would like to ask Hispanic employees or Spanish-speaking customers. Choose from these questions or form your own questions relating to your job. Share two questions with the group.

WHO? = ¿QUIÉN?   ¿Quién es tu jefe? = Who is your boss?
There are three ways of saying what: **#1 WHAT? = ¿CUÁL?**   *Use with open-ended answers.*   ¿Cuál es tu número de teléfono? = What is your phone number?   ¿Cuál es tu dirección? = What is your address?
#2 WHAT? = ¿QUÉ? Use when the answer is a specific item.   ¿Qué hora es? = What time is it?   ¿Qué es esto? = What is this?
#3 WHAT? = ¿CÓMO? = How or what did you just say?   ¿Cómo te llamas? = What is your name? (How are you called?)   ¿Cómo estás? = How are you?   ¿Cómo se dice _____ en español? = How do you say _____ in Spanish?
WHERE? = ¿DÓNDE? ¿De dónde eres? = Where are you from?   Soy de _____ = I'm from _____
WHEN? = ¿CUÁNDO? ¿Cuándo entraste? = When did you come in?   ¿Cuándo es tu cumpleaños? = When is your birthday?
WHY? = ¿POR QUÉ?   ¿Por qué llegaste tarde? = Why did you arrive late?
BECAUSE = PORQUE   Llegué tarde porque hay un problema con mi carro. =   I arrived late because there is a problem with my car.
HOW MUCH/MANY? = ¿CUÁNTO/ CUÁNTA?   ¿Cuánto tiempo más para terminarlo? = How much time until it is finished?   ¿Cuántos años tiene _____? = How old is _____?

32 = TREINTA Y DOS

In each lesson there will be general information on the various Spanish-speaking countries and cultural considerations. It's important to realize not all Spanish-speakers come from México. All of these Hispanic countries have unique histories, traditions and cultures. These sections will highlight a few of the famous folks and traditional foods, although there are many more that can be found on the Internet. The sample information provided will serve as a way of comparing and contrasting the countries. Here is a brief description of what this information means in each lesson:

- La Moneda Nacional signifies the name of the currency. You will notice some of the countries use the U.S. dollar.

- Los Lugares Para Visitar means the places to visit. This will include some of the major cities and famous attractions associated with the country.

- La Población signifies population.

- La Gente Famosa = the famous people

- La Comida = the food

- El Ingreso Anual = the annual income per capita in terms of U.S. dollars also known as the Gross National Income (GNI). Some people are surprised when they compare what the average worker in the United States makes with the salary of workers in other countries. According to sources at the World Bank in 2007, the average worker in the United States made $46,040 while workers in some Latin American countries make less than $2,000 a year! The World Bank is the source for this type of information throughout this book. Population estimates are from the United Nations.

España = Spain

- **La Moneda Nacional: Euro**
- **Los Lugares Para Visitar:**
  - **Madrid**—*La capital, Museo Nacional del Prado (museum), Palacio Real (Royal Palace), Puerta del Sol (Center of the City)*
  - **Sevilla**—*Cathedral, Alcázar (Palace)*
  - **Barcelona**—*Las Ramblas (Street), La Sagrada Familia (Church), Plaza de Colón (Columbus), Barrio Gótico (Gothic neighborhood)*
  - **Toledo**—*Cathedral*
  - **Granada**—*Alhambra (Palace and Fortress)*
  - **San Sebastián**—*Basque region, La playa = the beach*
- **La Población: 44.2 million**
- **La Gente Famosa:**
  - **Rey Juan Carlos I** *(born 1938) Crowned as King of Spain in 1975*
  - **Reina Sofía** *(born 1938) Crowned as Queen of Spain in 1975*
  - **Penélope Cruz Sánchez** *(born 1974) Actress*
  - **(José) Antonio (Domínguez) Banderas** *(born 1960) Actor*
  - **Francisco Franco** *(1892–1975) Dictator 1939-1975*
  - **Francisco de Goya** *(1746–1828) Artist*
  - **Pablo Picasso** *(1881–1973) Artist*
  - **Antoni Gaudí** *(1852–1926) Architect (La Sagrada Familia Church in Barcelona)*
  - **Hernán Cortés** *(1485–1547) Conquistador of the Aztecs*
  - **Francisco Pizarro** *(c.1500) Conquistador of the Incas*
  - **Isabel de Castilla** *(1451–1504)* and **Ferdinand II de Aragón** *(1452–1516) Queen and King of Spain*
- **La Comida:**
  - **Paella** = *yellow saffron rice mixed with seafood, peas and/or chicken*
  - **Tortilla Española** = *an egg and potato omelet, made with two onions, four potatoes and six eggs (Recipe starting on page 182, Lesson 9)*
  - **Tapas** = *appetizers - The name tapa comes from "tapar" to cover.*
  - **Jamón Serrano** = *dry-cured thinly sliced ham*
  - **Vino** = *wine from La Rioja and other areas*
  - **Aceite de Oliva** = *olive oil - Spain produces approximately 36% and consumes 20% of the global supply.*
  - **Turrón** = *almond marzipan bark candy*
- **El Ingreso Anual = Annual Income (GNI): $29,450 per year**

33 = TREINTA Y TRES

Read these three trivia statements about Spain. Two sentences are true and one is false. Guess which one is not true. The previous cultural section does not contain the answers, so check the Answer Key to find out why one of them is not culturally correct.

INTERESTING THINGS = COSAS INTERESANTES:

1. _____ Flamenco dancers usually use castanets and are accompanied by a guitarist.

2. _____ Picasso had a "Green Period" where he painted various subjects with shades of green paint.

3. _____ Construction on La Sagrada Familia Church in Barcelona began in 1882 and may finish around 2026. The word gaudy comes from the ornate, garish style of the church's designer, Antoni Gaudí.

FOOD = COMIDA:

1. _____ If you order a "Tortilla con queso" in Spain you would get something like a Quesadilla with a flour taco shell.

2. _____ Some Tapas are Calamares fritos (fried squid), Pulpo (Octopus), Olivas (Olives), Croquetas (potato rolls) and Chorizo sausage. Some bartenders cover or "tapar" your drink with a plate of tapas to keep the flies away from your beverage.

3. _____ Calamares en su tinta = Squid in its own ink can turn your mouth black as you eat it.

34 = TREINTA Y CUATRO

One of the great joys of studying Spanish is the discovery of the great diversity of the language. There are some differences and unique phrasing in each country, which adds to the variety of Spanish words. For example, carro is car in México; coche is car in Spain, but pig in Guatemala. A tortilla, which is a flour shell in México, is a potato omelet in Spain. Taco is a food in México. A taco is the heel of a shoe in Argentina and tacones are high heels. A taco in Chile is a traffic jam. In Costa Rica parents tell their children not to say "tacos" which means "bad words." This book does not contain any "tacos," so you will have to learn those on your own. Many people have already learned a few bad words in Spanish while working in kitchens, so we will concentrate on "clean" conversations.

Native speakers often identify a person's origin by listening to their accent or slang. We have the same concept in English. The English spoken in the United States, Australia and the United Kingdom is different but is still considered English. The same is true in the Spanish-speaking countries. Castilian Spanish from Spain tends to be the most formal and proper. In places bordering México, "Spanglish" words combining English and Spanish are used more frequently. "Spanglish" is also used in some restaurant environments. We will show some of the common vs. proper ways of saying each phrase in the upcoming chapters.

When you listen to a native speaker from Spain, they may use the "th" sound for "S" for example, "gracias" would sound like *(Grah-thee/ahs)*. As your Spanish improves, you may be able to determine which country someone is from just by listening to their accent.

When meeting people from different Spanish-speaking countries it may be fun to write down and practice their unique slang expressions. Just as in English, there are always different ways and styles of saying the same thing. The best way to learn Spanish is to memorize one way of saying a phrase and then add more ideas/concepts as your skill level advances. The phrases in this book will generally be understood in all of the Spanish-speaking countries and also in your favorite restaurants.

35 = TREINTA Y CINCO

Write the letter of the corresponding English phrase on the line next to the Spanish phrase.

1. _____ Más rápido.
2. _____ La sopa está fría, caliéntala.
3. _____ Hazlo de nuevo sin cebollas.
4. _____ Atrás.
5. _____ No está correcto.
6. _____ El plato está caliente.
7. _____ No hay cangrejo.
8. _____ Apúrate.
9. _____ Con permiso.
10. _____ ¿Cuánto tiempo más para el aperitivo?
11. _____ Necesito la ensalada para la mesa quince.
12. _____ Sin nueces, hay una alergia.
13. _____ ¿Recibiste la orden para la mesa diez y ocho?
14. _____ Pon la mayonesa aparte.
15. _____ Faltan las papas fritas.

A. *(ah)* Remake it without onions.
B. *(beh)* Behind.
C. *(seh)* Without nuts, there is an allergy.
D. *(deh)* The plate is hot.
E. *(eh)* I'm missing the fries.
F. *(ehf-feh)* Did you get the ticket for table eighteen?
G. *(heh)* This is wrong.
H. *(ah-cheh)* How much longer for the appetizer?
I. *(eeee)* Hurry.
J. *(hoh-tah)* I need the salad for table fifteen.
K. *(kah)* Put the mayonnaise on the side.
L. *(ehl-leh)* Faster.
M. *(ehm-meh)* Excuse me.
N. *(ehn-neh)* The soup is cold, warm it up.
Ñ. *(ehn-ñyeh)* There is no crab.

36 = TREINTA Y SEIS

Spanish is often referred to as a "Romance Language." All Latin-based languages like Italian, French and Portuguese are considered "Romance Languages." One possible reason for this is because all nouns have a gender. They are all either masculine or feminine.

The four ways of saying "the," invented just to confuse us

In Spanish the "el" before the noun makes the word masculine. For example, el libro means the book. In Spanish the "la" before the word makes the word feminine. For example, la casa means the house. If the noun is plural, then the article changes to "los" if it is masculine or "las" if it is feminine. For example, los libros means the books and las casas means the houses.

	SINGULAR	PLURAL
MALE	el	los
FEMALE	la	las

el mesero = the male server la mesera = the female server	los meseros = the servers (at least 1 male) las meseras = the servers (all females)
el gerente = the male manager la gerente = the female manager	los gerentes = the managers (at least 1 male) las gerentes = the managers (all females)

How do you know which one to use?

Normally if a noun ends in the letter o it's masculine, and if it ends in the letter a it's feminine. However, that is not always the case. For example, el día, el problema and la mano are just a few examples where there are exceptions to the rule.

- Masculine nouns frequently end in –o –os –l –ma
- Feminine nouns frequently end with –a –as –dad –tad –tud –ción –sión
- Nouns ending in –ista and –e, can use either el, la, los, or las depending on gender.

Now practice what you've learned. Fill in the blanks with either el, la, los, or las.

1. _____ apio   2. _____ hermana   3. _____ hermanos   4. _____ limón

5. _____ calabazas 6. _____ cuchillos 7. _____ cuenta   8. _____ uvas

9. _____ mitad   10. _____ cucharas 11. _____ tenedores 12. _____ atún

37 = TREINTA Y SIETE

Translate these phrases. Write the English for the first seven phrases and write the Spanish for the last eight phrases. This may be done as an exam or as homework for the next lesson. When finished check your answers in the Answer Key.

1. ¿Recibiste la orden para la mesa diez y ocho? _____

2. Atrás. _____

3. Pon la mayonesa aparte. _____

4. No hay cangrejo. _____

5. Con permiso. _____

6. Apúrate. _____

7. Hazlo de nuevo sin cebollas. _____

8. I need the salad for table 15. _____

9. The soup is cold, warm it up. _____

10. How much longer for the appetizer? _____

11. Without nuts, there is an allergy. _____

12. The plate is hot. _____

13. This is wrong. _____

14. I'm missing the fries. _____

15. Faster. _____

38 = TREINTA Y OCHO

Play the game of "Toma Todo". Each player chooses 10 flashcards he or she would like to practice. These may be from any of the words and phrases in Lessons 1 and 2. The first person to run out of flashcards loses the game. When one person says them in Spanish, the other player could try to say them in English without peeking at the back of the flashcard.

IF YOU ROLL A 1 - TOMA 1 = TAKE 1 You take one from the center and say it in Spanish.

IF YOU ROLL A 2 - TOMA 2 = TAKE 2 You take two from the center and say them in Spanish.

IF YOU ROLL A 3 - PON 1 = PUT 1 You put one in the center and say it in Spanish.

IF YOU ROLL A 4 - PON 2 = PUT 2 You put two in the center and say them in Spanish.

IF YOU ROLL A 5 - TODOS PONEN = EVERYONE PUTS ONE. EACH player has to put one in the center and say it in Spanish

IF YOU ROLL A 6 - *TOMA TODO* = TAKE EVERYTHING. ¡Jackpot! Take all the pieces from the center and as an extra bonus you don't have to say anything.

39 = TREINTA Y NUEVE

Cut the flashcards on the following page apart, or make your own. Keep the flashcards in a plastic bag, envelope, or in your wallet and practice as much as possible during the week. Place one phrase a day on your refrigerator, mirror, or computer and learn a few at a time. Strive to find at least five minutes each day to review them, especially if you are waiting for someone or arrive early somewhere. Save all the flashcards to use during the games later in the book.

The plate is hot.	Excuse me. Behind.	There is no crab.
Hurry. Faster.	This is wrong. Remake it without onions.	Put the mayonnaise on the side.
Without nuts, there is an allergy.	The soup is cold, warm it up.	I'm missing the fries.
How much longer for the appetizer?	Did you get the ticket for table 18?	I need the salad for table 15.

No hay cangrejo. (No Eye Kahn-greh-hoh.)	Con permiso. (Kohn Pehr-mee-soh.) Atrás. (Ah-trahs.)	El plato está caliente. (Ehl Plah-toh Ehs-tah Kah-lee/ehn-teh.)
Pon la mayonesa aparte. (PohN Lah Mah-yoh-neh-sah Ah-pahr-teh.)	No está correcto. (No Ehs-tah Koh-rrehk-toh.) Hazlo de nuevo sin cebollas. (Ahs-loh Deh Noo/eh-voh Seen Seh-boh-yahs.)	Apúrate. (Ah-POOH-rah-teh.) Más rápido. (Mahs RAH-pee-doh.)
Faltan las papas fritas. (Fahl-tahn Lahs Pah-pahs Free-tahs.)	La sopa está fría, caliéntala. (Lah Soh-pah Ehs-tah FREE-ah, Kah-lee/EHN-tah-lah.)	Sin nueces, hay una alergia. (Seen Noo/eh-sehs, Eye Oon-ah Ah-lehr-hee/ah.)
Necesito la ensalada para la mesa quince. (Neh-seh-see-toh Lah Ehn-sah-lah-dah Pah-rah Lah Meh-sah Keen-seh.)	¿Recibiste la orden para la mesa diez y ocho? (Reh-see-bees-teh Lah Ohr-dehn Pah-rah Lah Meh-sah Dee/eh-see/oh-cho?)	¿Cuánto tiempo más para el aperitivo? (Qwahn-toh Tee/ehm-poh Mahs Pah-rah Ehl Ah-peh-ree-tee-voh?)

CHAT WITH THE BUSERS

GOALS: In this lesson you will learn about these topics: a front of the house server communicating with a buser, gender differences, machismo, Hispanic families, supervising Latino employees, expressing likes and dislikes, describing your family, your job, your age, México, historical perspectives, resetting the dining room area, alphabet and a server requesting help from a buser.

40 = CUARENTA

Read these phrases and answers from Lessons 1 and 2. Change them to fit your own personal information. The pronunciation guide for these phrases is in the Glossary on pages 271-290.

1. ¿Cómo estás? Estoy ocupada y cansada. = I am very busy and tired.
   Estoy _____

2. ¿Cómo te llamas? Me llamo _____

3. ¿Cuál es tu apellido? Mi apellido es Pospishil. _____

4. ¿Recibiste la orden con las papas fritas? Sí, recibí la orden. También tiene_____

5. ¿Cuánto tiempo más para el aperitivo? Viene en _____

41 = CUARENTA Y UNO

Guess the English translation of these family members to fill in the blanks. For more family words see Extra Vocabulary-Lesson 3 on page 211.

1. mamá/madre= _____
2. papá/padre =_____
3. hijo = _____
   (mi-jo is slang for mi hijo and means sweetie/darling)
4. hija =_____
   (mi-ja is slang for mi hija and means sweetie/darling)
5. esposo = _____
6. esposa = _____ (The plural "esposas" means handcuffs)

42 = CUARENTA Y DOS

The accents and gender of a word do make a difference in Spanish. For example, el papá means dad. However, la papa means potato and el Papa means the pope. A crowd may chant, "¡Viva El Papa!" This means long live the Pope. If they chanted, "¡Viva la papa!" this would mean long live the potato. The expression "ni papa" means you don't know any Spanish—not even the word potato. Luckily you will now know papa is potato in Latin America and patata is potato in Spain. If someone asks if you speak Spanish, answer with "ni papa" and you might get a big smile.

43 = CUARENTA Y TRES

Have one person say the lines for Diego Rivera and the other person say the lines for Frida Kahlo. Then switch roles. If you have a group, have two people present this as a skit.

Diego Rivera: Hola, Frida.

Frida Kahlo: Hola Diego, ¿Cómo estás?

Diego Rivera: Estoy mal. La comida del almuerzo está fría.

Frida Kahlo: Caliéntala.

Diego Rivera: Falta la carne y no hay pescado.

Frida Kahlo: Ándale. Entonces, vete a pescar.

Diego Rivera: Ay, Ay, Ay, no quiero. ¿Cuánto tiempo más para la cena?

Frida Kahlo: Por lo menos tres horas. Hasta luego, voy a pintar.

Diego Rivera: No entiendes. Tengo hambre y sed.

Frida Kahlo: Yo voy a pintar. Si quieres comer, vete a tu restaurante favorito.

New words = Palabras nuevas:

Entonces, vete a pescar. = Then, go fishing.

pintar = to paint

por lo menos = at least

Tengo hambre y sed. = I am hungry and thirsty.

44 = CUARENTA Y CUATRO

These five phases will help a server communicate with a buser. Read the statements out loud and then play charades. By choosing any phrase in the book to act out. The rest of the students can guess the phrases in Spanish. When you begin to try out your Spanish skills, sometimes you will get yourself into confusing situations. When speaking with a Spanish-speaking employee use what you already know and try out your detective skills to guess the rest. Relax and have fun because many Hispanics are honored that you are trying to learn their language and relieved that they aren't relying on their own English skills.

1. Table 13 needs service. =
   La mesa 13 necesita servicio.
   (Lah Meh-sah Treh-seh Neh-seh-see-tah Sehr-vee-see/oh.)

2. Will you clean table seven for me? =
   ¿Puedes limpiarme la mesa siete?
   (Pweh-dehs Leem-pee/ahr-meh Lah Meh-sah See/eh-teh?)

3. Clear the big plates. =
   Quita los platos grandes.
   (Kee-tah Lohs Plah-tohs Grahn-dehs.)

4. Put this in a "to-go" box. =
   Ponlo en una caja para llevar.
   (PohN-loh Ehn Oon-nah Cah-hah Pah-rah Yeh-vahr.)

5. Follow me with this tray. =
   Sígueme con esta bandeja.
   (See-geh-meh Kohn Ehs-tah Bahn-deh-hah.)
   Note: you could add; Walking the entrée to table 12. =
   Caminando el plato principal de la mesa 12.
   (Cah-mee-nahn-doh Ehl Plah-toh Preen-see-pahl Deh Lah Meh-sah Doh-seh.)

45 = CUARENTA Y CINCO

In many Hispanic countries, family is very important. Asking and taking interest in the Hispanic employee's family is a great way to build rapport. Latin America is still a machismo society, meaning males have a lot of influence in the family. This, however, is slowly changing in the younger generations. It is still very common to work together toward the good of the entire extended family and not emphasize individual goals. In the kitchen, Latinos are usually great team members and may even overly agree with their supervisor.

Historically in Latin America, respect for the boss is a given. The manager makes the decisions and the workers carry out the orders. Workers don't want to look bad in front of their coworkers, so they try to avoid conflict. Be aware that shyness and lack of eye contact are signs of respect, not disrespect. Sometimes an employee would rather keep his or her job than report an accident or a mistake. As a solution, managers may want to ask for feedback privately instead of bringing up problems in front of the group. Characteristics of self-sufficiency, competitiveness and independence at college age are all more common in the United States. However, the workplace in Latin America is changing to be more competitive in a global economy, and risk taking, questioning of authority and adherence to deadlines are on the rise. There are always exceptions to the rule. Some Hispanic employees—especially those who were raised in the United States—may demonstrate a blend of both cultures.

46 = CUARENTA Y SEIS

In workplaces today many employees and customers express their likes and dislikes. To say, "I like something" in Spanish, use "me gusta" or "me gustan." See more examples on the following page.

Play a game to practice with your group. The first person says, "Me gusta o Me gustan _____." The next person will add on by saying, "Me gusta _____ y a (Julia) te gusta _____." Continue to add on for the rest of the group. Lo siento = Sorry for the last person that has to repeat them for everybody.

To like = Gustar:

Read this chart and then answer the four questions below in your own opinion, using either me gusta or no me gusta.

I like the chocolate. = Me gusta el chocolate.	I don't like the chocolate. = No me gusta el chocolate.
I like the chocolates. (more than one chocolate) = Me gustan los chocolates.	I don't like the chocolates. (more than one chocolate) = No me gustan los chocolates.
He/She/You (formal) likes the chocolate. = Le gusta el chocolate.	Do you like chocolate?= ¿Te gusta el chocolate?

1. ¿Te gusta la comida aquí? = the food here_____
2. ¿Te gusta el café con leche? = coffee with milk _____
3. ¿Te gusta tu trabajo? = job _____
4. ¿Te gustan los libros? = books (use gustan)_____
   _____

Next, ask a partner the same four questions. They will answer in Spanish with either Me gusta = I like or No me gusta = I don't like. Write your partner's answer on the following lines.

1. ¿Te gusta la comida aquí? _____
2. ¿Te gusta el café con leche? _____
3. ¿Te gusta tu trabajo? _____
4. ¿Te gustan los libros? _____

For more practice with Gustar and Indirect/Direct Object pronouns there are some exercises at the end of the book in Extra Grammar-Lesson 3. If these grammar concepts are too confusing, concentrate on the flashcards and phrases from these lessons and just keep practicing. Conversing with native speakers is the best way to build up your skills.

47 = CUARENTA Y SIETE

Read these phrases out loud using the pronunciation column on the right. Leave this chart blank, the following pages will have spaces for you to fill in your own information.

ENGLISH:	SPANISH:	PRONUNCIATION GUIDE:
My name is _____.	Me llamo _____.	*Meh Yah-moh _____.*
His/Her name is _____.	Se llama _____.	*Seh Yah-mah _____.*
I live in Omaha.	Yo vivo en Omaha.	*Yo Vee-voh Ehn Oh-mah-hah.*
She lives in _____.	Ella vive en _____.	*Eh-yah Vee-veh Ehn _____.*
He lives in _____.	Él vive en _____.	*L Vee-veh Ehn _____.*
I work in _____.	Yo trabajo en _____.	*Yo Trah-bah-hoh Ehn _____.*
She works in _____.	Ella trabaja en _____.	*Eh-Yah Trah-bah-hah Ehn _____.*
He works in _____.	Él trabaja en _____.	*L Trah-bah-hah Ehn _____.*
He/She doesn't work, but goes to school.	No trabaja, pero va a la escuela.	*No Trah-bah-hah Pehr-oh Vah Ah Lah Ehs-qweh-lah*
I am _____ years old.	Yo tengo _____ años.	*Yo Tehn-goh _____ Ah-ñyohs.*
She is _____ years old.	Ella tiene _____ años.	*Eh-yah Tee/eh-neh _____ Ah-ñyohs*
He is _____ years old.	Él tiene _____ años.	*L Tee/eh-neh _____ Ah-ñyohs.*
I like _____.	Me gusta _____.	*Meh Goose-tah _____.*
He/She likes _____.	Le gusta _____.	*Leh- Goose-tah _____.*

THE FAMILY PROJECT = EL PROYECTO DE LA FAMILIA:

Create your own family project. To begin, read these two sample descriptions. If you have a group, have each person read one sentence out loud.

- Me llamo Julia. Yo vivo en Omaha. Yo trabajo en la universidad y en mi casa. Yo tengo 38 años. Tengo dos hijos. Me gusta viajar y hablar por teléfono.

- Mi hermana se llama Carrie. Ella vive en San Francisco. Ella trabaja con música. Ella tiene 36 años. Le gustan los gatos.

Now, fill in these blanks for yourself and four of your family members or friends, even including your pets. You can use the chart on page 51 and the extra vocabulary from pages 211 through 213 to help you. For the next meeting, you will tell the group in Spanish about your "family." Bring in family pictures or create a computer presentation. If you would rather tell about a famous family like the Kennedys or the Brady Bunch, bring in a picture of them instead. Practice during the week by sharing this with your own family.

Me llamo _____. Yo vivo en _____.
                   name   city

Yo trabajo en _____.
              workplace

Yo tengo _____ años. Me gusta _____.
         #   something you like

~~~~~~

Mi _____ se llama _____. Vive en _____.
  family member/friend   name   city

Trabaja en _____.
          workplace

Tiene _____ años. Le gusta _____
       #   something he/she likes

Mi _____ se llama _____. Vive en _____.
_{family member/friend}   _{name}   _{city}

Trabaja en _____.
_{workplace}

Tiene _____ años. Le gusta _____
_#   _{something he/she likes}

~~~~~~~~~~~~~~~~~~~~~~~~~~~~~~~~~~~~~~

Mi _____ se llama _____. Vive en _____.
_{family member/friend}   _{name}   _{city}

Trabaja en _____.
_{workplace}

Tiene _____ años. Le gusta _____
_#   _{something he/she likes}

~~~~~~~~~~~~~~~~~~~~~~~~~~~~~~~~~~~~~~

Mi _____ se llama _____. Vive en _____.
_{family member/friend}   _{name}   _{city}

Trabaja en _____.
_{workplace}

Tiene _____ años. Le gusta _____
_#   _{something he/she likes}

48 = CUARENTA Y OCHO
México—Estados Unidos Mexicanos

- La Moneda Nacional: **Mexican Peso**

- Los Lugares Para Visitar:
  - ★ **México City D.F. (Distrito Federal)** *La capital*
    - Population of Mexico City is 9 million
    - Zócalo-town center with Catedral Nacional
    - Ruinas del Templo Mayor = Aztec ruins
    - Museo Nacional de Antropología-Piedra del Sol = Aztec Calendar
    - Teotihuacan = pyramids of the Sun and Moon
  - ★ **Alcapulco/ Cancún** *La Playa = the beach, Chichén Itza Mayan ruins*
  - ★ **Oaxaca** *Chocolate and Mole Monte Albán, Mitla Zapotec ruins*
  - ★ **Guanajuato** *Silver, Museo Casa Diego Rivera, Museo de las Momias*

- La Población: **106.5 million**

- La Gente Famosa:
  - ★ **Diego Rivera** *(1886–1957) Artist*
  - ★ **Frida Kahlo** *(1907–1954) Artist*
  - ★ **Octavio Paz** *(1914–1998) Nobel Prize for Literature 1990*
  - ★ **Sor Juana Inés de la Cruz** *(c. 1650) Famous writer*
  - ★ **Francisco "Pancho" Villa** *(1878–1923) Revolutionary*
  - ★ **Emiliano Zapata** *(1879–1919) Revolutionary*
  - ★ **Moctezuma** *(c. 1500) Last Inca Ruler*
  - ★ **La Malinche/Doña Mariana** *(c.1500) Woman translator for Cortés*

- La Comida:
  - ★ **Tacos** = *soft corn tortilla filled with meat or seafood*
  - ★ **Frijoles** = *beans*
  - ★ **Tortillas** = *flat, round, thin, unleavened bread made of corn or flour, recipe in Lesson 9*
  - ★ **Mole Poblano** = *a brown sauce made with ground nuts or seeds, Mexican chocolate, dried chilies, garlic, onions, and spices*
  - ★ **Enchiladas** = *tortillas rolled with meat inside and baked while covered in sauce. Recipe on page 182.*
  - ★ **Chapulines** = *roasted crickets*
  - ★ **Salsas, Guacamole** = *avocado smashed with chile and spices*
  - ★ **Tequila** = *alcoholic drink made from the Maguey (Agave) plant*

- El Ingreso Anual = Annual Income (GNI): **$8,340 per year**

49 = CUARENTA Y NUEVE

Read these three trivia statements about México. Two sentences are true and one is false. Guess which one is not true. The previous cultural section does not contain the answers, so check the Answer Key to find out why one of them is not culturally correct.

INTERESTING THINGS = COSAS INTERESANTES:

1. _____ The National Cathedral in México City was built on top of Aztec ruins.

2. _____ Frida Kahlo was married to Diego Rivera and they lived in La Casa Azul = The Blue House in México City.

3. _____ The Aztecs had a dream that they should build México City on the spot where they found an eagle holding a cactus in its mouth.

FOOD = COMIDA:

1. _____ Mole sauce can be verde (green), amarillo (yellow), negro (black), coloradito/rojo (red) and is served over chicken.

2. _____ You can shop at some stores in México and pay with Chocolate (Cacao) beans.

3. _____ Tequila was originally made near the town of Tequila, México, in the state of Jalisco.

50 = CINCUENTA

Family rapport is highly valued in the Hispanic culture. Here are some questions that will help you get to know your employees. Practice these with a partner and then try them out with co-workers or any Spanish speaking friends.

Use the chart on p. 51 to help you answer the questions. The English translations for these sentences are in the Answer Key. Answers will vary.

1. ¿Tienes familia aquí? Sí, tengo familia aquí.
   No, no tengo familia aquí.

2. ¿Cuántas personas hay en tu familia?
   Hay _____ personas en mi familia.

3. ¿Cómo se llaman tus hijos? Mis hijos se llaman_____.

4. ¿Cuántos años tienen tus hijos? Mis hijos tienen _____ años.

5. ¿Cómo está la familia? Mi familia está_____.

6. ¿Qué te gusta hacer? Me gusta _____.

7. ¿Dónde vives? Vivo en _____.

8. ¿De dónde eres? Soy de _____.

9. ¿Cuánto tiempo has estado aquí?
   He estado aquí por _____ años.

10. ¿Te gusta tu trabajo? Sí, me gusta mi trabajo.
    No, no me gusta mi trabajo.

51 = CINCUENTA Y UNO

Practice these three Spanish phrases that will help a server tell a buser to reset the dining room area and prepare the tables for customers. In the third phrase substitute the Extra vocabulary from p. 211 for the two chairs that are missing. Example: Two forks are missing.

1. Fold the napkins. Roll the silverware. =
   Dobla las servilletas. Envuelve los cubiertos.
   (Doh-blah Lahs Sehr-vee-yeh-tahs.) (Ehn-vwehl-veh Lohs Koo-bee/ehr-tohs.)

2. Watch me. Set the table like this. =
   Mírame. Pon la mesa así.
   (MEE-rah-meh.) (PohN Lah Meh-sah Ah-SEE)

3. Two chairs are missing. =
   Faltan dos sillas.
   (Fahl-tahn Dohs See-yahs.)

52 = CINCUENTA Y DOS

Circle the English choice that matches the Spanish phrase.

1. **Pon la mesa así.**
   a. Put the table over there.
   b. The table has bread.
   c. The table needs claning.
   d. Set the table like this.

3. **Mírame.**
   a. Watch me.
   b. María likes me.
   c. Marry me.
   d. The mirror needs cleaning.

2. **Faltan dos sillas.**
   a. It is your fault, see ya.
   b. We are missing two servers.
   c. Two chairs are missing.
   d. Two seats are broken.

4. **Envuelve los cubiertos.**
   a. Involve the customers.
   b. Roll the curtains.
   c. Roll the silverware.
   d. Wrap up the crablegs.

53 = CINCUENTA Y TRES

Read or sing el alfabeto = the alphabet out loud using the following pronunciation guide to help you. Note: The letters CH, LL, RR used to be considered as separate letters in the Spanish alphabet, until the Real Academia Española eliminated them in the 1990's.

THE ALPHABET = EL ALFABETO:

A	*ah*	Ñ	*ehn-ñyeh*
B	*beh*	O	*oh*
C	*seh*	P	*peh*
D	*deh*	Q	*koo*
E	*eh*	R	*air-reh*
F	*ehf-feh*	S	*ehs-seh*
G	*heh*	T	*teh*
H	*ah-cheh*	U	*oo*
I	*eee* OR *(eee Latina)* *(Latina literally means the Latin Eee)*	V	*veh* OR *(oo-veh)*
J	*hoh-tah*	W	*doh-bleh-veh* OR *(doh-bleh-oo)* *(In Spain = oo-veh doh-bleh)*
K	*kah*	X	*eh-kees*
L	*ehl-leh*	Y	*yeh* OR *(ee-gree-eh-gah)* *(Griega literally means the Greek Eee)*
M	*ehm-meh*	Z	*seh-tah*
N	*ehn-neh*		

The Piñata Game = El juego de la piñata:

Here are two games to practice with the alphabet. With a partner, spell each other's Spanish names or middle names or favorite Spanish word. Ask your partner, "¿Cómo se escribe esto? = How do you spell that?" One person spells and the partner writes down the letters, until they guess the word.

Play a game called Piñata. This game is like hangman. Each person thinks of a Spanish phrase from Lessons 1–3 and writes down the exact number of lines to correspond to each letter in the phrase. The difference is you start with a 7-point star piñata and fill in one of each of the triangles for each wrong guess. The first person to fill their piñata loses the game. Latin Americans have been using candies and small toys to fill up piñatas for many years. Piñatas may have originated in Europe with a painted clay pot filled with candies and coins. A star-shaped piñata probably represented the Star of Bethlehem at Christmas time and is still used in the December Posadas celebrations. Now there are many designs from animals to cartoon characters. Find Web sites showing different styles of piñatas. To make your own piñata, see directions on the internet. In Cuba they attach strings to the piñata and instead of using a bat, everyone grabs a string and pulls the piñata apart.

54 = CINCUENTA Y CUATRO

¡AY AY AY! = Uh oh! Is their coffee cup empty over there? Does your ice need a refill? Are you looking for the manager? Need someone to watch your station? Read these four phrases that servers may want to use to request help from a buser.

1. Table 26 needs decaffeinated coffee. Also, take bread to them. =
   La mesa 26 necesita café descafeinado. También, llévales pan.
   (Lah Meh-sah Veh/een-teh-ee-seh/ace Neh-seh-see-tah Cah-feh Dehs-cah-feh/ee-nah-doh.) (Tahm-bee/ehn Yeh-vah-lehs Pahn.)

2. Bring me more ice. =
   Traeme más hielo.
   (Trah/eh-meh Mahs Ee/eh-loh.)

3. Have you seen the manager? =
   ¿Has visto al gerente?
   (Ahs Vees-toh Ahl Heh-rehn-teh?)

4. You're in charge of my area. I am going to the bathroom. =
   Allí te encargo mi área. Voy al baño.
   (Ah-YEE Teh Ehn-kahr-goh Mee AH-ree-ah.) (Voy Ahl Bah-ñyoh.)

55 = CINCUENTA Y CINCO

Write the letter of the corresponding English phrase on the line next to the Spanish phrase.

1. _____ Traeme más hielo.
2. _____ ¿Puedes limpiarme la mesa seis?
3. _____ Allí te encargo mi área.
4. _____ ¿Has visto al gerente?
5. _____ La mesa 26 necesita pan. Llévales pan a ellos.
6. _____ Sígueme con esta bandeja.
7. _____ Voy al baño.

A. *(ah)* You're in charge of my area.
B. *(beh)* Have you seen the manager?
C. *(seh)* I am going to the bathroom.
D. *(deh)* Table 26 needs bread. Take bread to them.
E. *(eh)* Follow me with this tray.
F. *(ehf-feh)* Bring me more ice.
G. *(heh)* Will you clean table six for me?

56 = CINCUENTA Y SEIS

You are a server training a new buser how to reset the table at your restaurant. What would you say in Spanish? Hint: Fill in the squares of the puzzle with letters from one of the Spanish phrases in 51 = cincuenta y uno.

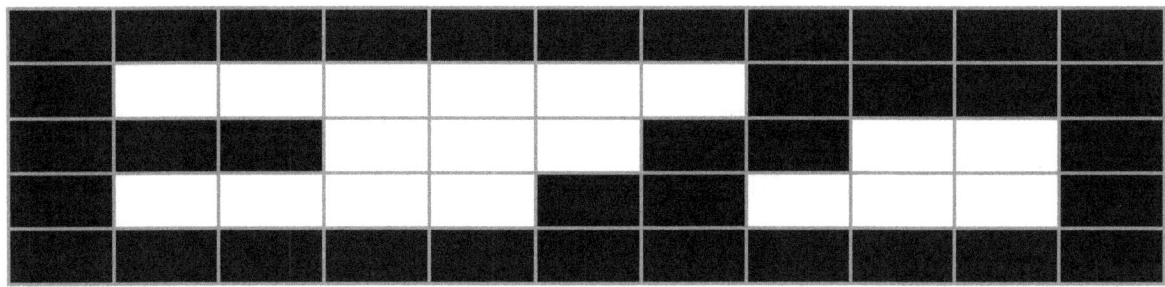

57 = CINCUENTA Y SIETE

Translate these phrases. Write the English for the first eight phrases and write the Spanish for the last nine phrases. This may be done as an exam or as homework for the next lesson. When finished check your answers in the Answer Key.

1. ¿Puedes limpiarme la mesa siete? _____
2. Mírame. _____
3. ¿Has visto al gerente? _____
4. La mesa 26 necesita café descafeinado. _____
5. Envuelve los cubiertos. _____
6. Pon la mesa así. _____
7. Ponlo en una caja para llevar. _____
8. También, llévales pan. _____
9. Bring me more ice. _____
10. Table 13 needs service. _____
11. Follow me with this tray. _____
12. You're in charge of my area. _____
13. Clear the big plates. _____
14. Two chairs are missing. _____
15. I am going to the bathroom. _____
16. Walking the entrée to table 12. _____
17. Fold the napkins. _____

58 = CINCUENTA Y OCHO

Cut apart the 20 flashcards on the following page to use for "Bingo" = "Lotería". Pick 16 flashcards and put them in any order to make four rows of 4. The "Bingo" Game Board is on the following page. Call out the phrases from 57 = cincuenta y siete in random order. Flip the card over when you hear the phrase called and keep going until you have four in a row turned over. Then yell, "¡LOTERÍA!" Note: The word lotería also means lottery in some countries. You may see people walking around the streets selling these tickets, hoping their numbers will be called on a certain day of the week. In some countries the unemployed, elderly and stay-at home moms get together in the neighborhood = barrio to play "Bingo" with their spare change.

To make this "Bingo" game even more challenging, add your other flashcards from Lessons 1 and 2. Then you would use the glossary to call out any phrases from Lessons 1–3 in any order. Another idea is to separate all of the flashcards with questions from Lessons 1–3. Use these question cards to interview Hispanic employees or Spanish-speaking friends during the week.

59 = CINCUENTA Y NUEVE

Cut the flashcards on page 65 or make your own. Keep the flashcards in a plastic bag, envelope, or in your wallet and practice as much as possible during the week. Place one phrase a day on your refrigerator, mirror, or computer and learn a few at a time. Strive to find at least five minutes each day to review them, especially if you are waiting for someone or arrive early somewhere. Save all the flashcards to use during the games later in the book.

"BINGO = ¡LOTERÍA!" BOARD

Table 13 needs service.	Will you clean table seven for me?	Clear the big plates.
Put this in a "to-go" box.	Walking the entrée to table 18. Follow me with this tray.	Fold the napkins. Roll the silverware.
Table 26 needs decaffeinated coffee. Also, take bread to them.	Two chairs are missing.	Watch me. Set the table like this.
Bring me more ice.	Have you seen the manager?	You're in charge of my area. I am going to the bathroom.

Quita los platos grandes. *(Kee-tah Lohs Plah-tohs Grahn-dehs.)*	¿Puedes limpiarme la mesa siete? *(Pweh-dehs Leem-pee/ahr-meh Lah Meh-sah See/eh-teh?)*	La mesa 13 necesita servicio. *(Lah Meh-sah Treh-seh Neh-seh-see-tah Sehr-vee-see/oh.)*
Dobla las servilletas. *(Doh-blah Lahs Sehr-vee-yeh-tahs.)* Envuelve los cubiertos. *(Ehn-vwehl-veh Lohs Koo-bee/ehr-tohs.)*	Sígueme con esta bandeja. *(See-geh-meh Kohn Ehs-tah Bahn-deh-hah.)*	Ponlo en una caja para llevar. *(PohN-loh Ehn Oon-nah Cah-hah Pah-rah Yeh-vahr.)*
Mírame. *(MEE-rah-meh.)* Pon la mesa así. *(PohN Lah Meh-sah Ah-SEE.)*	Faltan dos sillas. *(Fahl-tahn Dohs See-yahs.)*	La mesa 26 necesita café descafeinado. *(Lah Meh-sah Veh/een-teh-ee-seh/ace Neh-seh-see-tah Cah-feh Dehs-cah-feh/ee-nah-doh.)* También, llévales pan. *(Tahm-bee/ehn Yeh-vah-lehs Pahn.)*
Allí te encargo mi área. *(Ah-YEE Teh Ehn-kahr-goh Mee AH-ree-ah.)* Voy al baño. *(Voy Ahl Bahn-yoh)*	¿Has visto al gerente? *(Ahs Vees-toh Ahl Heh-rehn-teh?)*	Traeme más hielo. *(Trah/eh-meh Mahs Ee/eh-loh.)*

CHAT WITH THE CLEANING CREW

GOALS: In this lesson you will learn about these topics: more practice with numbers, communicating with the cleaning staff; the Mayan number system; cleaning the bathroom and/or kitchen areas; three very useful verbs: Tener, Querer and Ir; cleaning the floors; and locating Central American countries: Guatemala, El Salvador, Honduras and Nicaragua.

60 = SESENTA

Begin with the family presentations from Lesson 3. Using 47 = cuarenta y siete, tell a partner in Spanish about yourself and four family members or friends. Show your family photos as you talk about each person. Then, share three sentences about your family to the entire group. Another idea is to have each partner introduce the other person to the group by sharing three sentences they learned about the partner's family.

61 = SESENTA Y UNO

Legends and myths are an important part of Hispanic culture. One of the best preserved is the tale of La Llorona, or the crying one, told throughout the Americas. The details vary a bit, but the essence of the story remains consistent.

A young woman falls in love with a man who is not her husband. She can't run away with him because she already has children with her husband. In her despair, she throws her kids in the river and drowns them. Unfortunately, this strategy didn't work out that well. The man she is having an affair with decides she is crazy and runs away. In La Llorona's despair she is forced to wander by the river (or any other body of water—including a wash basin) to search for her missing children.

In her grief you might hear her crying out, "¿Dónde están mis hijos?" = Where are my kids? This cautionary tale works for a lot of different groups. Women are warned not to have affairs and to be good mothers. Young children are warned to avoid being alone at night, being near the water, and behaving badly. If they violate any of these rules, La Llorona could claim them. Sleep tight.

62 = SESENTA Y DOS

Ask these questions with a partner and write the partner's answers on the line provided. Spell your name using the alphabet on p. 58.

1. ¿Cómo te llamas? _____
2. ¿Cuál es tu apellido? _____
3. ¿Cuántas personas hay en tu familia? _____
4. Any other questions from Lessons 1–3. _____

63 = SESENTA Y TRES

Read aloud these three phrases that can help you communicate with the cleaning staff. For the location of the trash sacks, brainstorm possible answers in Spanish using the direction words below. See Page 214 for more uniform vocabulary. For example, another word for apron is delantal.

1. Put on the gloves and the apron. =
   Ponte los guantes y el mandil.
   (PohN-teh Lohs Gwahn-tehs Ee Ehl Mahn-deel.)

2. Take out (empty) the trash. =
   Saca la basura.
   (Sah-cah Lah Bah-soo-rah.)

3. Where are the trash bags? =
   ¿Dónde están las bolsas de basura?
   (DohN-deh Ehs-tahn Lahs Bohl-sahs Deh Bah-soo-rah?)

- 🌎 right = derecha
- 🌎 left = izquierda
- 🌎 here = aquí/acá
- 🌎 there = allá
- 🌎 over there = allí
- 🌎 near the = cerca de (more direction words on p. 154)

64 = SESENTA Y CUATRO

Circle the English choice that matches the Spanish phrase. Hint: A few of the phrases are from Lesson 3.

1. **¿Dónde están las bolsas de basura?**
    a. Where do I put the trash?
    b. Where are the trash cans?
    c. Where are the trash bags?
    d. Do you have any trash?

2. **Ponte los guantes.**
    a. Put on the gloves.
    b. Put on your uniform.
    c. Put the grapes on the salad.
    d. Put out the fire.

3. **Quitan los menús.**
    a. Take the item off the menu.
    b. Remove the big plates.
    c. Take menus to them.
    d. Remove the menus.

4. **Saca la basura.**
    a. Take out the bowls.
    b. Empty the trash.
    c. Sacks for trash are over there.
    d. Put the bones in the trash.

5. **La mesa 13 necesita servilletas.**
    a. Is there a reason to learn this?
    b. Table 13 needs service.
    c. Table 13 needs napkins.
    d. Table 13 needs smiles.

6. **Ponte el mandil.**
    a. Put on your apron.
    b. Put that on the mantel.
    c. Clean the fireplace.
    d. Put your apron on the hook.

7. **Faltan dos tazas de café.**
    a. Two chairs are missing.
    b. Two coffee mugs are missing.
    c. Two coffee pots are missing.
    d. We are missing the decaf coffee pot.

8. **Traeme una toalla.**
    a. Take out the towels.
    b. Take the towel over there.
    c. I need three towels.
    d. Bring me a towel.

65 = SESENTA Y CINCO

One of the great Pre-Columbian civilizations was the Mayan Empire. Math is one area in which they made many contributions. The Mayans were the first people to use the concept of zero. Zero was depicted in the Mayan writing system with a drawing of a seashell. Below are the Mayan numbers 1–19 which were originally formed by using sticks and stones.

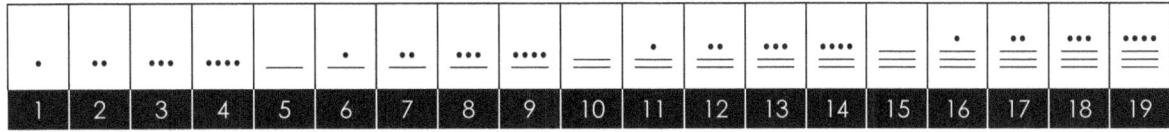

Now invent five of your own math problems using the Mayan numbers.

For example, _____ + ••• = •••

1. _____

2. _____

3. _____

4. _____

5. _____

66 = SESENTA Y SEIS

Use these five phrases to communicate with your cleaning staff about the bathroom or even kitchen areas. Read them out loud using the pronunciation guide. Which one would you use the most at your workplace? Try to memorize that one right now.

1. Clean the bathroom right away. =
   Limpia el baño ahora mismo.
   (Leem-pee/yah Ehl Bah-ñyoh Ah-oh-rah Mees-moh.)

2. Did you finish cleaning? =
   ¿Terminaste de limpiar?
   (Tehr-mee-nahs-teh Deh Leem-pee-ahr?)

3. Use the disinfectant. =
   Usa el desinfectante.
   (Oo-sah Ehl Dehs-een-fehk-tahn-teh.)

4. Fill up the soap dispenser. =
   Llena la jabonera.
   (Yeh-nah Lah Hah-boh-neh-rah.)

5. The bathroom needs toilet paper. =
   El baño necesita papel higiénico.
   (Ehl Bah-ñyoh Neh-seh-see-tah Pah-pehl Ee-hee/eh-nee-koh.)

Note: Papel higiénico is used in Latin America as the proper term for toilet paper, but papel del baño is more commonly heard in Mexico. Due to plumbing issues in some countries, you may see this sign; Toilet paper is thrown in the trash never in the toilet = El papel higiénico se tira en el cesto de basura, nunca en el inodoro. *(Ehl Pah-pehl Ee-hee/eh-nee-koh Seh Tee-rah Ehn Ehl Cehs-toh Deh Bah-soo-rah, Noon-kah Ehn Ehl Een-oh-dohr-oh.)*

67 = SESENTA Y SIETE

Write the letter of the corresponding English phrase on the line next to the Spanish phrase.

1. _____ Llena el jabón para las manos.

2. _____ ¿Terminaste de limpiar?

3. _____ ¿Dónde están las bolsas de basura?

4. _____ Limpia el baño ahora mismo.

5. _____ El baño necesita papel higiénico.

6. _____ Ponte los guantes para fregar.

7. _____ Saca las toallas sucias.

8. _____ Usa el desinfectante.

A. *(ah)*   The bathroom needs toilet paper.

B. *(beh)*   Use the disinfectant.

C. *(seh)*   Take out the dirty towels.

D. *(deh)*   Where are the trash bags?

E. *(eh)*   Clean the bathroom right away.

F. *(ehf-feh)*   Did you finish cleaning?

G. *(heh)*   Put on the gloves to scrub.

H. *(ah-cheh)*   Fill up the hand soap.

68 = SESENTA Y OCHO

If you have taken a Spanish class before, you have probably encountered verbs. Verbs are action words that are always changing—just like life. For example, in English we change "I have" to "she has." Let's look at three very useful verbs and how they change depending on the subject of the sentence. We will look at these seven subjects. For more information like the formal you = usted and vosotros = y'all *(only used in Spain)*, buy a grammar book.

SINGULAR SUBJECTS:	PLURAL SUBJECTS:
I = Yo You (informal) = Tú You (formal) = Usted He = Él She = Ella	We = Nosotros They = Ellos

Read the chart out loud and then do the activities to practice with the verb.

TO HAVE = TENER:

I have. = Yo tengo.	We have. = Nosotros tenemos.
You have. = Tú tienes. (Informal, singular)	
He has. = Él tiene. She has. = Ella tiene. Mary Ellen has. = María Elena tiene. You have. = Usted tiene. (formal, singular)	They have. = Ellos tienen. Anna and Francis have. = Ana y Francisco tienen. You have. = Ustedes tienen. (formal, plural)

Common phrases using the verb tener:

Here are some typical expressions with the verb tener. Choose two phrases that fit for you right now and share them with a partner.

- to be thirsty = tener sed
- to be hungry = tener hambre
- to be tired = tener sueño
- I am _____ years old. = Tengo _____ años.
- to be cold = tener frío
- to be hot = tener calor
- to be scared = tener miedo
- to have to = tener que
- to be in a hurry = tener prisa

Fill in the blank with the correct form of the verb tener using the previous boxes to help you. Find the answers and the English translations in the Answer Key.

1. Yo _____ 40 años.
2. ¿Tú _____ un trapo o unas toallas de papel?
3. Nosotros _____ mucho trabajo.
4. Araceli _____ hambre.
5. Yo _____ frío.
6. Ellos no _____ calor.
7. Ella _____ sueño.
8. Franco _____ prisa.
9. Melchor y Carolina no _____ sed.
10. Tú _____ que reciclar las botellas de plástico.

69 = SESENTA Y NUEVE

Read the chart out loud and then do the activities to practice with the verb. Remember that these verbs are in the present tense.

TO WANT = QUERER:

I want. = Yo quiero.	We want. = Nosotros queremos.
You want. = Tú quieres. (informal)	
He wants. = Él quiere. She wants. = Ella quiere. Eve wants. = Eva quiere. You want. Usted quiere (formal)	They want. = Ellos quieren. Rose and James want. = Rosa y Santiago quieren. You want. = Ustedes quieren. (formal, plural)

Fill in the blank with the correct form of the verb querer using the previous chart to help you. Find the answers and the English translations for these sentences in the Answer Key.

1. Yo _____ cocinar.

2. Ella _____ regar las plantas.

3. ¿Tú _____ probar un chile relleno?

4. Catalina _____ aprender un poco español.

5. Ellos _____ tener mejor servicio.

6. Nosotros no _____ fumar.

70 = SETENTA

Read the chart out loud and then do the activities to practice with the verb. This verb may also be used to talk about things that are going to happen in the future.

GOING TO = IR A:

I am going to = yo voy a	we are going to = nosotros vamos a
you are going to = tú vas a (informal)	
he is going to = él va a she is going to = ella va a Gilbert is going to = Gilberto va a you are going to = usted va a (formal, singular)	they are going to = ellos van a Ellen and John are going to = Elena y Juan van a you are going to = ustedes van a (formal, plural)

Fill in the blank with the correct form of the verb ir a using the previous chart to help you. Find the answers and the English translations for these sentences in the Answer Key.

1. Yo _____ a pulir las cucharas.

2. Eliana _____ a Guatemala.

3. Los clientes _____ a pagar sus cuentas.

4. Ella _____ a cambiar el foco.

5. ¿Tú _____ a trabajar mañana?

6. Nosotros _____ a tener la reunión hoy.

71 = SETENTA Y UNO

Read these four Spanish phrases out loud. These will help you communicate to cleaning staff about the floor.

1. Vacuum the dining room. =
   Aspira el comedor.
   (Ahs-pee-rah Ehl Koh-meh-dohr.)
   Note: Some people may say; "Pasa la aspiradora por el comedor."

2. Sweep outside. =
   Barre afuera.
   (Bah-rreh Ah-fweh-rah.)

3. Mop the kitchen floor. =
   Trapea el piso de la cocina.
   (Trah-peh-ah Ehl Pee-soh Deh Lah Koh-see-nah.)

4. Caution. Wet floor. =
   Cuidado. Piso mojado.
   (Qwee-dah-doh. Pee-soh Moh-hah-doh.)
   Note: "¡Cuidado!" can also mean, "Be careful! and/or "Watch out!")

72 = SETENTA Y DOS

Now you have an opportunity to practice. Find these Spanish phrases in the word search and then write the English phrases on the lines. The words in each of the phrases are joined together without spaces and there are no punctuation marks. The Spanish phrases are from 71 = setenta y uno. ¡Buena suerte! = Good luck!

LESSON 4: CHAT WITH THE CLEANING CREW

A	G	H	T	I	E	M	F	L	J	S	M	O	B	C
E	N	T	L	I	M	P	I	A	H	O	S	R	E	M
N	D	B	U	S	C	A	P	A	L	I	B	R	C	N
T	M	O	J	A	D	O	E	R	P	I	D	O	O	A
R	G	U	S	U	T	A	L	J	U	L	I	A	M	U
C	D	E	T	I	F	H	I	K	L	M	P	O	E	J
Z	A	T	R	E	S	C	M	A	S	U	E	S	D	Y
S	R	M	A	R	E	S	E	O	I	C	E	R	O	A
L	A	S	P	I	R	A	D	O	R	A	C	E	R	S
Z	N	E	E	P	R	E	D	E	S	C	U	A	T	O
M	I	S	A	R	L	A	H	O	R	A	T	M	A	R
L	C	E	N	O	C	U	I	D	A	D	O	N	B	O
U	O	S	L	B	R	A	D	L	E	R	R	A	B	M
E	C	S	A	R	E	U	F	A	V	M	E	S	T	A
E	L	E	N	A	A	N	D	J	A	D	E	N	T	E
G	E	A	Z	R	Q	O	O	J	R	G	C	U	M	P

WORD SEARCH = BUSCAPALABRAS

LIMPIA= _____

ASPIRA= _____

COMEDOR = _____

TRAPEA= _____

COCINA= _____

CUIDADO= _____

PISO= _____

MOJADO= _____

BARRE = _____

AFUERA = _____

73 = SETENTA Y TRES

Have one person say the lines for Rigoberta Menchú and the other person say the lines for Rubén Darío. Then switch roles. If you have a group, have two people present this as a skit.

Rubén Darío: Hola. Buenos días.
Rigoberta Menchú: Hola. El baño está muy sucio. Hay que limpiarlo.
Rubén Darío: Muy bien. Ponte los guantes y limpia el baño. Usa el desinfectante. El baño necesita papel higiénico.
Rigoberta Menchú: ¿Y el piso?
Rubén Darío: Trapea el piso del baño y aspira el comedor. También tienes que barrer afuera.
Rigoberta Menchú: Con permiso. Cuidado. El piso está mojado.
Rubén Darío: ¿Terminaste de limpiar?
Rigoberta Menchú: No, pero no soy Cenicienta. (= Cinderella) Me voy para mi casa. Renuncio a esta posición. (= I quit) Yo no quiero trabajar aquí. Adiós.
Rubén Darío: Ay, ay, ay. Adiós.

Work with a partner or individually to write your own conversation or role play with a typical work situation. Include questions, problems, solutions and/or phrases from Lessons 1–4. Present this new conversation in front of the group.

74 = SETENTA Y CUATRO

Families in Central America = América Central rely on each other even if they move far away from their country. You may see T-shirts, flags, photos, and medallions on display. Paychecks are wired back to Latin America to help with family expenses. Some Spanish-speakers enjoy talking about where they are from, and some Spanish learners don't quite remember the names and locations of the Central American countries on a map. (See the map on page 24.)

An easy way to know the locations is to remember the phrase, "My grandma happily eats nine chile peppers." In this mnemonic, the first letter of each word represents a Spanish-speaking country starting in México, and continuing from the North down to the South: M = México, G = Guatemala, H = Honduras, E = El Salvador, N = Nicaragua, C = Costa Rica, P = Panamá. "My brave grandma happily..." would add the English-speaking country of Belize, formally British Honduras.

75 = SETENTA Y CINCO

Read the information about these four Central American countries.

EL PAÍS	GUATEMALA	EL SALVADOR	HONDURAS	NICARAGUA
LA MONEDA NACIONAL	Quetzal	U.S. Dollar/Colón	Lempira	Córdoba
LOS LUGARES PARA VISITAR	**Guatemala City** • *La capital* **Antigua** • *Colonial City* • *Volcanoes to climb* **Tikal National Park** • *Mayan Ruins* **Lake Atitlán** • *Deepest lake in Central America*	**San Salvador** • *La capital* **Tazumal** • *Mayan Ruins* **Los Cobanos** • *Fishing* **Llopango market** • *Shopping*	**Tegucigalpa** • *La capital* **Copán Ruinas** • *Mayan Ruins* **Bay Islands** **San Pedro Sula** • *History Museum*	**Managua** • *La capital* **Granada and León** • *Colonial Cities* **Lake Nicaragua** • *Volcanoes* • *7 active, 50 total*
LA POBLACIÓN	13.4 million	6.9 million	7.1 million	5.6 million
LA GENTE FAMOSA	**Rigoberta Menchú Tum (Born 1959)** • *Human rights Activist* • *Nobel Prize Winner 1992* **Ricardo Arjona (Born 1964)** • *Singer*	**Óscar Romero (1917–1980)** • *Archbishop and murdered during Civil War* **Christy Turlington (Born 1969)** • *Half Salvadoran, Supermodel*	**Lempira (Died 1537)** • *War captain of the Lencas and fought against the Spanish* **Robert Sosa (Born 1930)** • *Poet* **Neida Sandoval (Born 1961)** *and* **Satcha Pretto (Born 1980)** • *Work with Univisión Television*	**Daniel Ortega (Born 1945)** • *President (1985–1990 & 2007)* **Rubén Darío (1867–1916)** • *Poet* **Giocanda Belli (Born 1948)** • *Novelist* • *Poet* **Violeta Chamorro (Born 1929)** • *First female president in Latin America (1990–1997)*
LA COMIDA	**Café** • *Coffee* **Pepián** • *Meat and veggie stew* **Licuado** • *Fruit juice*	**Pupusas** • *Thick, corn tortilla* **Sopa de Pata** • *Soup* **Yuca Frita** • *Fried yucca*	**Tostones** • *Twice fried plantains* **Anafres** • *Bean/cheese dip served with chips*	**Gallo Pinto** • *Red beans and rice* **Pan de Coco** • *Coconut bread* **Mondongo** • *Tripe / intestine stew*
EL INGRESO ANUAL = ANNUAL INCOME (GNI)	$2,400 per year	$2,850 per year	$1,600 per year	$980 per year

76 = SETENTA Y SEIS

Read these three trivia statements about Guatemala, El Salvador, Honduras and Nicaragua. Two sentences are true and one is false. Guess which one is not true. The previous cultural section does not contain the answers, so check the Answer Key to find out why one of them is not culturally correct.

INTERESTING THINGS = COSAS INTERESANTES:

1. _____ Lake Nicaragua is called "Mar Dulce" = Sweet Sea. It is a freshwater lake with no tuna fish or sharks.

2. _____ Rubén Darío's real name is Félix Rubén García Sarmiento. He is known as the father of the modernismo literary movement.

3. _____ Tikal, Guatemala was a large, ancient Mayan civilization city that included about 3,000 structures.

FOOD = COMIDA:

1. _____ Anafres bean dip from Honduras is served in a clay pot with hot coals underneath.

2. _____ If you ordered El Salvadorian Sopa de Pata, you may find yucca, plantains, cow's stomach and cow's feet along with some lemon juice and spices in your dish.

3. _____ Tamales in Nicaragua are called Nacatamales. Shredded pork, mashed potatoes and corn are wrapped in corn husks.

77 = SETENTA Y SIETE

Translate these phrases. Write the English for the first seven phrases and write the Spanish for the last six phrases. This may be done as an exam or as homework for the next lesson. When finished, check your answers in the Answer Key.

1. Saca la basura. _____

2. El baño necesita papel higiénico. _____
_____

3. Cuidado. _____

4. ¿Dónde están las bolsas de basura? _____
_____

5. Trapea el piso de la cocina. _____
_____

6. Limpia el baño ahora mismo. _____
_____

7. Usa el desinfectante. _____

8. Sweep outside. _____

9. Did you finish cleaning? _____

10. Vacuum the dining room. _____
_____

11. Fill up the soap dispenser. _____

12. Wet floor. _____

13. Put on the gloves. _____

78 = SETENTA Y OCHO

Play a game called, "¿Which one is the lie? = ¿Cuál es la mentira?" *(Qwahl Ehs Lah Mehn-tee-rah?)* Create three new sentences in Spanish using the vocabulary from this chapter. The trick is to write two true sentences and one false sentence. You may want to use the extra vocabulary from pages 213-219 or the previous chapters to help you form your sentences. For example:

1. Limpia el pescado. = Clean the fish.

2. Aspira la mantequilla. = Vacuum the butter.

3. La panadera necesita el extintor. = The baker needs the fire extinguisher.

In this case, the second sentence would be false. After you have written your sentences in both Spanish and English, then read ONLY the Spanish phrases aloud to your class or co-workers. See if they can guess which one is the lie = mentira. Choose any three from the verb list below to get started.

- Ponte…
- Saca…
- Trapea…
- Limpia…
- Usa…
- Barre…
- Aspira…
- Llena…
- El baño necesita…
- ¿Dónde está…?

79 = SETENTA Y NUEVE

Cut the flashcards on the following page apart, or make your own. Try playing the game called "Toma Todo". The directions are on page 42. Save all the flashcards to use during the games later in the book. The more you practice with the flashcards, the faster you will learn Spanish.

Put on the gloves and the apron.	Where are the trash bags?	Take out (empty) the trash.
Vacuum the dining room.	Mop the kitchen floor.	Caution. Wet floor.
Clean the bathroom right away.	Did you finish cleaning?	The bathroom needs toilet paper.
Fill up the soap dispenser.	Use the disinfectant.	Sweep outside.

Saca la basura. (Sah-cah Lah Bah-soo-rah.)	¿Dónde están las bolsas de basura? (DohN-deh Ehs-tahn Lahs Bohl-sahs Deh Bah-soo-rah?)	Ponte los guantes y el mandil. (PohN-teh Lohs Gwahn-tehs Ee Ehl Mahn-deel.)
Cuidado. (Qwee-dah-doh.) Piso mojado. (Pee-soh Moh-hah-doh.)	Trapea el piso de la cocina. (Trah-peh-ah Ehl Pee-soh Deh Lah Koh-see-nah.)	Aspira el comedor. (Ahs-pee-rah Ehl Koh-meh-dohr.)
El baño necesita papel higiénico. (Ehl Bah-ñyoh Neh-seh-see-tah Pah-pehl Ee-hee/eh-nee-koh.)	¿Terminaste de limpiar? (Tehr-mee-nahs-teh Deh Leem-pee-ahr?)	Limpia el baño ahora mismo. (Leem-pee/yah Ehl Bah-ñyoh Ah-oh-rah Mees-moh.)
Barre afuera. (Bah-rreh Ah-fweh-rah.)	Usa el desinfectante. (Oo-sah Ehl Dehs-een-fehk-tahn-teh.)	Llena la jabonera. (Yeh-nah Lah Hah-boh-neh-rah.)

LESSON 5 LECCIÓN

TIME FOR A CHAT WITH THE MANAGER

GOALS: In this lesson you will learn about these topics: telling time in Spanish, daily routine (reflexive verbs), manaña, tardiness, holidays and fiestas, months of the year/days of the week, scheduling phrases, Aztec Calendar, weather, manager phrases to communicates with employees, legends and myths, Costa Rica, Panamá, the verbs "to be," and Ser versus Estar.

80 = OCHENTA

Try to fill out this solicitud de empleo = job application in Spanish. Remember the English translation is found in the Answer Key.

Datos Personales:

_____
Nombre (Apellido, Nombre)

_____
Número de Teléfono

_____
Dirección/Domicilio

_____
Número de Seguro Social

_____
Intereses y Habilidades Especiales

Educación:

_____
Nombre de la Escuela   Fechas

¿Te graduaste? ☐ Sí ☐ No?

Último Trabajo:

_____
Nombre del Lugar   Puesto

Salario Final _____

Referencias:

_____
Nombre   Número de Teléfono

Años de Conocer _____

_____
Firma del Solicitante   Fecha

81 = OCHENTA Y UNO

What time is it? = ¿Qué hora es? *(Keh Oh-rah Ehs?)* Using the number chart from 26 = veintiséis in Lesson 2, you will be able to tell time in Spanish. In traditional Spanish customs, during the first half of every hour, you will add the minutes to 30. During the second half of every hour, you will subtract the minutes from the next hour.

For example:

2:00	Son las dos. This means it is 2 o'clock.
2:05	Son las dos y cinco. Y means "and," This literally means, "It is 2 o'clock and five minutes."
2:15	Son las dos y cuarto. Cuarto means quarter past. Cuatro means 4.
2:27	Son las dos y veinte y siete or veintisiete.
2:30	Son las dos y media. After 30 minutes past the hour, you subtract from the next hour.
2:35	Son las tres menos veinticinco. Menos means minus. This literally means, It's 3 minus 25. In other words it's 25 minutes until 3 o'clock.
2:50	Son las tres menos diez.

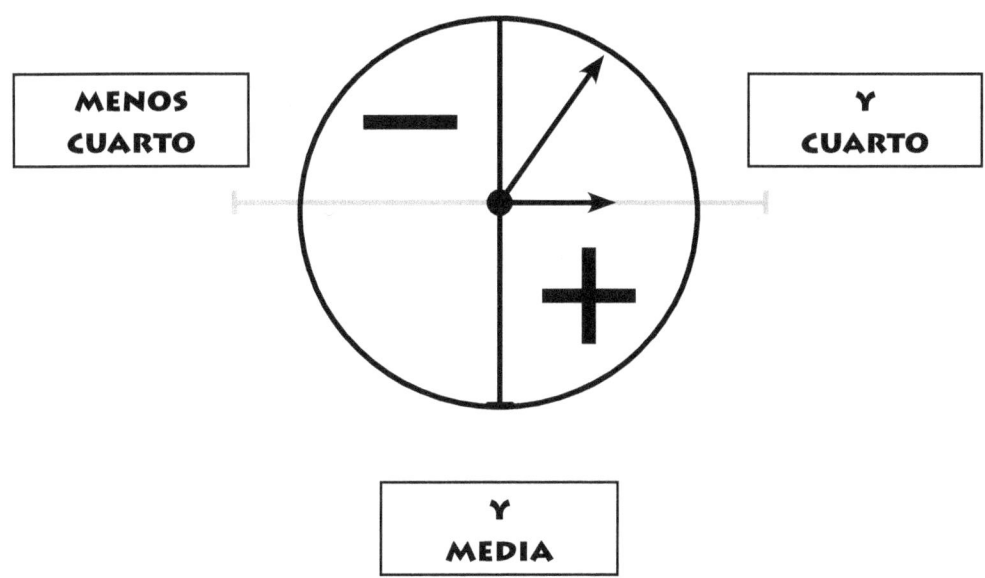

82 = OCHENTA Y DOS

What is your typical day like? Fill in the blanks with the correct time.
Note: a.m. = de la mañana and p.m. = de la tarde/de la noche.

1. _____ Es la una. (Use "es" because it's the first hour/singular.)
2. _____ Son las dos. (Use "son" for the rest of the hours because they are plural.) There will be more about this in 96 = noventa y seis.
3. _____ Son las tres.
4. _____ Son las cuatro.
5. _____ Son las cinco y cuatro.
6. _____ Son las seis y cuarto.
7. _____ Son las siete y media. *(Ee Meh-dee-ah)*
8. _____ Son las ocho y media.
9. _____ Son las nueve menos veinte.
10. _____ Son las diez menos cuarto. *(Qwahr-toh)*
11. _____ Son las once menos diez.
12. _____ Son las doce menos cinco.

Now fill in the blanks with your own information. Share the next six answers with a partner. For more information on reflexive verbs see Extra Grammar-Lesson 5.

13. Me levanto (I get up) a las _____
14. Yo como el desayuno (I eat breakfast) a las _____
15. Yo cocino el almuerzo (I cook lunch) a las _____
16. Trabajo (I work) a las _____
17. Yo como la cena (I eat dinner) a las _____
18. Me acuesto (I go to bed) a las _____

83 = OCHENTA Y TRES

"Mañana" is one of the first words you must be familiar with when traveling or working in Latin America. It means both "tomorrow" and "morning". If someone tells you a project will get done mañana, it may be finished sometime in the future but not necessarily tomorrow. Historically, in Latin America and other parts of our world, people aren't tied to the clock. Relationships, rather than punctuality, are more of a priority. In the United States, appointments and deadlines are scheduled in advance. Tardiness is considered impolite and you may even be fired. While the culture in the United States is influencing the global marketplace in this respect, some Hispanic companies are still on their traditional schedules. For example, a bank in Spain may be closed from noon until three for a siesta every afternoon.

This relaxed attitude about time is also shown in social situations. If you are given an invitation for a party at 7 p.m., the party may actually begin around 10 p.m. Many parties = fiestas are celebrated throughout the year. A way to build rapport is to ask Hispanic customers or employees how they are celebrating the upcoming holidays. Research more about Hispanic holidays on the Internet. Typical holidays and celebrations to be aware of include the following:

- January 6th marks the day of the Three Kings and many Latino children have candy or other gifts placed in their shoes while they sleep.

- Mardi Gras = Carnaval is a celebration around Ash Wednesday. In Puerto Rico and the Dominican Republic they make elaborate masks.

- Holy Week = Semana Santa. Parades and parties often are held on Fat Tuesday. In Spain, groups of friends coordinate costumes and dress up in themes. For example, they might all be witches, babies or soccer players.

- In México, November 1st–2nd is known as Day of the Dead = Día de los Muertos. This is essentially like Memorial Day. Families leave a trail of marigold flowers and build altars with sugar skulls to honor the deceased.

- Independence Days are some of the biggest celebrations in each country, with parades and festivals in the town square. For example, Independence Day in México is September 16th. (Many people confuse this with Cinco de Mayo.)

- Cinco de Mayo is a celebration of the victory of one Mexican/ French battle in 1862. Cinco de Mayo is actually a bigger celebration in the United States, demonstrating Mexican-American pride.

84 = OCHENTA Y CUATRO

Say the months aloud using the pronunciation guide to help you.

THE MONTHS OF THE YEAR = LOS MESES DEL AÑO:

1. January = enero *(Eh-neh-roh)*
2. February = febrero *(Feh-breh-roh)*
3. March = marzo *(Mahr-zoh)*
4. April = abril *(Ah-breel)*
5. May = mayo *(Mah-yoh)*
6. June = junio *(Who-nee/oh)*
7. July = julio *(Who-lee/oh)*
8. August = agosto *(Ah-gohs-toh)*
9. September = septiembre *(Sehp-tee/ehm-breh)*
10. October = octubre *(Oct-too-breh)*
11. November = noviembre *(Noh-vee/ehm-breh)*
12. December = diciembre *(Dee-see/ehm-breh/DCM-breh)*

To play this game, you will need a partner and two dice. The goal is to be the first person to roll each number from 2 through 12. 2 = febrero, 3 = marzo, 4 = abril, etc. Since you are unable to roll a 1, cross off #1 January. When you roll a 4, cross off #4 April = abril from the list and say, "abril." Now pass the dice to your partner. The next time you roll a 4, you will just say abril and pass the dice to your partner, but you won't be able to cross anything off. The winner is the first person to cross off all of the numbers from 2 through 12. Another way to play is to give each person a pair of dice and have the whole group do this at the same time.

85 = OCHENTA Y CINCO

Say the days of the week aloud using the pronunciation guide to help you. Try writing your weekly schedule in Spanish.

THE DAYS OF THE WEEK = LOS DÍAS DE LA SEMANA:

- Monday = lunes *(Loo-nehs)*
  (Many calendars in Latin America start with Monday)

- Tuesday = martes *(Mahr-tehs)*

- Wednesday = miércoles *(Mee-EHR-koh-lehs)*

- Thursday = jueves *(Who/eh-vehs)*

- Friday = viernes *(Vee/ehr-nehs)*

- Saturday = sábado *(SAH-bah-doh)*

- Sunday = domingo *(Doh-mean-goh)*

Circle the English choice that matches the Spanish phrase.

1. **enero**
   a. June
   b. March
   c. May
   d. January

2. **octubre**
   a. September
   b. August
   c. October
   d. July

3. **jueves**
   a. Thursday
   b. Monday
   c. Saturday
   d. Sunday

4. **miércoles**
   a. Tuesday
   b. Saturday
   c. Thursday
   d. Wednesday

86 = OCHENTA Y SEIS

Look outside and check the weather. Ask a partner what the weather is like and then listen to the answer. Use the pronunciation guide to help you.

THE WEATHER = EL CLIMA

What is the weather like today? = ¿Cómo está el clima hoy?
(Koh-moh Ehs-tah Ehl Clee-mah Oh/ee?)

- It's windy. = Hace viento.   (Ah-seh Vee/ehn-toh.)
- It's hot. = Hace calor.   (Ah-seh Kah-lore.)
- It's sunny. = Hace sol.   (Ah-seh Sohl.)
- It's cold. = Hace frío.   (Ah-seh FREE-oh.)
- Rain. = Llueve.   (You/eh-veh.)
- Snow. = Nieva.   (Nee/eh-vah.)
- It's cloudy. = Está nublado.   (Ehs-tah Noo-blah-doh.)

If the sun is out and you are hot, use this expression, "Yo tengo calor." Do not use, "Estoy caliente," because it would mean I am hot in a good-looking, sexual way. Along the same lines, if it's the middle of winter and you are cold, then say this phrase, "Yo tengo frío" and not "Estoy frío." Note: El tiempo means both "the time" and "the weather" depending on the context.

In pairs play the game of charades. Take turns having one partner act out a weather word or a month of the year, and the other person will guess in Spanish. In a group, divide into teams. One person from each team would come to the front of the room to act out the word, and the rest of the team shouts out the answers. The first team to correctly guess the answer would get a point for their team.

87 = OCHENTA Y SIETE

Calendar phrases may be used if a manager is asking an employee about scheduling. Ask a partner the questions and invent an answer in Spanish. Use the month list from page 92 and the days of the week list from page 93 to help you with the Spanish.

1. What days can you work? =
   ¿Cuáles días puedes trabajar?
   (Qwahl-ehs Dee-ahs Pweh-dehs Trah-bah-hahr?)

2. Your schedule is Thursday through Saturday from 3:00 to 10:00. =
   Tu horario es de jueves a sábado de 3:00 a 10:00.
   (Too Oh-rah-ree/oh Ehs Deh Who/eh-vehs Ah SAH-bah-doh Deh Trehs Ah Dee/ehs.)

3. What time did you come in? =
   ¿A qué hora entraste?
   (Ah Keh Oh-rah Ehn-trahs-teh?)

4. Can you come in early? Can you stay late? =
   ¿Puedes venir temprano? ¿Puedes quedarte tarde?
   (Pweh-dehs Veh-neer Tehm-prah-noh?)
   (Pweh-dehs Keh-dahr-teh Tahr-deh?)

5. Did you already clock in/clock out? =
   ¿Ya marcaste la entrada/la salida?
   (Yah Mahr-kahs-teh Lah Ehn-trah-dah/Lah Sah-lee-dah?)

Note: "Ponchar" is Spanglish for "punch in/clock in." The correct Spanish would be either "marcar," "fichar" "timbrar" or "registrar," but in restaurants many people use "ponchar." The phrase heard most often is, "Did you punch in?" = "Ya ponchaste la entrada?" *(Yah Pohn-chas-teh Lah Ehn-trah-dah?)* What other examples of "Spanglish" have you heard in the culinary world? Discuss these and make a list of some examples.

88 = OCHENTA Y OCHO

Answer the questions below with either Cierto or Falso. (True/False) Use the previous vocabulary to help you. Answers are on page 256.

- Yesterday = Ayer *(Ah-yehr)*
- Tomorrow/Morning = Mañana *(Mah-ñyah-nah)*
- Today = Hoy *(Oh/ee)*
- The next month = El próximo mes *(Ehl Prohx-see-moh Mehs)*
- The last week = La semana pasada *(Lah Seh-mahn-nah Pah-sah-dah)*

1. Hoy es martes. ¿Ayer fue viernes?(fue = was) _____
2. Hoy es domingo. ¿Ayer fue sábado? _____
3. Hoy es miércoles. ¿Mañana será jueves? (será = will be)_____
4. Son las siete. ¿A qué hora entraste, a las ocho? _____
5. Hoy es enero. ¿El próximo mes será octubre? _____

Paychecks = Cheques de pago:

A note about salary = el sueldo: in some companies, direct deposit is free and there is a fee for a paper paycheck, but some Spanish-speakers may still prefer the actual check. In your group, brainstorm what some of their reasons might be. Here are some phrases to help you to translate the direct deposit form and explain the benefits of using it if you know someone that might be interested.

- Do you have a checking or savings account ?= ¿Tiene una cuenta de cheques o ahorros?
- Do you want to save money with direct deposit? = ¿Quiere ahorrar dinero con depósito directo?
- name of the bank = nombre del banco
- name(s) on the account = nombre(s) en la cuenta.
- the 9 digit routing number = el número de ruta de 9 dígitos
- the account number = el número de cuenta
- the check number = el número de cheque

89 = OCHENTA Y NUEVE

These seven phrases are phrases that managers could use with their employees. Read them aloud.

1. Fill out these papers. =
   Llena estos papeles.
   (Yeh-nah Ehs-tohs Pah-peh-lehs.)

2. What is your phone number and address? =
   ¿Cuál es tu número de teléfono y dirección?
   (Qwahl Ehs Too NOO-meh-roh Deh Teh-LEH-foh-noh Ee Dee-rehk-see/ohn?)

3. Is everything O.K.? =
   ¿Está todo bien?
   (Ehs-tah Toh-doh Bee/ehn?)

4. Good job. =
   Buen trabajo.
   (Bwhen Trah-bah-hoh.)

5. The boss wants to talk to you. =
   El jefe quiere hablar contigo.
   (Ehl Heh-feh Kee/eh-reh Ah-blahr Kohn-Tee-goh.)

6. It's important to arrive on time. =
   Es importante llegar a tiempo.
   (Ehs Eem-pohr-tahn-teh Yeh-gahr Ah Tee/ehm-poh.)

7. Do you need anything else? Do you have questions? =
   ¿Necesitas algo más? ¿Tienes preguntas?
   (Neh-seh-see-tahs Ahl-goh Mahs?) (Tee/eh-nehs Preh-goon-tahs?)

90 = NOVENTA

Write the letter of the corresponding English phrase on the line next to the Spanish phrase.

1. _____ ¿Está todo bien?

2. _____ ¿A qué hora entraste?

3. _____ Llena estos papeles.

4. _____ Es importante llegar a tiempo.

5. _____ ¿Cuáles días puedes trabajar?

6. _____ Tu horario es de jueves a sábado de 3:00 a 10:00.

7. _____ El jefe quiere hablar contigo.

8. _____ ¿Cuál es tu número de teléfono?

9. _____ ¿Necesitas algo más?

10. _____ Buen trabajo.

11. _____ ¿Puedes venir temprano?

12. _____ ¿Ya marcaste la entrada?

A. *(ah)* Do you need anything else?

B. *(beh)* What days can you work?

C. *(seh)* What time did you come in?

D. *(deh)* Did you already clock in?

E. *(eh)* Your schedule is Thursday through Saturday from 3:00 to 10:00.

F. *(ehf-feh)* Is everything O.K.?

G. *(heh)* What is your phone number?

H. *(ah-cheh)* Good job.

I. *(eeee)* Fill out these papers.

J. *(hoh-tah)* Can you come in early?

K. *(kah)* It's important to arrive on time.

L. *(ehl-leh)* The boss wants to talk to you.

91 = NOVENTA Y UNO

Complete the crossword puzzle with words from the 12 Spanish phrases in 90 = noventa. There are no punctuation marks. Find the opposite translation. If the clue is in Spanish, then write the English phrase. If the clue is in English, then write the Spanish phrase. Check your answers in the Answer Key when you are finished. ¡Buena suerte!

HORIZONTAL
2 HORA
4 TODO
6 HORARIO
8 TEMPRANO
10 TRABAJO

VERTICAL
1 PAPERS
3 WHAT/WHICH
5 BOSS
7 PHONE
9 TO ARRIVE
11 EXIT
13 QUESTION

92 = NOVENTA Y DOS

Many Ancient Mesoamerican cultures created their own calendar and number systems. México is the home of two of the greatest Pre-Columbian empires, the Aztec and the Mayas. A great contribution of the Aztecs was the Aztec Calendar. On December 17, 1790, workers found a huge 26-ton stone buried faced down. When they turned it over, they discovered many hieroglyphs surrounding a mask of fire. The Aztecs didn't have an alphabet, but they communicated through these hieroglyphs. Historians discovered this Piedra del Sol = Sun Stone was used as an Aztec calendar.

The stone had the information to calculate a 365-day calendar year, which was helpful in agriculture and also a 260-day ritual cycle. Adding these two together created the 52-year century. Each of the 18 periods had 20 days represented by animals and other glyphs. For example, Day One was crocodile, Day Two was wind, Day Five was serpent, etc. The Sun Stone = La Piedra del Sol is on display at the Museo Nacional de Antropología in México City.

THE AZTEC CALENDAR / SUN STONE = PIEDRA DEL SOL, IS ON DISPLAY IN MEXICO CITY.

93 = NOVENTA Y TRES

Read the information about these final two Central American countries.

EL PAÍS	COSTA RICA	PANAMÁ
LA MONEDA NACIONAL	Colón	U.S. Dollar/Balboa
LOS LUGARES PARA VISITAR	**San José** • *La capital* • *Teatro Nacional* • *Gold museum)* **Arenal** • *Active Volcano/Hot Springs* **Poás/Iruazú** • *Volcanoes/Craters* **Manual Antonio National Park** **Monteverde Cloud Forest** **Tamarindo and Playa Langosta** • *Beaches*	**Panama City** • *La capital* • *Panama canal and the Miraflores locks* • *Casco Antiguo/Viejo is a World Heritage site* **San Blás-Islands** • *Home of the Kunas and molas* **Pearl Islands=Las Perlas** **Bocas del Toro** • *Rainforest and Beach* **Colón** • *Caribbean port* **Boquete** • *Volcán Barú - Chiriquí*
LA POBLACIÓN	4.5 million	3.3 million
LA GENTE FAMOSA	**Laura Chinchilla (Born 1959)** • *Elected President in 2010* **Óscar Arias (Born 1941)** • *Nobel Peace Prize Winner 1985* • *He helped to end Civil Wars in several Central American countries.* • *President (1986-1990) & (2006-2010)* **Pancha Carrasco (1826-1890)** • *First woman in the military*	**Manuel Noriega (Born 1934)** • *Dictator of Panamá (1983-1989)* • *In 1989 he began serving jail time in Florida for cocaine trafficking, racketeering, and money laundering.* **Rod Carew (Born 1945)** • *In baseball hall of fame* **Rubén Blades (Born 1948)** • *Singer, songwriter, actor* **Gloria Guardia (Born 1940)** • *Novelist, journalist*
LA COMIDA	**Gallo Pinto** • *Black beans and rice usually flavored with cilantro and served with Huevos revueltos = Scrambled eggs* **Flan de Coco** • *Coconut flan* **Café con leche** • *= Coffee with milk* **Fresco de frutas** • *Fruit salad*	**Tamales** • *Corn meal dough wrapped in banana leaves* **Patacones de plátano** • *Fried plantains* **Sancocho** • *Stew* **Ceviche** • *Lemon fish* **Empanandas** • *Pastry pockets with filling*
EL INGRESO ANUAL = ANNUAL INCOME (GNI)	$5,560 per year	$5,510 per year

94 = NOVENTA Y CUATRO

Read these three trivia statements about Costa Rica and Panamá. Two sentences are true and one is false. Guess which one is not true. The previous cultural section does not contain the answers, so check the Answer Key to find out why one of them is not culturally correct.

INTERESTING THINGS = COSAS INTERESANTES:

1. _____ In Costa Rica, "Pura Vida" (Pure Life) means great or cool.

2. _____ It takes 18 hours and only costs about $18 to go by bus from San José, Costa Rica, to Panamá City, Panamá.

3. _____ In order to see the red lava balls cascading down the active volcano Arenal, you should go during the day.

FOOD = COMIDA:

1. _____ Empanadas in Panamá may have meat, chicken, cheese, and even a raisin in there.

2. _____ The Ceviche fish dish is cooked in the oven for 3 hours.

3. _____ Fresco de Frutas fruit salad in Costa Rica may contain papaya, banana, and pineapple with strawberry syrup poured on top.

95 = NOVENTA Y CINCO

Have one person say the lines for employee Óscar Arias and the other person say the lines for Boss/Manager Laura Chinchilla. If you have a group, have two people present this as a skit.

Laura Chinchilla:	Buenas tardes Óscar. Quiero hablar contigo.
Óscar Arias:	Buenas tardes Jefe Laura. ¿Está todo bien?
Laura Chinchilla:	Sí, no hay problema. Aquí está tu evaluación. Buen trabajo. Llena estos papeles, por favor.
Óscar Arias:	¿Firmo aquí?
Laura Chinchilla:	Perfecto, firma allí. ¿Cuál es tu número de teléfono?
Óscar Arias:	Mi número de teléfono es (402) 555-6789.
Laura Chinchilla:	Bueno. ¿Para verificar, cuál es tu dirección?
Óscar Arias:	Mi dirección es Calle 13 Suroeste 4321. ¿Necesitas algo más, Gerente Laura?
Laura Chinchilla:	¿A qué hora entraste? ¿Ya marcaste la entrada?
Óscar Arias:	Por supuesto. Entré a las 12:15.
Laura Chinchilla:	Es importante llegar a tiempo. Tu horario es de martes a domingo de 12 a 7. ¿Puedes venir más temprano mañana?
Óscar Arias:	Voy a intentarlo. Quiero cambiar mi horario, porque no tengo carro.
Laura Chinchilla:	¿Cuáles días puedes trabajar?
Óscar Arias:	Puedo trabajar martes, jueves, viernes y domingo de 1 a 7 de la noche.
Laura Chinchilla:	Está bien. Buen trabajo. Si no tienes preguntas, puedes regresar a trabajar. Gracias. Voy a mi casa. ¡Hasta mañana!
Óscar Arias:	¡Hasta mañana!

New words = Palabras nuevas:

¿Firmo aquí? = Do I sign here?	Firma allí.= Sign there.
No tengo carro. = I don't have a car.	Por supuesto. = Of course.
Quiero cambiar. = I want to change.	Voy a intentarlo. = I will try.

96 = NOVENTA Y SEIS

One of the more confusing aspects of the language for new students is the fact that there are two verbs translated as "to be." The two verbs are ser and estar. They have very specific uses.

The verb estar is used to describe temporary things like weather, health and location. Estar is also used when saying "-ing" words. Examples: Estoy comiendo. = I am eating. ¿Estás trabajando? = Are you working? For most other "to be" phrases, you will use the verb ser. Ser is used to describe more permanent. Examples: She is tall. = Ella es alta. I am from Costa Rica = Soy de Costa Rica. These things won't usually change. As you keep practicing the use of ser or estar will become natural during your conversation. For present progressive (–ing) see Extra Grammar-Lesson 5.

To be = Ser or Estar:

Here are two examples of the difference in meaning between ser and estar:

Ser: Mi jefe es malo. = My boss is bad, as in a bad nature or character.

Estar: Mi jefe está malo. = My boss is feeling bad or sick.

Ser: Yo soy lista. = I am smart.

Estar: Yo estoy lista. = I am ready.

The following pages will help you to remember when to use each verb. Keep in mind that ser is more permanent and estar is more temporary.

START WITH CHOICE #1, SER: To help you remember when to use ser, memorize the acronym DOT COM, -the first letter of each of these six categories:

Date: Hoy es martes. = Today is Tuesday. No es el 17 de junio. = It is not June 17th. Es el 29 de noviembre. = It is the 29th of November.

Occupations: Él es un cocinero. = He is an cook.

Time: Es la una y media. = It is 1:30. No son las once y cuarto. = It is not 11:15.

Characteristics that are permanent:
La maestra es alta. = The female teacher is tall.
Yo soy una mujer. = I am a woman.

Origin/Nationality:
Chocolate es un producto de México. = Chocolate is a product from México.
Yo soy de los E.E.U.U. (Estados Unidos) de América. = I am from the United States of America.

Mine/Possession: La receta es de Diego. = The recipe is Doug's.
La merienda es de Rosita y Juanito. = The snack is Rosie and Johnny's.

TO BE (MORE PERMANENT) = SER:

I am. = Yo soy.	We are. = Nosotros somos.
You are. = Tú eres. (informal)	
He is. = Él es. She is. = Ella es. Adam is. = Adán es. You are. Usted es. (formal, singular)	They are. = Ellos son. Abraham and Nolan are. = Abrahán y Manolo son. You are. = Ustedes son. (formal, plural)

CHOICE #2, ESTAR: To help you remember when to use estar, memorize the acronym WELL,- the first letter of each of these four categories:

Weather: Está nublado. = It is cloudy.

Emotion or a change from previous condition:
El maestro está cansado. = The male teacher is tired.
La cantinera está despedida. = The female bartender is fired.

Locations: Tú estás en la clase de español. = You are in Spanish class.

Lifestyle/Health: Yo estoy enfermo. = I am sick. (male)
Yo estoy casada. = I am married. (female)

TO BE (CHANGING) = ESTAR:

I am. = Yo estoy.	We are. = Nosotros estamos.
You are. = Tú estás. (informal)	
He is. = Él está. She is. = Ella está. Michael is. = Miguel está. You are. = Usted está. (formal)	They are. = Ellos están. Cindy and Tom are. = Cintia y Tomás están. You are. = Ustedes están. (formal, plural)

Now it is time to practice the difference between ser and estar. Look carefully at the subject and meaning of each sentence and then decide if you will use ser and estar. Refer to the charts to help you. Check your answers in the Answer Key.

1. Nosotros _____ trabajando tiempo extra. (overtime)

2. Tú _____ enojado. (mad)

3. Nosotros _____ rubios. (blond)

4. La Llorona _____ una leyenda. (legend)

5. _____ las ocho y media.

6. Celeste y Mateo _____ bien.

97 = NOVENTA Y SIETE

Translate these phrases. Write the English for the first eight phrases and write the Spanish for the last seven phrases. This may be done as an exam or as homework for the next lesson.

1. Buen trabajo. _____

2. Tu horario es de jueves a sábado de 3:00 a 10:00. _____

3. Es importante llegar a tiempo. _____

4. Puedes quedarte tarde? _____

5. Llena estos papeles. _____

6. ¿Ya marcaste la salida?_____

7. ¿Cuál es tu número de teléfono? _____

8. ¿Tienes preguntas? _____

9. What days can you work? _____

10. The boss wants to talk to you. _____

11. What time did you come in? _____

12. Can you come in early? _____

13. Is everything O.K.? _____

14. Did you already clock in? _____

15. Do you need anything else? _____

98 = NOVENTA Y OCHO

Play either "Tic-Tac-Toe" or "Around the World" (directions below in 99 = noventa y nueve). To play the "Tic-Tac-Toe" = "Tres en Raya" game, you and your partner will only need to share one "Tic-Tac-Toe" board found in 18 = dieciocho-Lesson 1. One person will need five small squares with an X written on each square, and the other person will need five squares with an O written on each square. To make it easier to see, use two different colors of paper for the small squares.

Choose nine flashcards from 99 = noventa y nueve and put the flashcards Spanish side up on the "Tic-Tac-Toe" board. Player X will go first, choosing a square that will help them to get three in a row. Player X will read the Spanish for that square and say what it means in English in order to cover it up with a "Bingo" X piece. Then it is Player O's turn. Player O will read the Spanish for the square and say what it means in English. Play until someone gets three in row = "Tres en Raya" or "Tic-Tac-Toe". To make it more difficult, put the English side up and say the answer in Spanish. ¡Buena suerte! = Good luck!

99 = NOVENTA Y NUEVE

Cut the flashcards on the following page apart, or make your own. Try playing the game called "Around the World". The host/teacher will say the phrase in English using the flashcards from Lessons 1-5. One student will stand behind the chair of another student. These two students are competing to be the first person to correctly say the phrase in Spanish. The rest of the group will be listening and waiting for their turn. The winner is the first of the two students that is able to shout out the phrase, even if they have to look it up in their book. The rest of the group is silent. The winner now advances to the next student on the right and those two try to say the phrase in Spanish. Play continues all the way "Around the Room/World". The person that defeats the most opponents is declared the winner.

What days can you work?	Your schedule is Thursday through Saturday from 3:00 to 10:00.	What time did you come in?
Can you come in early? Can you stay late?	Did you already clock in/ clock out?	Fill out these papers.
What is your phone number and address?	Is everything O.K.?	Good job.
The boss wants to talk to you.	It's important to arrive on time.	Do you need anything else? Do you have questions?

¿A qué hora entraste? *(Ah Keh Oh-rah Ehn-trahs-teh?)*	Tu horario es de jueves a sábado de 3:00 a 10:00. *(Too Oh-rah-ree/oh Ehs Deh Who/eh-vehs Ah SAH-bah-doh Deh Trehs Ah Dee/ehs.)*	¿Cuáles días puedes trabajar? *(Qwahl-ehs Dee-ahs Pweh-dehs Trah-bah-hahr?)*
Llena estos papeles. *(Yeh-nah Ehs-tohs Pah-peh-lehs.)*	¿Ya marcaste la entrada/ la salida? *(Yah Mahr-kahs-teh Lah Ehn-trah-dah/ Lah Sah-lee-dah?)*	¿Puedes venir temprano? *(Pweh-dehs Veh-neer Tehm-prah-noh?)* ¿Puedes quedarte tarde? *(Pweh-dehs Keh-dahr-teh Tahr-deh?)*
Buen trabajo. *(Bwhen Trah-bah-hoh.)*	¿Está todo bien? *(Ehs-tah Toh-doh Bee/ehn?)*	¿Cuál es tu número de teléfono y dirección? *(Qwahl Ehs Too NOO-meh-roh Deh Teh-LEH-foh-noh Ee Dee-rehk-see/ohn?)*
¿Necesitas algo más? *(Neh-seh-see-tahs Ahl-goh Mahs?)* ¿Tienes preguntas? *(Tee/eh-nehs Preh-goon-tahs?)*	Es importante llegar a tiempo. *(Ehs Eem-pohr-tahn-teh Yeh-gahr Ah Tee/ehm-poh.)*	El jefe quiere hablar contigo. *(Ehl Heh-feh Kee/eh-reh Ah-blahr Kohn-Tee-goh.)*

LESSON 6 LECCIÓN

CHAT WITH THE LINE COOKS

GOALS: In this lesson you will learn about these: conquistadors, why Spanish is spoken throughout the Americas, back of the house kitchen phrases, communication styles, Colombia, Ecuador, Venezuela, cooking phrases for on the line and regular present tense –ar verb conjugation.

100 = CIEN

Use the Extra Vocabulary: Kitchen equipment and Extra Vocabulary: Utensils found in the back of this book to draw a map of your kitchen in Spanish. If you are not currently working in a restaurant then draw a map of your dream kitchen. Another idea is to place Spanish labels near 25 Kitchen appliances and utensils for all of the Back of the House staff to learn.

101 = CIENTO UNO

Spanish is spoken throughout South America. However, Portuguese is spoken in the country of Brazil. The Treaty of Tordesillas created on June 7, 1492, divided the newly discovered territory between Spain and Portugal. This treaty tried to squeeze all other European countries out of the new lands that were being discovered. Therefore, most of the Americas speak Spanish.

The Spanish spoken in the Americas most closely resembles the Spanish spoken in the south of Spain. This is where many of the sailors and conquistadors came from. Two famous conquistadores are Hernán Cortés, the conqueror of the Aztecs, and Francisco Pizarro, the conqueror of the Incas. There are still variations and slang words that differ in each region; for example, in Argentina, "yo me llamo" sounds like, "*Shoh Meh Shah-moh*" due to the close proximity of Portuguese spoken by neighboring Brazil. The Spanish in Argentina is also heavily influenced by the Italian immigrants that settled in Argentina.

102 = CIENTO DOS

Read the sample schedule, then answer the questions below. Note: This restaurant is closed on Sundays. Answers are on page 258.

	LUNES	MARTES	MIÉRCOLES	JUEVES	VIERNES	SÁBADO
JULIA	DÍA LIBRE	5-9	11-8	9-6	11-8	11-8
FRANCISCO	7-5	7-5	7-5	DÍA LIBRE	7-5	7-5
JUAN	3-9	9-3	DÍA LIBRE	3-9	3-9	3-9
ELENA	12-8	DÍA LIBRE	9-9	12-9	12-9	8-8

103 = CIENTO TRES

Decide if this translation is Cierto = True or Falso = False. If the answer is false, then write the correct answer on the line. Check your answers in the Answer Key. Hint: overtime/over 40 hours = horas extras and part-time = medio tiempo.

1. Elena tiene que trabajar el lunes. _____

2. Juan trabaja por veinte horas esta semana. _____

3. Juan puede cambiar con Julia el martes. _____

4. Francisco y Elena tienen horas extras. _____

5. Francisco trabaja muy tarde en la noche. _____

6. Julia trabaja medio tiempo. _____

104 = CIENTO CUATRO

Practice these Spanish phrases that deal with the kitchen/ back of the house. These will help communicate with Hispanic line cooks.

1. I need a new one, on the fly. =
   Necesito uno nuevo, al vuelo.
   (Neh-seh-see-toh Oo-no Noo/eh-voh, Ahl Vweh-loh.)

2. Have the chef taste it. =
   Deja que el chef lo pruebe.
   (Deh-hah Keh Ehl Chehf Loh Proo/eh-beh.)

3. It's missing salt. =
   Le falta sal.
   (Leh Fahl-tah Sahl.)

4. First In, First Out. FIFO =
   Primero en Entrar, Primero en Salir. PEPS
   (Pree-meh-roh Ehn Ehn-trah, Pree-meh-roh Ehn Sah-leer.)

5. What is this? Label it with the name and date. =
   ¿Qué es esto? Márcalo con nombre y fecha.
   (Keh Ehs Ehs-toh?) (Mahr-kah-loh Kohn Nohm-breh Ee Feh-cha.)

6. I want the chicken breast ready by 11:30. =
   Quiero la pechuga de pollo lista a las 11:30.
   (Key/air-oh Lah Peh-choo-gah Deh Poh-yoh Lees-tah Ah Lahs Ohn-seh Ee Meh-dee-ah.)

7. It's burning. =
   Se está quemando.
   (Seh Ehs-tah Keh-mahn-doh.)

8. Train the new person. =
   Entrena a la persona nueva.
   (Ehn-treh-nah Ah Lah Pehr-soh-nah Noo/eh-vah.)

105 = CIENTO CINCO

Write the letter of the corresponding English phrase on the line next to the Spanish phrase.

1. _____ Necesito uno nuevo.

2. _____ Le falta sal.

3. _____ Quiero la pechuga de pollo lista a las 11:30.

4. _____ PEPS

5. _____ al vuelo

6. _____ Entrena a la persona nueva.

7. _____ Deja que el chef lo pruebe.

8. _____ ¿Qué es esto?

9. _____ Se está quemando.

10. _____ Primero en Entrar, Primero en Salir.

11. _____ Márcalo con nombre y fecha.

12. _____ Necesito el lomo de puerco listo a las 11:30.

A. *(ah)* Train the new person.

B. *(beh)* FIFO

C. *(seh)* on the fly

D. *(deh)* What is this?

E. *(eh)* It's burning.

F. *(F --feh)* I want the chicken breast ready by 11:30.

G. *(heh)* It's missing salt.

H. *(ah-che)* First In, First Out.

I. *(eeee)* Label it with the name and date.

J. *(hoh-tah)* I need a new one.

K. *(kah)* Have the chef taste it.

L. *(ehl-leh)* I need the pork loin ready at 11:30.

106 = CIENTO SEIS

A customer has just said, "El pescado tiene demasiada sal." You need a new fish entrée very quickly. What would you say to the line cooks? Fill in the squares of the puzzle with letters from one of the Spanish phrases in 104 = ciento cuatro.

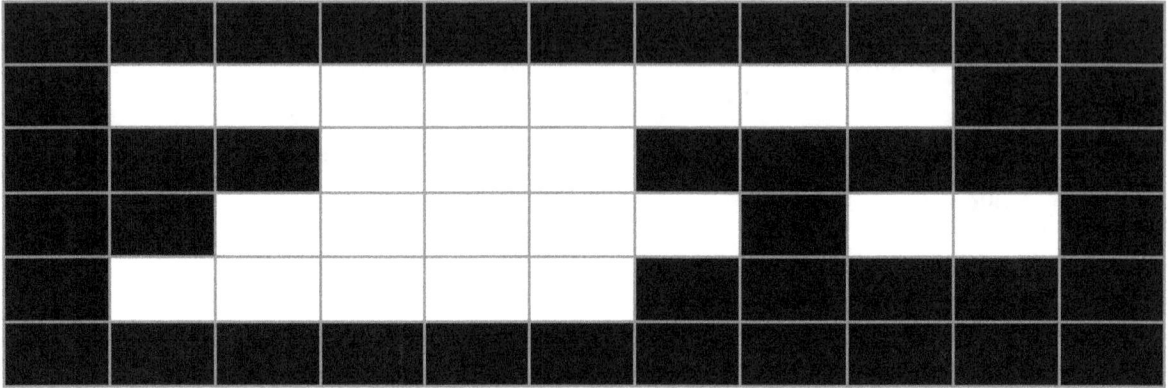

107 = CIENTO SIETE

Communication styles vary in different cultures. For example, a bilingual line cook, Juanito, may spend time a great deal of time talking with someone that is interested in learning Spanish. Juanito would feel rude if he tried to rush the person and get back to cooking, even if there was a lot of work to be done. Many people in the United States are known for accomplishing goals even at the cost of being very direct and blunt. Other cultures stereotype this attitude as the "Ugly American."

Latino culture is similar to other cultures around the world in that it is very important to save face and cooperate with other people. However, this causes Latinos to often say "yes" when they really mean "no." Latino employees generally will open up and tell you what they really mean only after they get to know you. Keeping this in mind, supervisors may want to ask individuals if anything is bothering them instead of waiting for someone to speak up in front of a group.

108 = CIENTO OCHO

Read the information about these three South American countries.

EL PAÍS	COLOMBIA	ECUADOR	VENEZUELA
LA MONEDA NACIONAL	Peso	U.S. Dollar	Bolívar
LOS LUGARES PARA VISITAR	**Santafé de Bogotá** • *La capital* • *Gold museum* **Zipaquirá salt mine** **Cartagena** • *Beachport* **Tatacoa desert** **Amazon jungle**	**Quito** • *La capital* **Guayaquil** **Islas Galápagos** = *Galápagos Islands* **Cuenca** • *Cathedral Monestery* **Amazon jungle**	**Caracas** • *La capital* **Salto Ángel / Canaima National Park** • *Waterfall* • *Cloud forest with 25,000 species of orchids* **Isla Margarita** • *Beaches*
LA POBLACIÓN	46.1 million	13.3 million	27.7 million
LA GENTE FAMOSA	**Fernando Botero (Born 1932)** • *Artist* **Álvaro Uribe (Born 1952)** • *President (Elected 2002)* **Shakira (Born 1977)** • *Singer* **Gabriel García Márquez (Born 1928)** • *Nobel prize for literature* **Elkin Patarroyo (Born 1947)** • *Nobel prize for science, discovered vaccine for malaria*	**Gerardo (Born 1965)** • *Singer "Rico Suave"* • *Record Producer* **Luis Miranda (Born 1932)** • *Painter* **Fanny Carrión de Fierro (Born 1939)** • *Literature* • *Poet* **Rafael Correa (Born 1963)** • *President (Elected 2007)* **Noralma Vera Arrata (Born 1936)** • *Prima Ballerina* **Rosalía Arteaga (Born 1956)** • *President in 1997 for three days*	**Simón Bolívar (1783–1830)** • *The Great Liberator* **Hugo Chavez (Born 1954)** • *President (Elected 1999)* **Luis Aparicio (Born 1934)** • *Baseball Hall of Fame* **Irene Sáez (Born 1961)** • *Miss Universe (1981)* • *Politician* **Carolina Herrera (Born 1939)** • *Fashion designer*
LA COMIDA	**Arepa** • *Thick corn tortilla* **Sancocho** • *Stew* **Café** = Coffee • *Fritanga* **Grilled meats, BBQ**	**Ceviche** • *Raw fish "cooked" by marinating in lemon juice, sometimes with tomato sauce* **Cassava** • *Yucca root* **Cuy** • *Fried guinea pig*	**Arepa** • *Bread made from corn* **Pabellón Criollo** • *Stewed and shredded meat with bananas, black beans and rice* **Pescado y Marisco** • *Fish and shellfish*
EL INGRESO ANUAL = ANNUAL INCOME (GNI)	$3,250 per year	$3,080 per year	$7,320 per year

109 = CIENTO NUEVE

Read these three trivia statements about Colombia, Ecuador and Venezuela. Two sentences are true and one is false. Guess which one is not true. The previous cultural section does not contain the answers, so check the Answer Key to find out why one of them is not culturally correct.

INTERESTING THINGS = COSAS INTERESANTES:

1. _____ In Zipaquirá, Colombia, the church is built entirely out of yucca roots.

2. _____ Angel Falls in Venezuela is the world's highest waterfall with a height of 3,212 feet.

3. _____ The Ecuadorian Galapágos Islands contributed to Darwin's theory of evolution.

FOOD = COMIDA:

1. _____ In Colombia, a fritanga may include grilled chicken, pig's feet, leg of lamb, blood sausage and chunchullo = fried cow intestines.

2. _____ In Venezuela, "pabellón a caballo" is stewed/shredded meat with a fried egg riding on top. "Pabellón con barandas" is made with fried plantains as side rails so the food does not fall off the plate. "Pabellón expreso" is a to-go plate.

3. _____ The cassava root (yucca) is used for making tapioca, flour, bioethanol, hay (animal feed) and ethno-medicine.

SOUTH AMERICA = AMÉRICA DEL SUR

To remember the Spanish-speaking countries of South America, you can use this phrase "Very Cool Extroverted Penguins Barely Participate Until Almost Chilled." In this mnemonic, the first letter of each word represents a Spanish-speaking country starting with V = Venezuela, C = Colombia, E = Ecuador, P = Peru, B = Bolivia, P = Paraguay, U = Uruguay, A = Argentina and C = Chile.
(See the map on page 24.)

110 = CIENTO DIEZ

Use these phrases for line cooks. Substitute other food words, p. 208.

1. Temp the steak to medium. =
   Prepara el bistec medio cocido.
   (Preh-pah-rah Ehl Bees-tehk Meh-dee/oh Koh-see-doh.)

2. Steam the vegetables. =
   Cocina los vegetales al vapor.
   (Koh-see-nah Lohs Veh-heh-tah-lehs Ahl Vah-pohr.)

3. Pan-fry the fish. =
   Fríe el pescado en el sartén.
   (FREE-eh Ehl Pehs-kah-doh Ehn Ehl Sahr-ten.)

4. Drain the potatoes. =
   Escurre las papas.
   (Ehs-koo-rreh Lahs Pah-pahs.)
   Note: The phrase, "Cola las papas," is from the word, colander = el colador.

111 = CIENTO ONCE

There is a lot of action on the line. These verbs help you give instructions. Complete 1-10 using the Extra Vocabulary, p. 208. Answers will vary.

1. Bake... = Hornea... _____
2. Boil/Simmer... = Hierve/a fuego lento... _____
3. Defrost... = Descongela... _____
4. Deliver... = Entrega... _____
5. Flip/Turn... = Voltea... _____
6. Grill... = Cocina a la parilla... _____
7. Sauté... = Saltea...(Note: Saltea also means to assault) _____
8. Add... = Añade... _____
9. Lightly fry/Brown... = Sofríe/Dora _____

112 = CIENTO DOCE

Do you need someone to bring you a certain pan or dish? Read these, then find more in Extra Vocabulary: Kitchen Equipment/ Appliances/ Pots/ Pans, p. 215.

- the baking sheet = la charola
- the bowl = el tazón
- the stock pot = la olla para caldo
- the sauce pan = la cacerola
- the sauté pan = el sartén

113 = CIENTO TRECE

Have three people say the lines for manager Shakira, Chef Simón Bolívar and the new trainee Gerardo "Rico Suave." Then switch roles.

Shakira: Hola Chef Bolívar. Por favor entrena al Sr. Suave, el chico nuevo.

Simón Bolívar: Hola Rico Suave. Me llamo Chef Bolívar. Prepara el bistec medio cocido.

Rico Suave: Chef, ayúdame, se está quemando.

Simón Bolívar: ¡Ay de mí! Necesito uno nuevo, al vuelo.

Shakira: Quiero los huevos revueltos listos a las 10:30. Deja que el chef los pruebe.

Simón Bolívar: Les falta sal y están fríos, caliéntalos.

Rico Suave: ¿Qué es esto? ¿Atún? Huele mal. = It smells bad.

Simón Bolívar: Tíralo a la basura. Primero en entrar, primero en salir. Marca el atún nuevo con nombre y fecha.

Shakira: ¿Recibiste la orden #42 para los camarones, el puré de papas, el coliflor, las habichuelas y el brócoli?

Simón Bolívar: Sí, apúrate, escurre las papas, fríe los camarones en el sartén y cocina los vegetales al vapor. Lo más rápido posible.

Rico Suave: Es demasiado trabajo, voy a mi casa a tomar una siesta. ¡Adiós!

114 = CIENTO CATORCE

Circle the English choice that matches the Spanish phrase. Use the four phrases from 112 = ciento doce.

1. **Fríe el pescado en el sartén.**
   a. Put the fish in the soup.
   b. Steam the fish.
   c. Fry the fish in the deep-fat fryer.
   d. Pan-fry the fish.

2. **Cocina el coliflor al vapor.**
   a. Cook the cauliflower.
   b. Steam the cauliflower
   c. Sauté the cauliflower.
   d. The cauliflower is too salty.

3. **Escurre las papas.**
   a. Drain the pasta.
   b. Drain the potatoes.
   c. Slice the potatoes.
   d. Stir the potatoes.

4. **Prepara el bistec medio cocido.**
   a. Temp the steak to medium.
   b. Temp the steak to well-done.
   c. Did you temp the steak?
   d. Prepare the steak and cook it.

115 = CIENTO QUINCE

In English and in Spanish, verbs must be matched with their subject. An English example is the verb to be. In English we say, "I am," "you are," and "he is." Some English verbs barely change when matching to their subject. Examples: "I speak." "He speaks." There isn't a lot of difference between speak and speaks. In our native language of English we conjugate without much thought.

However, as many people have taken high school Spanish may attest, you have to conjugate, conjugate and conjugate some more to pass the class. In this lesson we will begin with present tense verbs ending in –ar, Lesson 7 will have more practice with -ar and add the –er/ -ir verbs. The purpose of this next exercise is to show the basics of conjugation so you can further your knowledge on your own. If you don't understand it, don't worry. We won't tell your high school teacher.

Present Tense -ar verbs:

To conjugate and change these verbs to match the subject, take off the -ar, then add the correct ending. Read the chart out loud and then do the activities to practice with the verb.

To speak = Hablar:

I speak. = Yo hablo. Add -o	We speak. = Nosotros hablamos. Add –amos
You speak. = Tú hablas. = Add - as	
He speaks. = Él habla. Add -a She speaks. = Ella habla. Add -a You speak. = Usted habla. Add -a (Usted is the formal you.)	They speak. = Ellos hablan. (Ellos = Masculine) Add -an They speak. = Ellas hablan. (Ellas = Feminine) Add -an You speak. = Ustedes hablan. Add -an (Ustedes is you plural and formal. Vosotros is used in Spain.)

Notice that in the left column of the chart all the subjects are singular. The right column is plural. For example, for the verb "cantar = to sing;" Andrew sings = Andrés canta. Now if Andrew's sister Emily begins singing, you will use the plural (ellos, ellas, ustedes) form and say Andrew and Emily sing = Andrés y Emilia cantan.

Little by little = Poco a poco:

Step by step you will get better at Spanish, but you have to keep practicing. Try filling out the endings for these four regular –ar verbs. Answers on page 259.

1. **Cocinar = to cook**
   Yo _____
   Tú _____
   Ellos _____

2. **Trabajar = to work**
   El bebé no _____
   Mateo y yo (nosotros) _____
   Ellos _____

3. **Limpiar = to clean**
   Yo _____
   Ella _____
   Carina y Miguel _____

4. **Cortar = to cut**
   Yo _____
   Nosotros _____
   Ellas _____

116 = Ciento dieciséis

To play this game, roll one die to conjugate a verb on the following lines. Then pass the die to your partner who will roll to conjugate a verb on their own paper. Alternate turns. If you already have that verb filled in, you will have to pass the die to your partner without conjugating. The first person to roll all six numbers and be the first one to conjugate all six verbs correctly wins. Answers are on page 259.

If you roll a 1   Yo _____. to wash = lavar

If you roll a 2   Tú _____. to arrive = llegar

If you roll a 3   Ella _____. to mix = mezclar

If you roll a 4   Él _____. to prepare = preparar

If you roll a 5   Nosotros _____. to watch= mirar

If you roll a 6   Ellos _____. to organize = organizar

117 = CIENTO DIECISIETE

Translate these phrases. Write the English for the first seven phrases and write the Spanish for the last six phrases. This may be done as an exam or as homework for the next lesson. When finished, check your answers in the Answer Key.

1. Márcalo con nombre y fecha. _____

2. Prepara el bistec medio cocido. _____

3. Quiero la pechuga de pollo lista a las 11:30. _____
_____

4. Deja que el chef lo pruebe. _____

5. Primero en Entrar, Primero en Salir. PEPS _____

6. Cocina los vegetales al vapor. _____

7. Entrena a la persona nueva. _____

8. It's burning. _____

9. It's missing salt. _____

10. Drain the potatoes. _____

11. I need a new one, on the fly. _____

12. Pan-fry the fish. _____

13. What is this? _____

THE MEASUREMENTS: LAS MEDIDAS

Here are some measurements in Spanish. Use these to help you translate one of your favorite recipes. Find ingredients and food words in the Extra Vocabulary section at the back of the book.

How much Does it Weigh? = ¿Cuánto Peso?	The recipe says... = La receta dice...
kilograms = los kilogramos	teaspoon = la cucharadita, la cucharilla
gram = el gramo	tablespoon = la cuchara, la cucharada
ounces = las onzas	one cup = una taza
pound = la libra	one half cup = una media taza
How much Volume? = ¿Cuánto Es La Capacidad?	one-third cup = un tercio de taza
liter = el litro	¼ cup = un cuarto de taza
milliliters = el mililitro	one-eighth = un octavo de taza
pint = la pinta	a pinch = una pizca
quart = el cuarto de galón	half = la mitad
gallon = el galón	dozen = la docena
What is the Temperature? = ¿Cuál Es la Temperatura?	How Long? = ¿Qué Tan Largo?
degrees = grados (Fahrenheit)	inch = la pulgada
Centigrades = centígrados (Celsius)	feet = el pie
below zero = bajo cero	centimeter = el centímetro

118 = CIENTO DIECIOCHO

To review the numbers from Lesson 2, we will play a "Bingo" game. Fill in all of the squares by writing the number and the Spanish word for the number. To play, read the group of numbers one at a time from the Answer Key page 260. For example, 81–90 = "ochenta y uno hasta noventa." Cover the square if you have written a number between 81 and 90 in the third square on the right. If you wrote the number 95 = noventa y cinco, you will have to wait to cover the third square on the right. The first person to get four in a row, will shout, "LOTERÍA."

_____ 11–20	_____ 51–60	_____ 81–100	_____ 201–400
_____ 21–30	_____ 61–70	_____ ¿Cuántos años tiene?	_____ 401–600
_____ 31–40	¿Cúando es su cumpleaños?= When is your birthday? (Day of the month)	Su número favorito = Your favorite number between 1–1,000	_____ 601–800
_____ 41–50	_____ 71–80	_____ 101–200	_____ 801–1,000

119 = CIENTO DIECINUEVE

Cut the flashcards on the following page apart and practice them as much as possible. Save all of the flashcards to use during the games later in the book. Use any question cards to interview Spanish-speaking friends or employees. For another "Bingo" game challenge, use the "Bingo" game board on page 64 and add your flashcards from Lessons 1–5. Use the glossary to call out any phrases from Lessons 1–5 in any order.

Have the chef taste it.	It's missing salt.	First In, First Out. FIFO
What is this? Label it with the name and date.	I want the chicken breast ready by 11:30.	It's burning.
I need a new one, on the fly.	Train the new person.	Temp the steak to medium.
Steam the vegetables.	Pan-fry the fish.	Drain the potatoes.

| Primero en Entrar, Primero en Salir. PEPS

(Pree-meh-roh Ehn Ehn-trah, Pree-meh-roh Ehn Sah-leer.) | Le falta sal.

(Leh Fahl-tah Sahl.) | Deja que el chef lo pruebe.

(Deh-hah Keh Ehl Chehf Loh Proo/eh-beh.) |
|---|---|---|
| Se está quemando.

(Seh Ehs-tah Keh-mahn-doh.) | Quiero la pechuga de pollo lista a las 11:30.

(Key/air-oh Lah Peh-choo-gah Deh Poh-yoh Lees-tah Ah Lahs Ohn-seh Ee Meh-dee-ah.) | ¿Qué es esto? (Keh Ehs Ehs-toh?)

Márcalo con nombre y fecha. (Mahr-kah-loh Kohn Nohm-breh Ee Feh-cha.) |
| Prepara el bistec medio cocido.

(Preh-pah-rah Ehl Bees-tehk Meh-dee/oh Koh-see-doh.) | Entrena a la persona nueva.

(Ehn-treh-nah Ah Lah Pehr-soh-nah Noo/eh-vah.) | Necesito uno nuevo, al vuelo.

(Neh-seh-see-toh Oo-no Noo/eh-voh, Ahl Vweh-loh.) |
| Escurre las papas.

(Ehs-koo-rreh Lahs Pah-pahs.) | Fríe el pescado en el sartén.

(FREE-eh Ehl Pehs-kah-doh Ehn Ehl Sahr-ten.) | Cocina los vegetales al vapor.

(Koh-see-nah Lohs Veh-heh-tah-lehs Ahl Vah-pohr.) |

LESSON 7 LECCIÓN

Prep, bake and chat

GOALS: In this lesson you will learn about these topics: phrases used in the prep area, exclamations, adjectives, colors, Inca Empire, phrases to use with baking, Bolivia, Perú, Chile and regular present tense –er/–ir verb conjugation.

120 = CIENTO VEINTE

Translate this recipe = receta into English. Then try writing your own recipe in Spanish. Use the Extra Vocabulary in the back of the book to help with any new words. Check your translation in the Answer Key on page 260.

Un Flan muy rico

1. Primero, haz el caramelo. Pon una taza de azúcar granulada en un sartén. Derrítela a fuego mediano. Revúelvela continuamente hasta que el azúcar se ponga líquida. Échala rápidamente en un molde para flan.

2. En una olla, suavemente revuelve tres huevos grandes. Añade una lata de leche evaporada, una lata de leche condensada, y una cucharada de vainilla. Revúelve un poco y échalo al molde que ya contiene el caramelo.

3. Pon el molde en un Baño María. Hornéalo por 45 minutos a 325 grados.

4. Enfríalo en el refrigerador toda la noche o por lo menos cuatro horas.

5. Antes de servirlo, quita el flan del molde. Simplemente voltéalo y deja el caramelo gotear arriba del flan.

6. Cómelo con una cuchara. Invita a tus amigos a disfrutarlo.

121 = CIENTO VEINTIUNO

Read aloud these six Spanish phrases that could be used in the Prep area. Use these phrases to help with food preparation and handling.

1. Slice the watermelon and put it in a container. =
   Rebana la sandía y ponla en un recipiente.
   (Reh-bah-nah Lah Sahn-dee-ah Ee PohN-lah Ehn Oon Reh-see/pee-ehn-teh.) Note: Container could also be a envase, vasija, contenedor, or receptáculo.

2. Wash and peel the carrots. =
   Lava y pela las zanahorias.
   (Lah-vah Ee Peh-lah Lahs Zah-nah-oh-ree/ahs.)

3. Chop six big red apples. =
   Pica seis manzanas rojas grandes.
   (Pee-kah Seh/ace Mahn-zah-nahs Roh-hahs Grahn-dehs.)

4. Make more salad with lettuce, cucumbers and tomatoes. =
   Haz más ensalada con lechuga, pepinos y tomates.
   (Ahs Mahs Ehn-sah-lah-dah Kohn Leh-choo-gah, Peh-pee-nohs Ee Toh-mah-tehs.)

5. Cover and put away the shrimp. =
   Cubre y guarda los camarones.
   (Koo-breh Ee Gwahr-dah Lohs Cah-mah-roh-nehs.)

6. Take the meat out of the freezer. =
   Saca la carne del congelador.
   (Sah-kah Lah Kahr-neh Dehl Kohn-heh-lah-dohr.)

122 = CIENTO VEINTIDÓS

Write the letter of the corresponding English phrase on the line next to the Spanish phrase.

1. _____ Cubre y guarda los camarones.
2. _____ Pica seis manzanas rojas grandes.
3. _____ Rebana la sandía y ponla en un recipiente.
4. _____ Pica finamente los hongos.
5. _____ Haz más ensalada con lechuga, pepinos y tomates.
6. _____ Rebana la naranja.
7. _____ Lava y pela las zanahorias.
8. _____ Saca la carne del congelador.

A. *(ah)* Make more salad with lettuce, cucumbers and tomatoes.
B. *(beh)* Wash and peel the carrots.
C. *(seh)* Slice the orange.
D. *(deh)* Take the meat out of the freezer.
E. *(eh)* Slice the watermelon and put it in a container.
F. *(ehf-feh)* Cover and put away the shrimp.
G. *(heh)* Finely chop the mushrooms.
H. *(ah-che)* Chop six big red apples.

123 = CIENTO VEINTITRÉS

There are many ways to say something is "cool" or that you really like something. Many Hispanic countries use ¡Qué bueno!, but different regions have their own styles. Examples: In Costa Rica it's "¡Pura Vida!" In Venezuela or Colombia it's "¡Qué Chévere!" In Spain it's translated as "¡Qué Guay!" In México it's "¡Qué Padre!" A general expression used in telenovelas = soap operas is "¡Qué Genial!" "¡Claro que sí!" and "¡Por supuesto!" are two common ways of saying, "Of course!"

One of the best things about learning the language is discovering all the differences among the Spanish-speaking countries. Trying to understand the slang is a good way to keep your skills sharp. It is easy, don't worry = no te preocupes.

124 = CIENTO VEINTICUATRO

Think back to elementary school English when the teacher explained that adjectives are words to describe nouns. One major difference between English and Spanish is the placement of the adjective. For example, in English we place the adjective in front of the noun and say, "The President lives in the White House." However, in Spanish we say, "El Presidente vive en la Casa Blanca (house white)." In Spanish you say what it is (noun) and then describe it (adjective). In Spanish the adjective follows the noun. This is the opposite of English. Another example is this: The President of Argentina lives in the pink house. = El Presidente de Argentina vive en la Casa Rosada (house pink).

Read these examples using los colores = the colors. For more examples of colors and adjectives see the Extra Vocabulary-Lesson 7.

THE COLORS = LOS COLORES:

verde = green
rojo/a = red
blanco/a = white

el brócoli verde = the green broccoli
la gelatina roja = the red jello
el vino blanco = the white wine

Use the colors to describe the nouns. Make sure they agree in number and gender.

1. (verde)   la menta _____   las cebollinas _____

    el espárrago _____   los nopales _____

2. (blanco/a) la leche _____   las camisas _____

    el bacalao _____   los huesos _____

3. (rojo/a)   la salsa de tomate _____   las frambuesas _____

    el arándano _____   los rábanos _____

125 = CIENTO VEINTICINCO

Now that you've practiced with the color adjectives, let's add some adjectives from the culinary world. Read these examples aloud and then answer the five questions.

el cocinero bueno =
    the good male cook
	los cocineros buenos =
	    the good servers (at least 1 male)

la cocinera buena =
    the good female server
	las cocineras buenas=
	    the good servers (all females)

el jefe simpático=
    the nice male boss
	los jefes simpáticos =
	    the nice bosses (at least 1 male)

la jefe simpática =
    the nice female boss
	las jefes simpáticas=
	    the nice bosses (all females)

Circle the correct choice. Check that the ending of the adjective matches the subject of the sentence. Remember to change the -o ending to -a ending for females and add the –s ending for more than one person. The answers are on page 261.

1. el cliente rico   or   el cliente rica (rich male customer)

2. los jarras pequeños   or   las jarras pequeñas (the small jars)

3. la cuenta caro   or   la cuenta cara (the expensive bill)

4. los servicios baratos   or   el servicios baratas (cheap services)

5. el ayudante perezosa   or   las ayuantes perezosas (lazy helpers)

- Many beginning Spanish students have a hard time with the words "Bien" and "Bueno." Bien is an adverb so it is used with action words = verbs. For example, "¿Cómo estás?" The response is, "Muy Bien." Bueno/a is an adjective so it is linked with nouns. For example, "el taco es bueno."

- **"I SPY" = "YO VEO"**: To play the game, one person thinks of an object they see in the room. The other person guesses adjectives and colors in Spanish until they identify the secret object. For example, "¿Es blanco? = Is it white?" For more adjectives see Extra Vocabulary-Lesson 7.

126 = CIENTO VEINTISÉIS

The great contributions of the Inca Empire should be celebrated. The road system, pony-express–style message deliveries, architecture and mason work still inspire travelers today. The Inca Empire thrived in and around Perú during the 1400–1500s and was destroyed by a combination of the Spanish conquistadores and smallpox.

Their capital, Cusco, was considered the navel/bellybutton or center of the earth. The city walls formed the shape of a puma when viewed from above. The puma was the animal representing their god of the earth. Machu Picchu, built high on a mountain top, looks like a condor when viewed from above. The condor was the animal that represented the god of the heavens.

Spanish conquistadors searched in vain for a third city in the shape of a serpent, called El Dorado = the golden one. One conquistador, Francisco de Orellana in his search for this lost city of gold, became the first person known to navigate the Amazon River all the way to the ocean. El Dorado remains as an Incan legend, just waiting to be discovered. Use your newly acquired Spanish skills to try to find it. Repeat after me, "¿Dónde está El Dorado?" = "Where is El Dorado?"

▲ MACHU PICCHU AERIAL VIEW

THE CITY OF ▶ MACHU PICCHU

127 = CIENTO VEINTISIETE

Here are six phrases to help communicate in the back of the house. Use these to give directions to the bakers and prep cooks in the kitchen or bakery.

1. Cut the dessert in eight portions. =
   Corta el postre en ocho porciones.
   (Kohr-tah Ehl Pohs-treh Ehn Oh-cho Pohr-see/ohn-nehs.)

2. Use this recipe. =
   Usa esta receta.
   (Oo-sah Ehs-tah Reh-seh-tah.)

3. Mix the dough. =
   Mezcla la masa.
   (Mehs-klah Lah Mah-sah.)

4. Bake it for 45 minutes at 350 degrees. =
   Hornéalo por 45 minutos a 350 grados.
   (Or-NEH-ah-loh Pohr Qwah-rent-tah Ee Seen-koh Mee-noo-tohs Ah Treh-see- N-tohs Seen-qwehn-tah Grah-dohs.)

5. Turn off the oven. Turn on the stove. =
   Apaga el horno. Enciende la estufa.
   (Ah-pah-gah Ehl Or-noh.) (Ehn-see/ehn-deh Lah Ehs-too-fah.)
   Note: Prende is also used for turn on the appliance.

6. Boil the water in the big pot. =
   Hierve el agua en la olla grande.
   (Ee/ehr-veh Ehl Ah-gwah Ehn Lah Oh/ee-yah Grahn-deh.)

128 = CIENTO VEINTIOCHO

Circle the English choice that matches the Spanish phrase.

1. **Mezcla la masa.**
   a. Mix a massive amount.
   b. Use the mixer.
   c. Mix the dough.
   d. Mix up the mayonnaise.

2. **Hierve el agua en la olla grande.**
   a. Boil the water in the big pot.
   b. Boil a lot of water.
   c. Put water in a big pan.
   d. Heat up the water in the big pot.

3. **Corta el postre en ocho porciones.**
   a. Cut the pasta in eight pieces.
   b. Cut the cake in ten portions.
   c. Chop the dessert in eight minutes.
   d. Cut the dessert in eight portions.

4. **Enciende la estufa.**
   a. Turn on the lights.
   b. Turn on the stove.
   c. Turn off the stove.
   d. Turn on the blender.

5. **Usa esta receta.**
   a. Use this recipe.
   b. Throw out this recipe.
   c. Use the register.
   d. I could use a recess.

6. **Hornéalo por 45 minutos a 350 grados.**
   a. Mix it for 45 minutes.
   b. Bake it for 45 minutes at 350 degrees.
   c. Put it in the oven for 54 minutes at 350 degrees.
   d. Refrigerate it for 45 minutes.

129 = CIENTO VEINTINUEVE

Read this short skit to review phrases from this lesson. Have three people say the lines for Back of the House Manager Tupac Amaru II, Baker Isabel Allende and Prep cook Jaime Escalante.

Tupac Amaru II: Isabel, Usa esta receta y mezcla la masa para el pan.

Isabel Allende: ¡Claro que sí! Un momento, tengo que encender el horno. (¡Claro que sí!= Of course!)

Tupac Amaru II: Hornéalo por 55 minutos a 550 grados.

Isabel Allende: No, no, baja la temperatura. Se va a quemar. ¿Hay instrucciones en español?

Tupac Amaru II: ¡Buena idea! La receta también viene en español.

Isabel Allende: Gracias. La receta dice hornéalo 45 minutos a 450 grados. Luego, corta el pan en 16 porciones.

Tupac Amaru II: Buen trabajo Isabel. Jaime, por favor haz más ensalada con lechuga, cebollas, pepinos y apio. Rebana el melón chico y ponlo en un recipiente.

Jaime Escalante: ¿Necesitas algo más?

Tupac Amaru II: Sí, lava y pela las ciruelas. Corta siete peras amarillas medianas. Cubre y guarda toda la fruta. Márcalo con nombre y fecha. Hierve el agua en la olla grande.

Jaime Escalante: Lo siento. Me olvidé de sacar los vegetales del congelador.

Tupac Amaru II: En nuestro restaurante los vegetales no están congelados, usamos frescos.

Jaime Escalante: En nuestro restaurante siempre hay mucho trabajo.

Answer these three questions to check if you understood the skit.

1. What did Tupac tell Isabel incorrectly? _____

2. What is Isabel making? _____

3. Why can't Jaime get the vegetables from the freezer? _____

130 = CIENTO TREINTA

Write a role play or short skit by yourself or with a partner. Think of some funny scenarios or interesting situations that have happened on the job. Use about 10 phrases for each person from all the lessons 1–7. For an extra challenge, add props and even memorize it. Present this role play next time or find someone to present it to at your workplace.

131 = CIENTO TREINTA Y UNO

Find these 14 words from the Spanish phrases in this lesson. Write the English next to each of the Spanish words. ¡Buena suerte! Good luck!

WORD SEARCH = BUSCAPALABRAS

A	T	E	S	A	R	E	B	A	N	A	I	O	T
S	E	N	G	I	V	C	A	C	A	S	A	M	S
E	B	A	A	Ñ	Ó	O	H	R	S	I	A	Q	R
S	P	C	Ú	O	A	C	E	I	M	S	L	L	C
A	C	E	T	L	I	T	U	M	A	E	M	O	P
V	F	S	E	A	D	A	R	B	D	L	M	A	I
N	E	P	K	V	O	A	A	Ñ	R	I	E	N	C
E	G	T	Ó	A	S	D	N	A	A	E	S	H	A
N	H	A	Í	E	A	T	E	N	U	T	O	I	E
E	D	A	I	L	N	O	L	C	G	V	R	E	R
D	W	L	A	V	T	R	E	C	E	T	A	R	N
A	U	S	E	C	U	E	R	D	E	L	E	V	A
J	N	O	S	P	E	D	N	E	I	C	N	E	R
E	N	I	R	E	C	I	P	I	E	N	T	E	A

REBANA _____   GUARDA _____

RECIPIENTE _____   ENCIENDE _____

PELA _____   PICA _____

LAVA _____   RECETA _____

SACA _____   MASA _____

ENSALADA _____   APAGA _____

CUBRE _____   HIERVE _____

132 = CIENTO TREINTA Y DOS

Read the information about these three South American countries.

EL PAÍS	BOLIVIA	PERÚ	CHILE
LA MONEDA NACIONAL	Boliviano	Nuevo Sol	Peso
LOS LUGARES PARA VISITAR	**Sucre** • *La capital oficial* **La Paz** • *La capital administrativa* **Isla del Sol** • *Island in Lake Titicaca that the Incas believe they descended from*	**Lima** • *La capital* • *Plaza Mayor* **Islas Flotantes** • *Floating Islands on Lake Titicaca* **Machu Picchu** • *Inca Ruins* **Cusco** • *Inti Raymi festival* **Nazca Lines** **Arequipa** • *Colca Canyon*	**Santiago** • *La capital* • *Cerro San Cristobál* **San Pedro de Atacama** • *Desert* **Chuquicamata** • *Copper mine* **Easter island** • *Moai stone figures* **Viña del Mar/ Valparaíso** • *Beach* **Patagonia** • *Rainforest and glaciers*
LA POBLACIÓN	9.5 million	27.9 million	16.6 million
LA GENTE FAMOSA	**Jaime Escalante (Born 1930)** • *Teacher that inspired the movie, Stand and Deliver* **Evo Morales (Born 1959)** • *Elected President 2006* **Marina Núñez del Prado (1910-1995)** • *Sculptress* **Jaime Laredo (Born 1941)** • *Violinist*	**Tupac Amaru II (1742–1781)** • *Leader of Indigenous uprising. Atahualpa (c.1500) Last Inca Emperor* **Alberto Fujimori (Born 1938)** • *President (1990–2000)* • *Currently serving a 6-year prison sentence for abuse of power* **Pachamama** • *An Andes, Incan goddess meaning "Mother Earth"*	**Bernardo O'Higgins (1778–1842)** • *Independence Leader* **Michelle Bachelet (Born 1951)** • *President 2006–2010* **Augusto Pinochet (1915–2006)** • *Dictator (1973–1990)* **Pablo Neruda (1904–1973)** • *Poet* • *Nobel Prize in Literature 1971* **Isabel Allende (Born 1942)** • *Novelist*
LA COMIDA	**Chicha** • *Alcoholic drink made from purple corn* **Humitas** • *A sweet tamale* **Pique Macho** • *Beef, sausage, fries, boiled eggs, peppers* **Salteña** • *Meat/ potato pastry*	**Cuy** • *Roasted guinea pig* **Inca Cola** • *Yellow carbonated soda* **Mazamorra Morada** • *Purple corn pudding* **Papas a la Huancaína** • *Potatoes in an ají pepper, creamy sauce* **Quinoa** • *A nutritional grain*	**Empanadas** • *Triangle shaped hamburger pie usually with an olive and hard boiled egg pieces* **Pastel de Choclo** • *Chilean Sheppard's pie* **Lúcuma /Chirimoya** • *South American Fruits sometimes made into ice cream*
EL INGRESO ANUAL = ANNUAL INCOME (GNI)	$1,260 per year	$3,450 per year	$8,350 per year

133 = CIENTO TREINTA Y TRES

Read these three trivia statements about Bolivia, Perú and Chile. Two sentences are true and one is false. Guess which one is not true. The previous cultural section does not contain the answers, so check the Answer Key to find out why one of them is not culturally correct.

INTERESTING THINGS = COSAS INTERESANTES:

1. _____ Lake Titicaca's floating islands are made from Totora reeds that taste like celery when eaten and need to be regularly replenished. Walking on the island is like being on a bed of hay that sinks slightly. The Uros tribe lives on the islands and has an escuela flotante school.

2. _____ Chilean Poet Pablo Neruda had a carousel horse in his circular room and a cloud chair with an ocean view at his La Sebastina house.

3. _____ Machu Picchu was constructed in the shape of a jaguar on top of a mountain, without using mortar between the stones.

COMIDA = FOOD:

1. _____ The name for Bolivian Salteñas comes from the salty flavor. Even though these pastries have meat and potatoes inside, they are eaten for breakfast.

2. _____ Cuy is roasted guinea pig served whole on the plate (little beady eyes, teeth, etc.).

3. _____ Perú has 35 varieties of maize (corn) and 2,000 varieties of potatoes.

134 = CIENTO TREINTA Y CUATRO

Languages typically need two things to form a sentence. You need a noun and a verb. In Spanish there are roughly 10,000 verbs. Don't worry; you will not have to learn them all in this lesson. We're saving them for the next lesson. Just kidding!

Remember from Lesson 6, all Spanish infinitive verbs end in the letters –ar, -er and –ir. The breakdown is about 9,000 verbs ending in the letters –ar. There are about 500 –er verbs and 500–ir verbs.

In Lesson 6 we discussed –ar verbs, this lesson will have –er and –ir. The great thing is the endings of all these verbs are conjugated in a pattern, and once you figure out the pattern, verb conjugation is fairly simple. Being able to change the endings of verbs to match the subject will help rapidly expand your ability to communicate in Spanish.

If you still don't understand, DO NOT PANIC! Focus on memorizing the phrases in this book. These phrases are enough to help you out in common restaurant situations, but the next step will be producing more of your own phrases and that means you will have to form sentences by conjugating verbs. ¡Vámonos! = Let's go!

PRESENT TENSE -ER VERBS:

To conjugate and change these verbs, take off the -er, then add the correct ending to match the subject. Read the chart out loud and then do the activities to practice with the verb. Notice in the left column of the chart all the subjects are singular. The right column is plural.

TO SELL = VENDER:

I sell. = Yo vendo. Add -o	We sell. = Nosotros vendemos. Add -emos
You sell. = Tú vendes. Add -es	
He sells. = Él vende. Add -e She sells. = Ella vende. Add –e You (formal) sell. = Usted vende. Add -e	They sell. = Ellos venden. Add -en They (all female) sell. = Ellas venden. Add –en You (plural) sell. = Ustedes venden. Add –en

TO EAT = COMER:

I eat. = Yo como.	We eat. = Nosotros comemos.
You eat. = Tú comes.	
He eats. = Él come. She eats. = Ella come. You eat. = Usted come. (formal)	They eat. = Ellos comen. They eat. = Ellas comen. (all female) You (plural) eat. = Ustedes comen.

Read the above example of another present tense -er verb. Complete the endings for these three regular –er verbs on the lines provided. Check your answers in the Answer Key on page 263.

1. **COMPRENDER = TO UNDERSTAND**
    Yo _____.
    Tú _____.
    Timoteo y Alicia _____.

2. **BARRER = TO SWEEP**
    Yo _____.
    Ella _____.
    Ellas _____.

3. **APRENDER = TO LEARN**
    Él _____.
    Nosotros _____.
    Ellos _____.

The rule breakers: There are always a few that do not follow the rules. Some verbs have a spelling change in the stem of the verb so the verb sounds better when it's conjugated. It's not to make your lives more difficult. These verbs have to be memorized. For more information about stem changing verbs or other irregular verbs, or to practice more present tense verbs, look in the Extra Grammar-Lesson 7 or buy a basic Spanish grammar book. Again, the purpose of this section is to expand your knowledge of basic Spanish concepts and not to frustrate you.

135 = CIENTO TREINTA Y CINCO

Present Tense -ir verbs:

Now that you have practiced with the –er verbs, here are the last type of infinitive verbs with –ir endings. To conjugate and change these verbs, take off the -ir, then add the correct ending. Read the chart out loud and then do the activities to practice with the verb. Check your answers in the Answer Key.

To live = Vivir:

I live. = Yo vivo. Add -o	We live. = Nosotros vivimos. Add -imos
You live. = Tú vives. Add -es	
He lives. = Él vive. Add -e She lives. = Ella vive Add -e You live. = Usted vive. Add -e	They live. = Ellos viven. Add -en They live. = Ellas viven. Add -en You (plural) live. = Ustedes viven. Add -en

Complete the endings for these three regular –ir verbs on the lines provided.

1. **AÑADIR = TO ADD**
    Yo _____.
    Tú _____.
    Julia y Francisco _____.

2. **RECIBIR = TO RECEIVE**
    Yo _____.
    Teresa _____.
    Ellas _____.

3. **ABRIR = TO OPEN**
    Él _____.
    Nosotros _____.
    Ellos _____.

136 = CIENTO TREINTA Y SEIS

Translate these phrases. Write the English for the first seven phrases and write the Spanish for the last seven phrases. This may be done as an exam or as homework for the next lesson. When finished check your answers on page 264.

1. Saca la carne del congelador. _____

2. Rebana la sandía. _____

3. Corta el postre en ocho porciones. _____

4. Cubre y guarda los camarones. _____

5. Apaga el horno. _____

6. Pica seis manzanas rojas grandes. _____

7. Mezcla la masa. _____

8. Wash and peel the carrots. _____

9. Bake it for 45 minutes at 350 degrees. _____

10. Use this recipe. _____

11. Turn on the stove. _____

12. Make more salad with lettuce, cucumbers and tomatoes. _____

13. Boil the water in the big pot. _____

14. Put it in a container. _____

137 = CIENTO TREINTA Y SIETE

To play this "Tic-Tac-Toe" game, you and your partner will share one board depicted here. Cut out the X and O pieces found on page 149. Put nine flashcards from page 149, Spanish-side up on the board. Player X will go first, choosing a square that will help to get three in a row. Player X will read the Spanish for that square and say what it means in English in order to cover it up with an X piece. Then it is Player O's turn. Player O will read the Spanish for the square and say what it means in English. Play until someone gets three in row, "Tres en Raya" or "Tic-Tac-Toe". To make it more difficult, put the English side up and say the answer in Spanish. ¡Buena suerte! = Good luck!

"Three in a Row" = "Tres en Raya" game board

138 = CIENTO TREINTA Y OCHO

Put some of the flashcards in order to make a typical restaurant conversation. Use this to help you with your role play you will present next time. Practice your conversation with coworkers this week. Post one of the flashcards near your computer screen, or bathroom mirror, in order to practice one new phrase each day.

Juanito:	**Elena:**
Juanito:	**Elena:**

139 = CIENTO TREINTA Y NUEVE

Cut the flashcards on the following page apart, or make your own. Keep the flashcards in a plastic bag, envelope, or in your wallet and practice as much as possible during the week. Place one phrase a day on your refrigerator, mirror, or computer and learn a few at a time. Strive to find at least five minutes each day to review them, especially if you are waiting for someone or arrive early somewhere. Save all the flashcards to use during the games later in the book.

LESSON 7: PREP, BAKE AND CHAT 149

Slice the watermelon and put it in a container.	Wash and peel the carrots.	Chop six big red apples.
Make more salad with lettuce, cucumbers and tomatoes.	Cover and put away the shrimp.	Take the meat out of the freezer.
Cut the dessert in eight portions.	Use this recipe.	Mix the dough.
Bake it for 45 minutes at 350 degrees.	Turn off the oven. Turn on the stove.	Boil the water in the big pot.

O
O
O
O
O
X
X
X
X
X

Pica seis manzanas rojas grandes. (Pee-kah Seh/ace Mahn-zah-nahs Roh-hahs Grahn-dehs.)	Lava y pela las zanahorias. (Lah-vah Ee Peh-lah Lahs Zah-nah-oh-ree/ahs.)	Rebana la sandía y ponla en un recipiente. (Reh-bah-nah Lah Sahn-dee-ah Ee PohN-lah Ehn Oon Reh-see-pee/ehn-teh.)
Saca la carne del congelador. (Sah-kah Lah Kahr-neh Dehl Kohn-heh-lah-dohr.)	Cubre y guarda los camarones. (Koo-breh Ee Gwahr-dah Lohs Cah-mah-roh-nehs.)	Haz más ensalada con lechuga, pepinos y tomates. (Ahs Mahs Ehn-sah-lah-dah Kohn Leh-choo-gah, Peh-pee-nohs Ee Toh-mah-tehs.)
Mezcla la masa. (Mehs-klah Lah Mah-sah.)	Usa esta receta. (Oo-sah Ehs-tah Reh-seh-tah.)	Corta el postre en ocho porciones. (Kohr-tah Ehl Pohs-treh Ehn Oh-cho Pohr-see/ohn-nehs.)
Hierve el agua en la olla grande. (Ee/ehr-veh Ehl Ah-gwah Ehn Lah Oh/ee-yah Grahn-deh.)	Apaga el horno. (Ah-pah-gah Ehl Or-noh.) Enciende la estufa. (Ehn-see/ehn-deh Lah Ehs-too-fah.)	Hornéalo por 45 minutos a 350 grados. (Or-NEH-ah-loh Pohr Qwah-rent-tah Mee-noo-tohs Ah Treh-see/ehn-tohs Seen-qwehn-tah Grah-dohs.)

CHAT ABOUT DISHWASING AND FIRST AID

GOALS: In this lesson you will learn about these topics: First Aid, Safety and Personal Hygiene phrases, giving and receiving directions, , Back of the house-Dishwasher phrases, bilingual employees, this/that/these/those, preterite past tense, language acquisition: English versus Spanish, Argentina, Uruguay, Paraguay and final project ideas.

140 = CIENTO CUARENTA

In Lesson 7 you wrote an original skit using the vocabulary from the previous lessons. This role play should use phrases from Lessons 1–7. Read through a partner's role play and see what you comprehend. Ask for clarification as needed. Next, present your skit in front of the entire group. Make notes during the other skits if you have any questions or phrases you don't understand.

141 = CIENTO CUARENTA Y UNO

Practice these four Spanish polite phrases that deal with First Aid, Personal Hygiene and Safety. Use the pronunciation guide to help you read them out loud.

1. Don't come to work if you are sick. =
   No vengas al trabajo si estás enfermo. Note: for a female use "enferma".
   (No Vehn-gahs Ahl Trah-bah-hoh See Ehs-tahs Ehn-fehr-moh.)

2. Wash your hands with soap. =
   Lávate las manos con jabón.
   (LAH-vah-teh Lahs Mah-nohs Kohn Hah-bohN.)

3. In case of emergency, call 911. =
   En caso de emergencia, marca 911.
   *(Ehn Kah-soh Deh ehm-mehr-hen-see/ah, Mahr-kah
   Noo/eh-veh Oo-no Oo-no.)*
   Note: 911 can also be said, 9-11. *(Noo/eh-veh- ohn-seh)*

4. Do you need a band-aid or an aspirin? =
   ¿Necesitas una curita o una aspirina?
   (Neh-seh-see-tahs Oo-nah Koo-ree-tah Oh Oo-nah Ahs-pee-ree-nah?)

142 = CIENTO CUARENTA Y DOS

Circle the English choice that matches the Spanish phrase.

1. **¿Necesitas aspirina?**
    a. Do you need a new job?
    b. Do you need a band-aid?
    c. Do you need an aspirin?
    d. I need three aspirin.

2. **¿Te cortaste el dedo?**
    a. Did you cut the dough?
    b. Does your finger hurt?
    c. Cut the dessert.
    d. Did you cut your finger?

3. **No vengas al trabajo si estás enfermo/a.**
    a. Don't come to work.
    b. Don't get sick.
    c. Don't come to work if you are sick.
    d. Cover your mouth when you cough.

4. **¿Necesitas un hospital?**
    a. Do you need help?
    b. Do you need a hospital?
    c. Where is the hospital?
    d. Are you hurt?

5. **En caso de emergencia, marca 911.**
    a. In case of emergency, call 911.
    b. In case of emergency, run.
    c. Call 911 right now.
    d. Don't prank call 911.

6. **¿Necesitas una curita?**
    a. Do you need a cure?
    b. Do you need a band-aid?
    c. Do you need an aspirin?
    d. I have a band-aid.

7. **Lávate las manos con jabón.**
    a. Wash your hands twice.
    b. Wash your hands with soap.
    c. Use the hand sanitizer.
    d. Wash your hands again please.

8. **¿Estás enfermo?**
    a. Did you get fired?
    b. Who is sick?
    c. Are you hurt?
    d. Are you sick?

143 = CIENTO CUARENTA Y TRES

Fill out the English for these four directions. Check your answers in the Answer Key.

1. norte _____
2. este _____
3. sur _____
4. oeste _____

Read these direction words and then do the activity.:

I NEED DIRECTIONS. = NECESITO DIRECCIONES.

- turn = dobla
- right = derecha
- left = izquierda
- straight = derecho
- up = arriba
- down = abajo

- back = atrás
- front = en frente
- here = aquí/acá
- there = allá
- over there = allí
- near the = cerca de

- street = calle
- three blocks = tres cuadras
- corner = esquina
- on the first floor = en el primer piso
- on the second floor = en el segundo piso
- on the third floor = en el tercer piso

Now give directions in Spanish from this room to the nearest restroom. If you have a group, each person could write directions from his/her area to the restroom.

Va = Go...

_____
_____
_____
_____
_____
_____

144 = CIENTO CUARENTA Y CUATRO

Read these eight Spanish phrases out loud. These phrases will help communicate with the back of the house dish washer = el lavaplatos.

1. Will you wash more forks? =
   ¿Puedes lavar más tenedores?
   (Pweh-dehs Lah-vahr Mahs Teh-neh-doh-rehs?)

2. Wash this again. It's dirty. =
   Lava esto otra vez. Está sucio.
   (Lah-vah Ehs-toh Oh-trah Vehs.) (Ehs-tah Soo-see/oh.)

3. Let it soak. =
   Déjalo remojando.
   (Deh-hah-loh Reh-moh-hahn-doh.)

4. Dry the wine glasses. =
   Seca las copas de vino.
   (Seh-kah Lahs Koh-pahs Deh Vee-noh.)

5. Give me a sharp knife. =
   Dame un cuchillo filoso.
   (Dah-meh Oon Koo-chee-yoh Fee-loh-so?)

6. Put (restock) the small cups in their place. =
   Pon las tazas pequeñas en su lugar.
   (PohN Lahs Tah-sahs Peh-keh-nyahs Ehn Soo Loo-gahr.)

7. The broken glass goes here. =
   Los vidrios rotos van aquí.
   (Lohs Vee-dree-ohs Roh-tohs Vahn Ah-kee.)

8. Is there something that is not working? =
   ¿Hay algo que no está funcionando?
   (Eye Ahl-goh Keh No Ehs-tah Foon-see/oh-nahn-doh?)

145 = CIENTO CUARENTA Y CINCO

Choose one of these three activities:

1. Write the directions in Spanish from your house to your favorite restaurant. Then present the information to a partner or the group.

2. Write a scavenger hunt guiding your partner somewhere in the building using direction words. (See p. 154)

3. Create a map of your dream kitchen. Use the map to give directions to an item you will use for cooking. See Extra Vocabulary for lists of kitchen appliances and utensils.

146 = CIENTO CUARENTA Y SEIS

It's a great time and a tremendous opportunity to be bilingual in the United States. Many companies are willing to hire and quickly promote those who know and understand both English and Spanish. Workers may even get paid more for being able to speak Spanish. In the United States the goal for many is to work their way up the corporate ladder. However, many traditional Latinos, if given the choice between more money and more job security, might pick the job security. Traditional Latino values of not giving direct opinions and not upsetting co-workers are not as valued in many U.S. companies and therefore some Hispanic may not be rewarded with promotions.

Cultural awareness and understanding will help retain your best Hispanic employees. Bilingual employees have even more opportunities as U.S. and Latin American companies are partnering together in the global marketplace. Now is the time to become bilingual. Keep studying Spanish and practicing your phrases!

147 = CIENTO CUARENTA Y SIETE

Complete the crossword puzzle with parts of each of the 12 Spanish phrases from this lesson. The words in each of the phrases are joined together without spaces or punctuation marks. ¡Buena suerte! = Good luck!

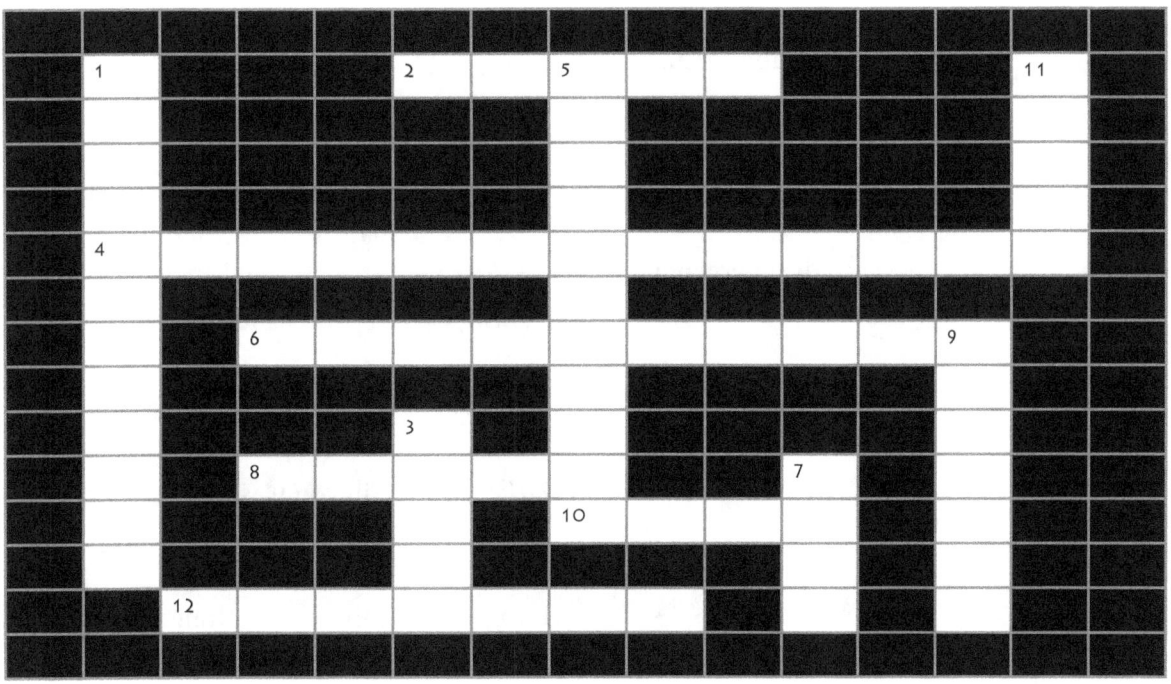

HORIZONTAL

2 SOAP
4 SMALL CUPS
6 EMERGENCY
8 HANDS
10 DRY
12 SICK

VERTICAL

1 NO ESTÁ FUNCIONANDO
3 CUCHILLO
5 VIDRIO ROTO
7 LAVA
9 ASPIRINA
11 TENEDORES

148 = CIENTO CUARENTA Y OCHO

Write the letter of the corresponding English phrase on the line next to the Spanish phrase.

1. _____ Lava esto otra vez. Está sucio.
2. _____ ¿Necesitas una curita?
3. _____ Los vidrios rotos van aquí.
4. _____ En caso de emergencia, marca 911.
5. _____ Déjalo remojando.
6. _____ No vengas al trabajo si estás enferma.
7. _____ ¿Hay algo que no está funcionando?
8. _____ ¿Puedes lavar más tenedores?
9. _____ Seca las copas de vino.
10. _____ Lávate las manos con jabón
11. _____ Dame un cuchillo filoso.
12. _____ Pon las tazas pequeñas en su lugar.

A. *(ah)* Restock the small cups.
B. *(beh)* Give me a sharp knife.
C. *(seh)* Wash this again. It's dirty.
D. *(deh)* Wash your hands with soap.
E. *(eh)* Dry the wine glasses.
F. *(ehf-feh)* Do you need a band-aid?
G. *(heh)* Will you wash more forks?
H. *(ah-che)* Is there something that is not working?
I. *(eeee)* The broken glass goes here.
J. *(hoh-tah)* Don't come to work if you are sick.
K. *(kah)* Let it soak.
L. *(ehl-leh)* In case of emergency, call 911.

149= CIENTO CUARENTA Y NUEVE

Have one person say the lines for server Eva Perón and the other person say the lines for dishwasher José de San Martín.

Eva Perón:	¿Puedes lavar más cucharas? ¿Hay algo que no está funcionando?
José de San Martín:	Sí. El lavaplatos no funciona. Tengo que lavar las cucharas a mano. Voy a tardar toda la noche.
Eva Perón:	Entonces, déjalas remojando. Ahora, seca las copas de vino.
José de San Martín:	¡Ay, caramba! Este vidrio está roto. Ay, me duele mi dedo.
Eva Perón:	¿Necesitas una curita? En caso de emergencia, marca 911.
José de San Martín:	Una curita es suficiente. Ay de mí, mi dedo no deja de sangrar. Voy a intentar lavar mis manos con jabón.
Eva Perón:	Mejor ve al doctor. No vengas al trabajo mañana tampoco. Descansa un día entero. Yo voy a lavar los platos.
José de San Martín:	Gracias, ahora voy a ir a ver al doctor. ¡Hasta luego!

150 = CIENTO CINCUENTA

Here is a chart to help you with this, that, these and those. Read the chart and then practice by translating the two sentences, check the answer key when you finish. For more on this and that, see page 235.

	THIS	THESE	THAT (Use with objects nearby)	THOSE (Use with objects nearby)	THAT (Use with objects farther away)	THOSE (Use with objects farther away)
MASCULINE	Este	Estos	Ese	Esos	Aquel	Aquello
FEMININE	Esta	Estas	Esa	Esas	Aquella	Aquella

1. (Pointing far away) That (female) server helps that (nearby) dishwasher with the those (nearby) sharp knives and these (nearby) hot plates.
   _____

2. These salads need those (nearby) onions, but make this salad without those (nearby) onions. _____

151 = CIENTO CINCUENTA Y UNO

A common question is, "Which language is easier to learn, Spanish or English?" The answer is both languages have challenging aspects, but anything can be learned if you are willing to put in the effort. English is a combination of Latin and Germanic rules. Since Spanish is based on Latin rules, there are similarities between English and Spanish. Other Latin based languages include French, Italian, Romanian, Catalan and Portuguese, just to name a few.

Another common question is, "Why shouldn't everyone learn English?" The answer is many people are trying to learn English. After these Spanish lessons, you realize learning another language is not that easy. English language fluency increases according to how many generations of the family have resided in the United States. For example, the Pew Hispanic Center in 2007 reported only 23% of first-generation Hispanics spoke English very well. This increased to 88% by the second generation and 94% of third or higher generations. In fact, many third-generation Hispanic/Chicanos may not even speak Spanish.

A great way to increase your level of Spanish is to find a native speaker and meet weekly for an "intercambio" or "exchange." Speak English for half of the time and Spanish for the other half. This will help you to increase your skills and practice the language during real conversations.

152 = CIENTO CINCUENTA Y DOS

It is great to live in the present, but sometimes you will need to chat in the past tense. These two verbs are both the same in the preterite past tense. Read the chart on the next page out loud and then do the following activities to practice with the verb. Check your answers on page 265.

To be = Ser + To go = Ir (Preterite Past Tense):

I was. I went. = Yo fui.	We were. We went. = Nosotros fuimos.
You were. You went. = Tú fuiste.	
He was. He went. = Él fue. She was. She went. = Ella fue. You were. You went. = Usted fue. (singular, formal)	They were. They went. = Ellos fueron. They were. They went. (all female) = Ellas fueron. You were. You went. (plural) = Ustedes fueron.

1. We were late yesterday. _____

2. I went to Spanish class on Tuesday. _____

3. Were you sick last Monday? _____

153 = CIENTO CINCUENTA Y TRES

To talk about completed actions in the past, you use the preterite tense. Read through the endings for the regular preterite tense and then complete the practice exercises.

To speak = Hablar (-ar preterite):

I spoke. = Yo hablé.	We spoke. = Nosotros hablamos.
You spoke. = Tú hablaste. (informal, singular)	
He spoke. = Él habló. She spoke. = Ella habló. You spoke. = Usted habló. (formal, singular)	They spoke. = Ellos hablaron. They spoke. (all female) = Ellas hablaron. You spoke. = Ustedes hablaron. (formal, plural)

TO EAT = COMER (-ER PRETERITE):

I ate. = Yo comí.	We ate. = Nosotros comimos.
You ate. = Tú comiste.	
He ate. = Él comió. She ate. = Ella comió. You ate. = Usted comió. (formal)	They ate. = Ellos comieron. They ate. (all female) = Ellas comieron. You ate. = Ustedes comieron.

TO LIVE = VIVIR (-IR PRETERITE):

I lived. = Yo viví.	We lived. = Nosotros vivimos.
You lived. = Tú viviste.	
He lived. = Él vivió. She lived. = Ella vivió. You lived. = Usted vivió. (formal)	They lived. = Ellos vivieron. They lived. (all female) = Ellas vivieron. You lived. = Ustedes vivieron.

Translate these phrases:

1. She lived in Argentina. _____
2. He spoke Spanish. _____
3. We ate empanadas. _____
4. They spoke English. _____
5. I ate a lot of meat. _____

If you would like more information on the regular and irregular preterite tense and imperfect past, see Extra Grammar-Lesson 8. The appendix has some practice exercises for the past tense. A more advanced grammar book or a college course would help you to learn even more.

154 = CIENTO CINCUENTA Y CUATRO

Read the information about these three South American countries.

EL PAÍS	ARGENTINA	URUGUAY	PARAGUAY
LA MONEDA NACIONAL	Peso	Peso	Guaraní
LOS LUGARES PARA VISITAR	**Buenos Aires** • *La Capital* • *La Casa Rosada = The Pink House is the presidential palace* • *Plaza de Mayo* • *Teatro Colón* • *Obelisco = Obelisk* **Iguazú** • *Waterfalls* **Pampas** • *Grasslands*	**Montevideo** • *La Capital* **Colonia de Sacramento** • *Calle de los Suspiros = Oldest Street of Sighs* • *Portón de Campo = City Gate* **Punta del Este** • *Beach*	**Asunción** • *La capital* **Itaipú Dam** • *One of the world's biggest hydroelectric dam* **Chaco** • *Rainforest* • *Butterflies* **Encarnación** • *Jesuit ruins*
LA POBLACIÓN	39.5 million	3.3 million	6.1 million
LA GENTE FAMOSA	**Eva Perón (1919–1952)** • *First Lady (1946–1952)* **Diego Maradona (Born 1960)** • *Soccer player* **José de San Martín (1778–1850)** • *Independence leader* **Juan Manuel de Rosas (1793–1877)** • *Ruler 1829–1852*	**José Gervasio Artigas (1764–1850)** • *Independence leader against Brazil and Portugal* **Virginia Patrone (Born 1950)** • *Painter* **Natalia Oreiro (Born 1977)** • *Singer, actress*	**Alfredo Strossner (1912–2006)** • *Dictator (1954–1989)* **Francisco Solano López (1826–1870)** • *Dictator and Leader of the War of Triple Alliance that Paraguay lost against Argentina, Brazil, and Uruguay* **Celeste Troche (Born 1981)** • *Golfer*
LA COMIDA	**Parrilla** • *Grilled meats* **Empanadas** • *Pastry pockets filled with meat inside* **Dulce de Leche** • *Sweet, carmelized condensed milk* **Dulce de Membrillo** • *Quince jam* **Italian Pasta Dishes**	**Asado** • *Grilled meats* **Chivito** • *Sandwich* **Alfajores** • *Cookies with dulce de leche in the middle* **Ñoquis/Gnocchis** • *Pasta dumplings* **Italian pasta dishes**	**Yerba Mate** • *Tea drunk with a metal or cane straw called a "bombilla"* **Tereré** • *Iced herbal tea* **Sopa Paraguaya** • *Soup of smashed corn, cheese, milk, and onions*
EL INGRESO ANUAL = ANNUAL INCOME (GNI)	$6,050 per year	$6,380 per year	$1,670 per year

155 = CIENTO CINCUENTA Y CINCO

Read these three trivia statements about Argentina, Uruguay and Paraguay. Two sentences are true and one is false. Guess which one is not true. The previous cultural section does not contain the answers, so check the Answer Key to find out why one of them is not culturally correct.

Interesting things = Cosas interesantes:

1. _____ The balcony of the "Casa Rosada" is where Eva Perón and her husband rallied their supporters known as the descamisados = shirtless. In the movie Evita, Madonna sang, "Don't cry for me Argentina," from the very same spot.

2. _____ Uruguay has never won a World Cup in fútbol = soccer.

3. _____ If you cross the Itapú dam by bus you will go from Paraguay to Brazil.

Food = Comida:

1. _____ Yerba Mate in Paraguay, Argentina and Uruguay is served in individual tea cups after the tea has been brewed for 24 hours.

2. _____ If you ordered a Pancho in Uruguay, you would get a hot dog. Salsa Golf is a condiment that might be on top of your hot dog if you are in Argentina.

3. _____ Since payday is traditionally the 30th of the month, people in Argentina and Uruguay eat Ñoqui's the day before, because they are cheap and filling.

156 = CIENTO CINCUENTA Y SEIS

Select one of these final projects. Either present these during the final lesson (page 192) and/or share them with Spanish-speaking employees or friends. Note: more project ideas are on page 166.

- **THE THEATER = EL TEATRO:** Role play a typical workplace exchange with a Spanish-speaking employee. Do this alone or with a partner and use props or exaggerate to make this funny. Each person should say about 10 lines. Have a native speaker check your script before your presentation.

- **THE IMPORTANT PHRASES = LAS FRASES IMPORTANTES:** Make your own list of 15 of the phrases you will use the most for your job. Type these in English and Spanish. (Add the pronunciation if it helps you.) Either take these from the phrases in the lessons or invent your own. Make a small "cheat sheet" to keep with you at work or make a poster to hang in the kitchen.

- **IN THE KITCHEN = EN LA COCINA:** Write out at least 12 sentences in Spanish for a cooking show script. This will be the steps to the recipe as you are preparing the food. Let us know in Spanish what ingredients you will be using. Either videotape this cooking show or demonstrate it live during Lesson 10.

- **THE MAP = EL MAPA:** Write out at least 12 sentences that give us a tour of your workplace. Use directional words, norte, sur, oeste, este, a la derecha, a la izquierda, etc. Design this map and print it from your computer or use a video camera and give us a walking tour in Spanish.

- **THE STORY = EL CUENTO:** This could be a mini-book with at least 12 sentences about any topic of your choice. It could be about Hispanic holidays, a trip, or even a book about a typical day.

- **THE MENU = EL MENÚ:** Make a menu for your dream restaurant. You should have at least four categories, such as beverages, appetizers, entrées and desserts, etc. You need to have five items in each category or 20 items total along with the prices. Write the name of the item and then a description. For example, a chicken breast with white rice and fried plantains = una pechuga de pollo con arroz blanco y plátanos fritos.

Note: Turn to the next page for more final project ideas.

🌐 **THE TRAVEL AGENCY = LA AGENCIA DE VIAJE:** You are a travel agent advertising your country so people will want to come to visit. You must make a brochure, poster or computer presentation about your country. Include a map of your country, pictures or drawings, newspaper clippings and anything else representing the country. You will need to include at least 12 sentences IN SPANISH describing the following:

1. The name of the country and the capital. Example: Mi país se llama _____ y la capital se llama_____.

2. The name of the money and how much one U.S. dollar equals. The exchange rate changes daily and can be found on the Internet.

3. The population and/or size of the country

4. What three things could a tourist do or see in your country?

5. What could a tourist try eating or what products could they buy as souvenirs?

6. What music, dance, typical sport, or famous artwork could they enjoy?

7. What is the government like? Any historical sites? (Use past tense if possible)

8. Who are some famous people from your country and why are they famous?

9. Describe the flag: Example: La bandera tiene los colores _____.) (Include an example of a flag)

10. What are some holidays your country celebrates?

11. What animals are native to your country?

12. What is the weather like in December in your country?

🌐 **HAVE ANY OTHER IDEAS? = ¿TIENE ALGUNA OTRA IDEA?:** Create any other project with at least 12 phrases in Spanish that will help you at your job. This project should be meaningful to you.

157 = CIENTO CINCUENTA Y SIETE

Translate these phrases. Write the English for the first seven phrases and write the Spanish for the last seven phrases. This may be done as an exam or as homework for the next lesson. When finished check your answers in the Answer Key.

1. ¿Necesitas una curita? _____

2. Seca las copas de vino. _____

3. Lávate las manos con jabón. _____

4. ¿Hay algo que no está funcionando? _____

5. Está sucio. _____

6. Los vidrios rotos van aquí. _____

7. ¿Puedes lavar más tenedores? _____

8. Don't come to work if you are sick. _____

9. Restock the small cups. _____

10. In case of emergency, call 911. _____

11. Give me a sharp knife. _____

12. Wash this again. _____

13. Do you need an aspirin? _____

14. Let it soak. _____

158 = CIENTO CINCUENTA Y OCHO

Play the game of "Toma Todo". Each player chooses 10 flashcards he or she would like to practice. These may be from any of the lessons 1–8. The first person to run out of flashcards loses the game. When one person says them in Spanish, the other player could try to say them in English without peeking at the back of the flashcard.

IF YOU ROLL A 1 - TOMA 1 = TAKE 1 You take one from the center and say it in Spanish.

IF YOU ROLL A 2 - TOMA 2 = TAKE 2 You take two from the center and say them in Spanish.

IF YOU ROLL A 3 - PON 1 = PUT 1 You put one in the center and say it in Spanish.

IF YOU ROLL A 4 - PON 2 = PUT 2 You put two in the center and say them in Spanish.

IF YOU ROLL A 5 - TODOS PONEN = EVERYONE PUTS ONE. EACH player has to put one in the center and say it in Spanish

IF YOU ROLL A 6 - *TOMA TODO* = TAKE EVERYTHING. ¡Jackpot! Take all the pieces from the center and as an extra bonus you don't have to say anything.

159 = CIENTO CINCUENTA Y NUEVE

Cut the flashcards on the following page apart, or make your own. Keep the flashcards in a plastic bag, envelope, or in your wallet and practice as much as possible during the week. Place one phrase a day on your refrigerator, mirror, or computer and learn a few at a time. Strive to find at least five minutes each day to review them, especially if you are waiting for someone or arrive early somewhere. Save all the flashcards to use during the games later in the book.

Don't come to work if you are sick.	Wash your hands with soap.	In case of emergency, call 911.
Do you need a band-aid or an aspirin?	Will you wash more forks?	Wash this again. It's dirty.
Let it soak.	Dry the wine glasses.	Give me a sharp knife.
Restock the small cups.	The broken glass goes here.	Is there something that is not working?

En caso de emergencia, marca 911. *(Ehn Kah-soh Deh Eh-mehr-hen-see/ah, Mahr-kah Noo/eh-veh Oo-no Oo-no.)*	**Lávate las manos con jabón.** *(LAH-vah-teh Lahs Mah-nohs Kohn Hah-bohN.)*	**No vengas al trabajo si estás enfermo/a.** *(No Vehn-gahs Ahl Trah-bah-hoh See Ehs-tahs Ehn-fehr-moh.)*
Lava esto otra vez. *(Lah-vah Ehs-toh Oh-troh Vehs.)* **Está sucio.** *(Ehs-tah Soo-see/oh.)*	**¿Puedes lavar más tenedores?** *(Pweh-dehs Lah-vahr Mahs Teh-neh-doh-rehs?)*	**¿Necesitas una curita o una aspirina?** *(Neh-seh-see-tahs Oo-nah Koo-ree-tah Oh Oo-nah Ahs-pee-ree-nah?)*
Dame un cuchillo filoso. *(Dah-meh Oon Koo-chee-yoh Fee-loh-so.)*	**Seca las copas de vino.** *(Seh-kah Lahs Koh-pahs Deh Vee-noh.)*	**Déjalo remojando.** *(Deh-hah-loh Reh-moh-hahn-doh.)*
¿Hay algo que no está funcionando? *(Eye Ahl-goh Keh No Ehs-tah Foon-see/oh-nahn-doh?)*	**Los vidrios rotos van aquí.** *(Lohs Vee-dree-ohs Roh-tohs Vahn Ah-kee.)*	**Pon las tazas pequeñas en su lugar.** *(PohN Lahs Tah-sahs Peh-keh-nyahs Ehn Soo Loo-gahr.)*

Travel Tips And Chat with Hispanic Customers

GOALS: In this lesson you will learn about these topics: Latin American schedules, restaurant etiquette, serving Hispanic customers, menus, Puerto Rico, Dominican Republic, Cuba and Equatorial Guinea, travel tips and recipes.

160 = CIENTO SESENTA

Read the paragraph silently to yourself and then have each person read one sentence aloud. Finally, answer the four questions to check your understanding. Look in the Answer Key, for an English translation of the paragraph and to check your answers.

Durante el verano pasado, mi familia fue a San Juan, Puerto Rico. Había muchos resturantes, iglesias, museos, edificios y gente. Había casí 1.6 millones de habitantes en el área de la capital. Nos gustaron El Morro y El Bosque Tropical "El Yunque." Comimos tostones, frijoles y arroz con pollo y bebimos piraguas. Finalmente mi familia le encantaba relajarse en la playa.

Using the previous paragraph, answer these four questions about the family's summer vacation last year.

1. Where did the family go last summer? _____

2. How big is the population in the capital? _____

3. What two tourist attractions did they like? _____
_____

4. What did they eat? _____

161 = CIENTO SESENTA Y UNO

Use the flash cards from the previous lessons and play a trivia/vocabulary game. Divide the group into two teams and pick one person to go first from each team or play this with partners. Someone will announce a phrase in English. Use the phrases on the flashcards or ask trivia questions about the 21 Spanish-speaking countries covered in each lesson. The first person to give the correct answer in Spanish gets a point. The winner is the person or the team that gets the most points at the end of 10 minutes. Use the Glossary for phrases. ¡Buena suerte! = Good luck!

162 = CIENTO SESENTA Y DOS

Ready to review? Make a sample menu with some of your favorite food items or translate the menu from your favorite restaurant. For more food words see the Extra Vocabulary section starting on page 206. Answers will vary. ¡Buen Provecho! = Enjoy your meal!

THE FOODS = LAS COMIDAS	THE DRINKS = LAS BEBIDAS
1. _____	1. _____
2. _____	2. _____
3. _____	3. _____
4. _____	4. _____
5. _____	5. _____

163 = CIENTO SESENTA Y TRES

Eating times and schedules vary in Latin America. Many businesses, museums and schools don't start until 9:00 a.m. The biggest difference is lunch = almuerzo. The main meal = la comida is eaten generally around 2:00 p.m. and consists of many courses. In fact, some shops and schools set their schedules around this meal so entire families can eat together. In some schools in Spain the children eat breakfast = desayuno and then go to school from 9:00 a.m. to 12:00 noon. After a three hour lunch break school resumes from 3:00 to 5:00 p.m. After school and work, a light snack = merienda is eaten.

Many Americans have been caught by surprise when restaurants are closed around 5:00 or 6:00 p.m. since no one is eating "supper" at that time. The last meal of the day is generally a light sandwich supper = cena around 9:00 or 10:00 at night. Generally people stay up much later in Latin American countries than in the United States, and parties last all night. For example, a wedding in Costa Rica had a timetable of 7:00 p.m. for the church service. At 8:00 p.m. the dancing at the reception started. The food was served at 10:00 p.m. The reception lasted until 5:00 a.m., then we went out for breakfast!

164 = CIENTO SESENTA Y CUATRO

Use these six Spanish restaurant server phrases with Hispanic customers or try ordering in Spanish at your favorite Latino restaurant. The polite usted form in these phrases is better for customer service. Note that Lessons 1-8 were in the tú form wheras Lesson 9 will be written in the usted form.

1. Welcome to our restaurant. = Bienvenidos a nuestro restaurante.
   (Bee/ehn-veh-nee-dohs Ah Noo/ehs-troh Rehs-tah/oo-rahn-teh.)

2. I recommend my favorite dish, the roast beef. =
   Yo le recomiendo mi plato preferido, la carne asada.
   (Yoh Leh Reh-koh-mee/ehn-doh Mee Plah-toh Preh-feh-ree-doh, Lah Kahr-neh Ah-sah-dah.)

3. How much does the plate of the day (prix fixe) cost? =
   ¿Cuánto cuesta el plato del día?
   (Qwahn-toh Qwehs-tah Ehl Plah-toh Dehl Dee-ah?)

4. It costs 16 dollars. = Cuesta 16 dólares.
   (Qwehs-tah Dee/eh-see-seh/ace DOH-lah-rehs.)

5. What would you like to drink and eat? = ¿Qué desea para tomar y comer?
   (Keh Deh-seh-ah Pah-rah Toh-mahr Ee Koh-mehr?)

6. I would like to order the flour tortillas. =
   Quiero pedir las tortillas de harina.
   (Key/air-oh Peh-deer Lahs Tohr-tee-yahs Deh Ah-ree-nah.)

165 = CIENTO SESENTA Y CINCO

Circle the English choice that matches the Spanish phrase.

1. **Cuesta 16 dólares.**
   a. It takes 16 hours.
   b. It costs 16 dollars.
   c. She is 16 years old.
   d. We have 16 doors.

2. **¿Cuánto cuesta el plato del día?**
   a. How many plates broke today?
   b. How many plates did you use today?
   c. What is on the prix fixe menu?
   d. How much does the plate of the day cost?

3. **Quiero pedir las tortillas de harina.**
   a. I would like more corn tortillas.
   b. I want more tortilla omelette.
   c. Are these flour or corn tortillas?
   d. I would like to order the flour tortillas.

4. **Yo le recomiendo mi plato preferido.**
   a. I recommend my favorite dish.
   b. I don't recommend any dishes here.
   c. What is your favorite dish?
   d. I recommend my favorite steak.

5. **¿Qué desea para comer?**
   a. When would you like to come over?
   b. What would you like to eat?
   c. I don't want to come to visit.
   d. What would you like to drink?

6. **Bienvenidos a nuestro restaurante.**
   a. Welcome to our world.
   b. This is a great restaurant.
   c. Welcome to our restaurant.
   d. Come back again to our restaurant.

166 = CIENTO SESENTA Y SEIS

Take turns using the phrases in 164 = ciento sesenta y cuatro to order from the mini-menu in 162 = ciento sesenta y dos. Have one person be the customer and the other will be the server. Here is a brief cultural note to help you. Lunches and dinners in the Spanish-speaking world are generally leisurely activities to be enjoyed. A traditional dinner includes several courses and chatting with your friends during the entire meal. In Latin American countries it's considered impolite for the waiter to give you the check until you specifically ask for the bill. Keep this in mind with your Hispanic customers. Likewise, if you are ready to pay, but you don't snap or signal to get your waiter's attention, you might be sitting and waiting for a long time.

167 = CIENTO SESENTA Y SIETE

Here are some phrases to help you when you travel in Latin America or when you need to finish serving Hispanic customers. These phrases are in the formal usted form which is better for customer service.

1. Cheers! Enjoy your meal. (Bon Appétit.) =
   ¡Salud! Buen provecho.
   (Sah-lood!) (Bwhen Proh-veh-cho.)
   Note: Salud also means Bless you!

2. The bill, please. =
   La cuenta, por favor.
   (Lah Qwehn-tah, Pohr Fah-vohr.)

3. Here is the bill. I will be the cashier whenever you're ready. =
   Aquí está la cuenta. Yo seré su cajera cuando usted esté listo.
   (Ah-kee Ehs-tah Lah Qwehn-tah.) (Yoh Seh-reh Soo Cah-heh-rah Qwahn-doh Oos-tehd Ehs-teh Lees-toh.)

4. Where is the bathroom? =
   ¿Dónde está el baño?
   (DohN-deh Ehs-tah Ehl Bah-ñyoh?)

5. Thank you for coming. =
   Gracias por venir.
   (Grah-see/ahs Pohr Veh-neer.)

6. Hope all goes well. =
   Que le vaya bien.
   (Keh Leh Vah-yah Bee/ehn.)

168 = CIENTO SESENTA Y OCHO

Write the letter of the corresponding English phrase on the line next to the Spanish phrase.

1. _____ Que le vaya bien.
2. _____ ¡Salud!
3. _____ Gracias por su paciencia.
4. _____ ¿Dónde está el chef?
5. _____ La cuenta, por favor.
6. _____ Aquí está la cuenta.
7. _____ ¿Dónde está el baño?
8. _____ Gracias por venir.
9. _____ Buen provecho.
10. _____ Yo seré su cajera cuando usted esté listo.

A. *(ah)* The bill, please.
B. *(beh)* I will be the cashier whenever you're ready.
C. *(seh)* Here is the bill.
D. *(deh)* Thank you for your patience.
E. *(eh)* Where is the bathroom?
F. *(ehf-feh)* Cheers! Bless you!
G. *(heh)* Thank you for coming.
H. *(ah-che)* Bon Appétit.
I. *(eeee)* Hope all goes well.
J. *(hoh-tah)* Where is the chef?

169 = CIENTO SESENTA Y NUEVE

An employee has just said, "Voy a México. Hasta luego." They are leaving for a week long vacation. How would you respond? Hint: Fill in the squares of the puzzle with letters from ONE of the Spanish phrases from page 176.

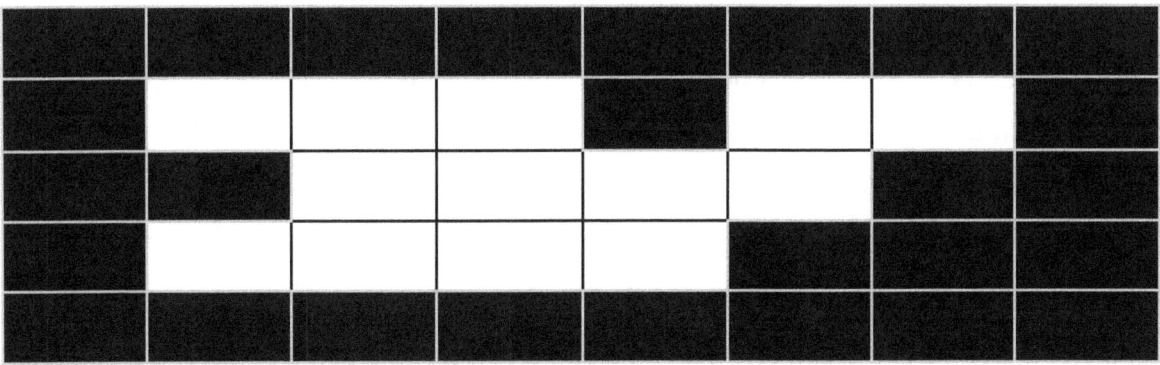

170 = CIENTO SETENTA

Have one person say the lines for Celia Cruz and the other person say the lines for Roberto Clemente. Then switch roles.

Celia Cruz:	Bienvenidos a nuestro restaurante. ¿Qué desea para tomar?
Roberto Clemente:	Quiero pedir dos vinos tintos.
Celia Cruz:	Aquí están sus vinos. ¡Salud! ¿Qué desea para comer? Yo le recomiendo mi plato preferido, el bistec.
Roberto Clemente:	Bueno, tengo hambre. ¿Cuánto cuesta el plato del día?
Celia Cruz:	Cuesta 38 dólares. Es muy rico y delicioso.
Roberto Clemente:	Es demasiado caro. No voy a comer. La cuenta, por favor.
Celia Cruz:	Aquí está la cuenta. Yo seré su cajera cuando usted esté listo. Gracias por venir.
Roberto Clemente:	Que le vaya bien.

171 = CIENTO SETENTA Y UNO

Working with a partner, fill in the blanks to write your own conversation. You may use the following skit as a guideline or write about a different restaurant situation. Present your new conversation to the group.

Estudiante #1:	Bienvenidos a _____ . ¿Qué desea para tomar?
Estudiante #2:	Quiero pedir _____
Estudiante #1:	Aquí están_____ ¡Salud! ¿Qué desea para comer? Yo le recomiendo mi plato preferido, _____
Estudiante #2:	Bueno, tengo hambre. ¿Cuánto cuesta el plato del día?
Estudiante #1:	Cuesta _____ dólares. Es muy rico y delicioso.
Estudiante #2:	Es demasiado caro. No voy a comer. La cuenta, por favor.
Estudiante #1:	Aquí está la cuenta. Yo seré su cajera cuando usted esté listo. Gracias por venir.
Estudiante #2:	Que le vaya bien.

172 = CIENTO SETENTA Y DOS

Read the information about these three islands and one Spanish-speaking country in Africa.

EL PAÍS	PUERTO RICO	DOMINICAN REPUBLIC	CUBA	EQUATORIAL GUINEA
LA MONEDA NACIONAL	U.S. Dollar	Dominican Peso	Cuban Peso	Franc
LOS LUGARES PARA VISITAR	San Juan • La capital El Moro • The fortress Las Cuevas de Camuy El Yunque • National park • Rainforest	Santo Domingo • La capital Las playas • 1,000 miles of white sand beaches Tres Ojos de Agua • Caves Amber coast	Havana • La capital • Forteleza = Fortress • Castillos = Castles • Gran Teatro • National Ballet	Malabo • La capital • This former Spanish colony in Africa gained independence in 1968
LA POBLACIÓN	3.9 million	9.8 million	11.3 million	520,000
LA GENTE FAMOSA	Ricky Martin (Born 1971) • Singer Roberto Clemente (1934–1972) • Baseball Player Luisa Capetillo (1879–1922) • Labor activist, women's rights	Juan Pablo Duarte (1813–1876) • Founding Father of the Republic Rafael Trujillo (1891–1961) • Dictator (1930–1961) Julia Alvarez (Born 1950) • Author	Celia Cruz (c.1925–2003) • Singer Fidel Castro (Born 1926) • Dictator (1959–2008) José Martí (1853–1895) • Poet • Writer Albita Rodriguez (Born 1962) • Singer	Francisco Nguema (1924–1979) • Dictator (1968–1979) Obiang Nguema (1942–Present) • Began as dictator (1979) Equatorial Guinea Women's National Soccer Team • Hosted and won the 2008 Women's African Football Championship
LA COMIDA	Frijoles Negros • Black bean Soup Arroz con Pollo • Chicken and rice Tostones • Twice fried plantains	Dominican Sancocho • Stew Mangú • Mashed plantain	Tostones • Twice fried plantains Frijoles Negros • Black beans Sandwich Cubano • Pork, ham and cheese sandwich	Arroz • Rice Pescado • Fish Malamba • Drink made from sugarcane Cassava • Yucca
EL INGRESO ANUAL = ANNUAL INCOME	$14,371 per year	$3,550 per year	$1,170 per year	$12,870 per year

173 = CIENTO SETENTA Y TRES

Read these three trivia statements about Puerto Rico, Dominican Republic, Cuba and Equatorial Guinea. Two sentences are true and one is false. Guess which one is not true. The previous cultural section does not contain the answers, so check the Answer Key to find out why one of them is not culturally correct.

INTERESTING THINGS = COSAS INTERESANTES:

1. _____ When you swim at night in the Bioluminescence Bay in Puerto Rico, the organisms light up as you move in the water.

2. _____ Yank tanks are classic cars in Cuba. Many were purchased from the U.S. before the 1959 embargo and are still running.

3. _____ Equatorial Guinea is located just north of Brazil.

FOOD = COMIDA:

1. _____ In the Dominican Republic, la bandera = the flag is a lunch of rice, red beans, plantains, meat and salad.

2. _____ In Puerto Rico, tostones are plantains that are usually toasted in a toaster oven.

3. _____ In Cuba, Ropa Vieja = Old clothes is a delicious meal of shredded steak in tomato sauce, black beans, yellow rice, fried yucca and plantains.

174 = CIENTO SETENTA Y CUATRO

Use the fact charts from all of the Latin American countries in lessons 1–9. Research some of the places to visit or the foods and write two true and one false statement. Have your partner or a Spanish-speaking employee guess which one is false.

175 = CIENTO SETENTA Y CINCO

After you have learned all these phrases, it is time to take a vacation. Here is some travel advice. When traveling, it is important to make sure your passport is protected at all times. This is the document that is the key for entering and leaving any country.

Before you leave, make copies of all important documents; leave a copy at home with a trusted friend and carry a copy in your suitcase. If something is lost or stolen, this copy will come in handy. Invest in a good travel wallet, which is like a pouch. These may be concealed under your clothes and hide items like a passport, credit cards, ATM cards and money. Fanny packs and back packs may be easily compromised by a determined thief. It may be a good idea to leave your jewelry and rings at home as they are not needed and will attract the wrong people.

Latin America is very enjoyable provided you don't forget to pack your common sense. The main thing is to enjoy yourself and be willing to practice your newly acquired Spanish. La práctica hace al maestro. = Practice makes perfect. By the way, there is no grammar section for this lesson. Take a break. You are on vacation!

176 = CIENTO SETENTA Y SEIS

Remember that during the next lesson you will present your final project. Project ideas were explained in 156 = ciento cincuenta y seis. Share them with Hispanic employees or Spanish-speaking friends. Here are over 20 recipe ideas to use next time for a final fiesta or find your own Hispanic recipe. Look at the recipes and decide what to make and bring. Write the name of the person who will bring each of these table setting products on the line next to the item.

WHO? = ¿QUIÉN?

plates = platos _____ napkins = servilletas _____

forks = tenedores _____ spoons = cucharas _____

knives = cuchillos _____ cups = vasos _____

The recipes = Las recetas:

1. **Tortilla de patatas (Spain):** A Tortilla de patatas is made with 2 onions, 4 potatoes and 6 eggs. Heat olive oil in a deep fat fryer. This can also be done in a skillet. Heat enough olive oil to cover the potatoes; this may be a cup or more of oil. Cut the potatoes and onions into small (1/2 inch) slices and fry them until brown. Lightly salt them to taste. In a separate bowl, stir the eggs a few times without beating them. Add the potatoes/onions to the eggs. Heat 1 tablespoon of olive oil in a skillet and add the egg/potato/onions mixture. Cook on medium heat for about 10 minutes. Top the skillet with a plate and flip it over. Heat 1 tablespoon of olive oil in the skillet and slide the "tortilla de patatas" back into the pan. Heat for about 5–10 minutes. Eat hot or cold. In Spain they use long baguette bread and put the "tortilla de patatas" inside as a sandwich. You will find one triangle piece of tortilla de patatas as a typical tapas dish. (See pages 36-37 for an explanation of tapas.)

2. **Tortillas/Pupusas/Arepas (Latin America):** It is easy to make your own tortillas. Buy "harina preparada para las tortillas" (tortilla flour). Take either the corn or white tortilla flour and then add the water and salt according to the package. Roll a ball and then shape them with a tortilla press. If you don't have a tortilla press, push a plate down on the dough to cut a circle or press the tortilla into a circle with your hands. Hint: You may want to use wax paper on each side of the dough ball to prevent it from sticking to the tortilla press. Finally, cook the tortilla on an electric skillet or pancake griddle for just a few minutes on each side. Finally, sprinkle them with cinnamon and sugar or top with salsa and cheese. To make pupusas or arepas follow the same steps, but make the dough thicker. ¡Qué rico! = How tasty!

3. **Gallo Pinto (Costa Rica):** In Nicaragua and Honduras, Gallo Pinto is usually made with red beans, whereas in Costa Rica, it is made with black beans. To make Gallo Pinto, heat 1 tablespoon of olive oil in a skillet. Sauté 1 chopped white onion and 2 cloves of garlic. Stir in one can of cooked black beans. (Do not drain.) Add 2 cups of cooked white rice and 1 teaspoon of Worcestershire sauce to the bean mix, and simmer for 5–10 minutes. Add a dash or two of crushed red pepper to taste. Chop some fresh cilantro and add that to the Gallo Pinto, but be careful because a small amount is very flavorful. Heat the mixture thoroughly and serve for breakfast with scrambled eggs.

4. **Cuban sandwiches (Cuba):** Slice one loaf of Cuban, Italian, or French bread into 4 parts. Split each part in half so that it is ready to fill. Spread mayonnaise or mustard on the bottom part of the bread. Stack the bread with sliced ham, roast pork, thin dill pickle slices and slices of Swiss cheese. Now add the top half of the bread. Brush with olive oil or butter. Put a heavy skillet on top of the sandwiches before grilling or baking in the oven. This will press them flat. Use a sandwich press for the same results. Bake them in the oven at 350 degrees until the cheese is melted.

5. **Mango gelatin (Central America):** Gelatin or flan or other kinds of pudding mixes may be found in a local grocery store or on the Internet. Some of the flavors are tembleque (a coconut dish), cajeta (like caramel), chocolate flan, walnut, sherry, piña (pineapple), peach and many more.

6. **Horchata (México):** Horchata, guanabana, tamarindo, sandía (watermelon), jamaica (hibiscus flower), mango and many other flavors of powdered drink mixes may be purchased from the grocery store. Klass Aguas Frescas brand makes many varieties. Simply mix with water to make a single serving or a pitcher full.

7. **Chicha/Mazamorra (Perú):** It is easy to make a purple corn pudding called Mazamorra and a purple corn drink called Chicha Morada. Both of these packaged mixes may be ordered from a Web site called La Bodega Peruana or other Web sites. Serve them with Inca Kola. It's a yellow carbonated soft drink tasting like bubble gum.

8. **Quesadillas (México):** Quesadillas are easy to make with a quesadilla maker or by folding one tortilla in half and cooking it on a sandwich-type grill. With a quesadilla maker, use two burrito-sized flour tortilla shells and fill them with your favorite meats and cheeses. Add salsa, black beans, corn and other spices. For a twist, make sweet, dessert quesadillas by adding cooked apples or slices of banana, cinnamon, and brown sugar to the plain tortillas and then cooking them. Serve with vanilla ice cream or whipped cream.

9. **Tostadas (México):** To make tostadas buy a package of tostada shells or fry your own. Spread with refried beans, then add chopped tomatoes and shredded lettuce. Top with Oaxacan or cheddar cheese, salsa and sliced avocados. Use any additional toppings as desired.

10. **Arroz con leche (Spain/Latin America):** To make this rice pudding, boil 4 cups of water with cinnamon. Add 2 cups of minute rice and cover for 5 minutes. Follow the package directions for other types of rice. Combine the rice with one can of sweetened condensed milk, one can of evaporated milk, a splash of vanilla, a dash of nutmeg and raisins. Add more rice to make a thicker pudding. Refrigerate for 1 hour and sprinkle cinnamon on top before serving.

11. **Sopapillas (México):** Mix together 1 teaspoon of salt, 2 teaspoons baking powder and 4 cups flour. Cut in 4 tablespoons of shortening. Measure 1 1/2 cups warm water and add to the dry ingredients. Mix the dough until it is smooth. Cover and let the dough rest for 20 minutes. Next, sprinkle flour onto a board and roll the dough until it is about 1/4 inch thick. Cut the dough into squares of about 3 inches. Add 2 quarts oil into a deep-fat fryer and heat to 375 degrees F. Use a candy thermometer to check that the oil is exactly 375 degrees so the sopapillas will puff up. Fry until golden brown, flipping them over halfway through. Put them on a plate with paper towels. Sprinkle with cinnamon and sugar. Serve them warm. Remember to reheat the oil to 375 between batches. This recipe makes about 2 dozen.

12. **Chicle = Chewing gum (Latin America):** Make your own chewing gum with a kit benefiting the chicleros in the rainforest. Chicleros are people who collect the sap from the chicle (gum) tree. Kits include the sap to melt and all of the ingredients. Kits to make your own gum can be found online.

13. **Chocolate (South America):** Chocolate comes from the cocoa bean pod, which may be found in the rainforests of Central and South America. Many companies sell authentic Latin American chocolates on the Internet and in Hispanic grocery stores. Make your own chocolate lollipops by melting chocolate chips and pouring them into any candy mold. Add lollipop sticks and freeze for about 10 minute. Kits to make your own chocolate candies from scratch can be found online.

14. **Chocolate caliente = Hot chocolate (México):** There are many different brands of Mexican Hot chocolate, that already have the cinnamon mixed into the bark. Blend the chocolate/cinnamon bark in the blender with hot milk to make a delicious drink in cold weather. Be sure to hold the top on the blender so the mixture doesn't fly out. Hot chocolate is even served for breakfast in Oaxaca, México.

15. **Dulces = Candies (Latin America):** One idea is to sample different candies from México, Spain and other countries. Latin Americans have been using candies and small toys to fill up piñatas for many years. Piñatas may have originated in Europe with a painted clay pot filled with candies and coins. A star-shaped piñata probably represented the Star of Bethlehem at Christmas time and is still used in the December Posadas celebrations. Now there are many designs from animals to cartoon characters. Find Web sites showing different styles of piñatas. To make your own piñata, start with an inflated balloon. Use newspaper dipped into liquid starch to cover the balloon. After it dries for a few days, decorate the piñata with tissue paper. Paint the tissue paper with watered down Elmer's glue to get it to stick to the piñata. Let this dry and then fill it with candy. In Cuba they attach strings to the piñata and instead of using a bat, everyone grabs a string and pulls the piñata apart.

16. **Pan Dulce = Sweet bread (Latin America):** "Pan Dulce" sweet breads are available at many bakeries or make your own. Check for Pan de los Muertos (The Bread of the Dead) the first few days of November. Look for the 3 Kings cakes (January 6) and Mardi Gras cakes (before Ash Wednesday). These cakes have a baby hidden inside and whoever finds the baby has to have the next fiesta. Sometimes they hide a coin inside the cake. Be careful while eating this one.

17. **Chicharrones (México):** Chicharrones are fried pork rinds. Buy them raw and they look like pasta wagon wheels. After you fry them, they puff up and may be dipped into salsa or sprinkled with cinnamon and sugar. It may be easier to buy them pre-cooked in bags usually located in the chip aisle at the grocery store.

18. **Tostones (Puerto Rico):** Tostones are fried plantains. The plantain looks like a huge banana, but it is really more like a potato so don't eat it raw. Heat 1/2 cup of oil in a skillet. Cut the plantain into circle slices. Fry the slices and then remove them from the skillet. Flatten them by smashing them with a plate or the bottom of a glass or use a "tostonera" from Puerto Rico. Dip the plantains in water, and then fry them again in the hot oil. Salt to taste and eat these while warm. Pre-packaged banana chips can be found in some grocery stores.

19. **QUESO FUNDIDO = CHEESE DIP (MÉXICO):** Cheese dip can be made by melting Velvetta and salsa together. Or use a can of tomatoes and add cooked ground beef. For a more authentic queso dip use Oaxacan cheese or any other fresh Mexican cheese that melts really well. Serve with chips.

20. **CHURROS (SPAIN):** Churros resemble long cinnamon sugar breadsticks. The dough may be made by combining 2 cups biscuit mix and 1 and 3/4 cups hot water. Stir for a few minutes. Roll the dough into long tubes or squeeze through a pastry bag. Fry 2 at a time in a deep fat fryer and then roll in a mixture of cinnamon and sugar. Eat warm. Other authentic churro recipes can be found on the internet.

21. **FLAN (LATIN AMERICA):** To make flan, put 1 cup of sugar in a saucepan and stir constantly on medium/low heat until liquid. Quickly pour the "caramel" to the bottom of a 10-inch pie plate or flan mold. In a separate bowl, stir 3 large eggs lightly. Add 1 can of evaporated milk, 1 can of sweetened condensed milk and 1 tablespoon of vanilla to the eggs. Gently stir to mix, do not beat. Pour into the pie plate or mold. Use a double boiler or put about 1 inch of boiling water in a larger pan and put the pie plate inside. This is called a Baño María = Maria's bath. Bake at 325 degrees for approximately 45 minutes. Refrigerate overnight or at least 4 hours and then flip over onto a serving dish allowing the caramel to drizzle across the top. It may be easier to buy a package of flan mix in the pudding aisle at the grocery store and just add milk.

22. **ENCHILADAS (MÉXICO):** To make enchiladas, start by browning one pound of hamburger. Add 3 ounces of cream cheese, 1 cup of salsa, 1/2 tablespoon of cumin, and 1 cup of shredded fiesta cheese to the hamburger. Grease a 9x13 pan. Put 3 spoonfuls of the hamburger mixture in one burrito-size tortilla and roll it up. About 6 burritos will fit in the pan. Then cover with 1 jar of enchilada sauce. Top with the remaining 1 cup of fiesta cheese and bake uncovered at 350 degrees F for 40 minutes.

23. **SALSA (LATIN AMERICA):** In a blender or food processor, combine 2 chopped green onions and 1 diced clove of garlic. Add cilantro, crushed red pepper and salt to taste. Add 2 1/2 cups of tomatoes fresh from the garden. Blend for a few seconds and serve with blue corn tortilla chips

24. **OTHER RECIPES:** You can find many other recipes in cookbooks or online. **¡BUEN PROVECHO! = ENJOY YOUR MEAL!**

177 = CIENTO SETENTA Y SIETE

Translate these phrases. Write the English for the first eight phrases and write the Spanish for the last seven phrases. This may be done as an exam or as homework for the next lesson. When finished check your answers in the Answer Key.

1. ¿Dónde está el baño? _____

2. Yo seré su cajera cuando usted esté listo. _____

3. Yo le recomiendo mi plato preferido, la carne asada. _____
   _____

4. La cuenta, por favor. _____

5. ¡Salud! _____

6. ¿Cuánto cuesta el plato del día? _____

7. Gracias por venir. _____

8. ¿Qué desea para tomar? _____

9. Welcome to our restaurant. _____

10. Here is the bill. _____

11. What would you like to eat? _____

12. Hope all goes well. _____

13. I would like to order the flour tortillas. _____

14. It costs 16 dollars. _____

15. Bon Appétit. _____

178 = CIENTO SETENTA Y OCHO

A conversation = Una conversación

Now that you have learned some phrases, it is time to create your own conversations. Finish the following sentences using a Spanish dictionary to help you. If you have a group, you all can share #1, then present #2, continuing on as time allows.

1. Me gusta _____
2. No me gusta _____
3. Yo soy _____
4. Yo estoy _____
5. Algún día, voy a... (a dream = un sueño) _____
6. Quiero tener _____
7. Mi comida favorita es _____
8. Mi trabajo es _____
9. Necesito _____
10. Aquí nadie sabe, pero en el pasado yo _____
11. Quisiera conocer (a person = una persona) _____
12. Este verano voy a _____
13. Nunca puedo _____
14. ¿Un viaje gratis? ¡Perfecto! Voy a _____
    con (with who? = ¿con quién?) _____

179 = CIENTO SETENTA Y NUEVE

Cut apart the 20 flashcards on the following page to use for "Lotería = Bingo". Pick any 16 flashcards from Lessons 1-9 and put them in any order to make four rows of 4. Use the phrases from the glossary to call out the phrases. Flip the card over when you hear the phrase called and keep going until you have four in a row turned over. Then yell, "¡LOTERÍA!" = "BINGO". Use the "Bingo" Game Board on page 64. Another idea is to separate all of the flashcards with questions from Lessons 1-9. Use these question to interview Spanish-speaking friends.

Welcome to our restaurant.	I recommend my favorite dish, the roast beef.	How much does the plate of the day cost?
Hope all goes well.	It costs 16 dollars.	What would you like to eat and drink?
The bill, please.	Here is the bill. I will be the cashier whenever you're ready.	I would like to order the flour tortillas.
Cheers! Enjoy your meal.	Where is the bathroom?	Thank you for coming.

¿Cuánto cuesta el plato del día? (Qwahn-toh Qwehs-tah Ehl Plah-toh Dehl Dee-ah?)	Yo le recomiendo mi plato preferido, la carne asada. (Yoh Leh Reh-koh-mee/ehn-doh Mee Plah-toh Preh-feh-ree-doh, Lah Kahr-neh Ah-sah-dah.)	Bienvenidos a nuestro restaurante. (Bee/ehn-veh-nee-dohs Ah Noo/ehs-troh Rehs-tah/oo-rahn-teh.)
¿Qué desea para tomar y comer? (Keh Deh-seh-ah Pah-rah Toh-mahr Ee Koh-mehr?)	Cuesta 16 dólares. Qwehs-tah Dee/eh-see-seh/ace Doh-lah-rehs.)	Que le vaya bien. (Keh Leh Vah-yah Bee/ehn.)
Quiero pedir las tortillas de harina. (Key/air-oh Peh-deer Lahs Tohr-tee-yahs Deh Ah-ree-nah.)	Aquí está la cuenta. Yo seré su cajera cuando usted esté listo. (Ah-kee Ehs-tah Lah Qwehn-tah. Yoh Seh-reh Soo Cah-heh-rah Qwahn-doh Oos-tehd Ehs-teh Lees-toh.)	La cuenta, por favor. (Lah Qwehn-tah, Pohr Fah-vor.)
Gracias por venir. (Grah-see/ahs Pohr Veh-neer.)	¿Dónde está el baño? (DohN-deh Ehs-tah Ehl Bah-ñyoh?)	¡Salud! (Sah-lood!) Buen provecho. (Bwhen Proh-veh-cho.)

LESSON 10 LECCIÓN

FUTURE CHATTING PROSPECTS

GOALS: In this lesson you will learn about these topics: final project presentations, proverbs, tongue twisters, 10 ideas to continue learning in the future, grocery store scavenger hunt and field trip, feedback form.

180 = CIENTO OCHENTA

Now that it is the final lesson, it is time to share your projects explained in 156 = ciento cincuenta y seis enjoy your food fiesta that was described in 176 = ciento setenta y seis. Present these final projects in front of the group and/or share them with your Hispanic employees.

Comments on final projects: _____

_____

_____

_____

_____

_____

_____

_____

_____

181 = CIENTO OCHENTA Y UNO

There are many dichos = proverbs in Spanish and English. Sometimes there are variations among countries and dialects. Read these examples of Spanish proverbs and write the letter on the line that matches with the equivalent English proverb.

THE PROVERBS = LOS DICHOS:

1. _____ Más vale tarde que nunca.

2. _____ A donde fueres, haz lo que vieres.

3. _____ Donde hay voluntad, hay un camino.

4. _____ A caballo regalado no se le mira el diente.

5. _____ Al mal tiempo, buena cara.

6. _____ A falta de pan, buenas son tortas.

7. _____ A lo hecho, pecho.

8. _____ Barriga llena, corazón contento.

9. _____ Cuando el río suena, agua lleva.

10. _____ Entre el dicho y el hecho hay un buen trecho.

11. _____ Dime con quién andas, y te diré quién eres.

12. _____ No todo lo que brilla es oro.

13. _____ Río que suena, piedras trae.

14. _____ Perro que ladra no muerde.

A. *(ah)* Where there is a will, there's a way (path).

B. *(beh)* Not everything that glitters is gold.

C. *(seh)* Better late than never.

D. *(deh)* A river that rumbles brings boulders. Any rumor has some truth.

E. *(eh)* To where you go, do the things you see. Also, when in Rome, do as the Romans do.

F. *(ehf-feh)* Don't look a gift horse in the mouth (or teeth).

G. *(heh)* Tell me who you're with and I'll tell you who you are. Also, birds of a feather flock together.

H. *(ah-che)* If there's no bread, cakes will do. Also, beggars can't be choosers.

I. *(eeee)* Full stomach, happy heart.

J. *(hoh-tah)* In the bad times, put on a good face.

K. *(kah)* A dog that barks doesn't bite. Also, his bark is worse than his bite.

L. *(ehl-leh)* Between word and deed, there's a wide trench. Also, easier said than done.

M. *(ehm-meh)* What's done is done, (take it on the chest). Also, face the music.

N. *(ehn-neh)* When the river makes noise, it's carrying water. Also, where there's smoke, there's fire.

182 = CIENTO OCHENTA Y DOS

Practice your pronunciation with these tongue twisters. Repeat them as quickly as possible.

TONGUE TWISTERS = TRABALENGUAS:

1. Pepe puso un peso en el piso del pozo. En el piso del pozo, Pepe puso un peso. = Pepe put a peso at the bottom of the well. At the bottom of the well, Pepe put a peso.

2. Erre con erre guitarra, erre con erre carril. Rápido corren los carros, cargados de azúcar del ferrocarril. = R with an R, guitar. R with an R, lane. The train cars go quickly, filled with sugar from the railroad.

3. Compadre, cómpreme un coco. Compadre, coco no compro, porque como poco coco como, poco coco compro. Pal, buy me a coconut. Pal, I don't buy coconuts, because I eat very few coconuts, I buy very few coconuts.

4. Tres tristes tigres tragaban trigo en un triste trigal. Three sad tigers swallowed wheat in a sad wheat field.

183 = CIENTO OCHENTA Y TRES

Now that you have made it to the final lesson of the book, realize this is just the first step. It's important to continue on with your success and really make Spanish a part of your daily life. The question is, "How do you continue the learning?" The most important thing is to work with your flashcards and practice, practice, practice. Another surefire way to continue your learning is to travel to a Spanish-speaking country and speak Spanish. Another way to guarantee your learning is to date a Spanish speaker who doesn't speak any English. However, these ways don't work for everybody. Especially for those who are broke and/or married.

There is a little more to do = Hay un poco más que hacer

Here are 10 suggestions to keep yourself and others enthusiastic about learning the language. Read these and then choose one that you will implement next week. Add it to your calendar to guarantee success.

1. **Study = Estudia:** Keep your study materials handy and use them often. Use a dictionary and make signs for basic items in the restaurant to teach new words. Customize phrase lists and laminate them for use at your work area. Pick your top 10 phrases to learn this month. Spend time to review some of your favorite activities in the book or complete anything you didn't get done in the past 10 weeks.

2. **Talk = Habla:** Create opportunities for speaking Spanish. Have Spanish-speaking employees explain various job situations or give kitchen tours. Ask these native speakers questions in Spanish and learn the appropriate response. Learn a new phrase a day. Listen to Spanish-speaking employees and try to understand their interactions with each other. Develop another role play using the phrases from Lessons 1–9.

3. **The classes = Las clases:** Provide refresher lessons. Not everybody is able to master the material during a 10-week lesson. Arrange follow up meetings, ask questions and practice with flashcards. Read more on the Spanish culture. Sign up for an online class or una clase at your local university. Many times community colleges have non-credit classes that are more conversational and less grammar based.

4. **A lunch in Spanish. = Un almerzo en español:** Organize a lunch led by a Spanish speaker. At first, just practice the phrases you learned. Then bring in other materials such as a bilingual picture dictionary. For further conversational practice, just speak in Spanish about your interests, current events, or what is happening at your workplace. Use the recipes from Lesson 9 to make a wonderful lunch. A set time works best, for example, the First Friday Fiesta might meet the first Friday of each month to chat in Spanish. Meet at work or go to your favorite Hispanic restaurant and order in Spanish.

5. **A special day = Un día especial:** Pick a day and incorporate Spanish as much as possible. Plan a specific day to practice your phrases. Greet others and ask questions in Spanish. If possible, have Spanish-speaking employees help with these activities and have a potluck lunch using the recipes in Lesson 9.

6. **FRIENDS = AMIGOS:** Look for a native speaker who would like to help you speak Spanish and practice together often. Find someone online to chat with in Spanish who actually lives in Latin America.

7. **THE LATIN LIFE = LA VIDA LATINA:** Bring in Spanish music with the English translations and learn some popular songs. Read the Spanish and the English translation as you listen to the song. Listen to a Spanish radio station in the car, or use the Internet to find authentic radio stations in each country. Watch movies in Spanish with the English subtitles. Bring in a Spanish children's book, practice reading to each other and see if you can follow along with the story. Watch one of the Spanish TV channels, maybe even a telenovela—a Spanish language soap opera. Unlike the English-language soap operas, the telenovelas only last for a few months and then the story ends— although not always happily ever after. Look up the news online and read newspapers from all over Latin America.

8. **THE CULTURE = LA CULTURA:** There is a lot of diversity in the Spanish-speaking world. Each country has its own unique phrasing, food and cultural history that adds to language enrichment. Find Hispanic cultural activities nearby, visit travel Web sites or read books about different Latin American countries. Better yet, travel to Latin America and spend a week at a language school. Costa Rica has a great school (ICLC) near San José, find out more on the internet.

9. **SEARCH = BÚSQUEDA:** Utilize the grocery store/scavenger hunt/ field trip form 184 = ciento ochenta y cuatro. Find a grocery store in your town with Hispanic products. Look for a bakery or other stores specializing in the needs of Latino customers. Go to the stores and try some of the diverse products available.

10. **TRY IT! = ¡INTÉNTELO!:** Try out your new skills. Write a bilingual article in your company's newsletter and make signs around the workplace in Spanish. The most important piece of advice is to continue communicating in Spanish. Don't worry if you make mistakes. Spanish speakers will generally help you with your Spanish, and they respect those willing to try to speak the language. Finally, remember "Donde existe voluntad, hay un camino. = Where there is a will, there is a way."

184 = CIENTO OCHENTA Y CUATRO

Take this paper to the grocery store in your town with the most Mexican/Latin American products. If you do not find all of the items at the store, search the Internet to answer the questions. See how many of these Spanish questions you understand, before you look at the English version that follows.

El supermercado: _____

La fruta y las verduras:

1. ¿De qué color son los nopales? Rojos o Verdes o Cafés_____

2. ¿Cómo se llaman algunos tipos de chiles? Se llaman chiles anchos, chiles _____ , chiles _____ .

3. ¿Cuánto cuesta una yuca? Una yuca cuesta $ _____ .

4. Los plátanos no son bananas. ¿Cuántos plátanos hay? Muchos o Pocos

5. ¿Cuánto cuesta alguna otra verdura o fruta de América Latina? _____ cuesta $_____ .
   (name of item = nombre)   (price = precio)

Los dulces:

6. ¿La marca del chocolate caliente es Abuelita o Mamá? _____

7. ¿Cuáles son los sabores de dos refrescos, gaseosas or jugos? Por ejemplo, los sabores son piña, tamarindo, _____ y _____.

8. ¿Cómo se llama un dulce de México? Se llama _____.

9. ¿Cúales son los tres tipos de papas o galletas. Los tipos son _____ , _____ y_____.

La comida típica:

10. ¿Cuáles son tres ingredientes en un mole? Los ingredientes son _____ y _____ y _____.

11. ¿Cuál es el símbolo del "Pan Bimbo?" _____

12. ¿Cuánto cuesta la harina preparada para tortillas o masa instantánea de maíz ? Cuesta $_____.

13. ¿Cuántas marcas de frijoles refritos hay? Hay #_____ marcas.

14. ¿Cúal es la diferencia entre tortillas y tostadas? _____

Las otras cosas:

15. ¿Cómo se llaman dos grupos de la música Mexicana? Se llaman _____ y_____.

16. ¿Cómo se llama una revista o periódico? Se llama _____

17. ¿Para lavar ropa se usa la marca _____?

La panadería:

Look for a bakery section or a nearby bakery. Ask these questions directly to an employee if the items are not labeled.

18. ¿Qué tipo de empanadas tienen hoy? _____

19. ¿Cuánto cuestan los churros? Cuesta $_____.

20. ¿De qué colores son los pan dulces que se llaman las conchas? Las conchas son _____ y _____.

El restaurante:

Vayan a un restaurante Latino y pidan su comida y bebida en Español.

The supermarket English version:

Remember to figure out as much as possible from the Spanish version, before you keep reading this page.

The fruits and vegetables:

1. What color are nopales=cactus? Red or Green or Brown _____

2. What are some names of different types of chiles? The names are wide chiles, _____ chiles and _____chiles.

3. How much does a yucca cost? A yucca costs $_____.

4. Plantains are not bananas. How many plantains are there? Many or Few

5. How much does another Latin American vegetable or fruit cost?
   _____ costs $_____ .
   Name of item   Price

The sweets:

6. The brand of hot chocolate is Grandma = Abuelita or Mom = Mamá?
   _____

7. What are the flavors of two refreshments, soda pops or juices? For example, the flavors are pineapple, tamarind, _____ and _____.

8. What is the name of a Mexican candy? The name is _____.

9. What are three types of potato chips or crackers/cookies? The types are _____, _____ and _____.

THE TYPICAL FOODS:

10. What are three ingredients in mole sauce? The ingredients are _____ and _____ and _____.

11. What is the symbol on "Bimbo" white bread? (Hint: It looks like the Pillsbury Dough boy.) _____

12. How much does prepared tortilla flour or instant corn tortilla dough cost? It costs $_____

13. How many brands of refried beans are there? There are #_____ brands.

14. What is the difference between tortillas and tostadas? _____

THE OTHER THINGS:

15. What are the names of two Mexican music groups? The names are _____ and _____.

16. What is the name of a magazine or newspaper? It is called _____.

17. To wash clothes you use the brand name _____.

THE BAKERY:

18. What type of empanadas do they have today? Hint: a pastry pocket with filling. They have _____.

19. How much do your churros cost? They cost $_____.

20. What colors are the sweet breads "the seashells?" The seashells are _____ and _____.

THE RESTAURANT:

Find a restaurant with cuisine from Latin America and celebrate your Spanish achievements. Use the vocabulary in Lesson 9 to help you order your food and drinks in Spanish. ¡Buena suerte! = Good luck!

185 = CIENTO OCHENTA Y CINCO

Use this feedback form to evaluate your learning. Share this with a co-worker, your boss, corporate trainers, or human resource managers and encourage others to learn Spanish using this book.

1. What five Spanish phrases will you use the most?
   _____
   _____
   _____
   _____

2. What activities helped you the most? _____
   _____
   _____
   _____

3. What cultural considerations will help you with your job? _____
   _____
   _____
   _____

4. What would you like to do differently next time you study Spanish? __
   _____
   _____
   _____

5. What would you still like to learn? _____
   _____
   _____
   _____

6. Any further questions or comments? _____
   _____
   _____
   _____

SUMMARY

Gracias.

Thank you for taking your time and putting in the effort to learn Spanish. Feel free to visit our Web site www.SpanishChatCompany.com to give us feedback, or ask questions. If you have any suggestions or changes for a future edition, just let us know. We would love to hear testimonials of how this *Culinary Spanish Chatbook* has helped you in your workplace. Keep practicing and keep smiling. Your journey has just begun. Enjoy the adventure! ¡Buen Viaje!

EXTRA VOCABULARY

This section contains extra vocabulary to enhance the lessons. The word "the" is implied on the English side and is not included in these lists. Also, back in the kitchen, English words sometimes are simply pronounced with a Spanish accent instead of using the correct Spanish. "El cooler" is an example of this "Spanglish." These are noted within the vocabulary along with the proper term. Please note that this list is not complete. If you need help, consult a dictionary or a Hispanic employee. If you have suggestions or ideas for changes, please visit our website at www.SpanishChatCompany.com.

EXTRA VOCABULARY FOR LESSON 1

Names = Nombres:

Women = Mujeres

Adriana	Elena	Maricarmen
Alejandra	Esmeralda	Maricela
Alicia	Ester	Marisol
Alma	Eva	Marta
Amalia	Gabriela	Mercedes
Ana	Gloria	Mónica
Andrea	Graciela	Olga
Ángela	Hilda	Paula
Beatriz	Inés	Rebeca
Blanca	Isabel	Raquel
Carmen	Juana	Rosa
Carolina	Julia	Sandra
Carlota	Laura	Sara
Cecilia	Liliana	Sofía
Clara	Linda	Susana
Cristina	Margarita	Teresa
Diana	María	Victoria
Dora	Maribel	Yolanda

Men = Hombres

Adán	Felipe	Marcos
Alberto	Félix	Mario
Alejandro	Fernando	Mateo
Alfonso	Francisco	Miguel
Alfredo	Gonzalo	Nicolás
Andrés	Gregorio	Oscar
Antonio	Guillermo	Pablo
Arturo	Héctor	Pedro
Bernardo	Jaime	Rafael
Carlos	Javier	Ramón
César	Jesús	Raúl
Daniel	Joaquín	Roberto
David	Jorge	Rubén
Diego	José	Samuel
Eduardo	Juan	Timoteo
Emilio	Julio	Tomás
Enrique	Luis	Victor
Ernesto	Manuel	

EXTRA VOCABULARY FOR LESSON 2

The numbers = Los números:

0 cero
1 uno
2 dos
3 tres
4 cuatro
5 cinco
6 seis
7 siete
8 ocho
9 nueve
10 diez
11 once
12 doce
13 trece
14 catorce
15 quince
16 diez y seis (dieciséis)
17 diez y siete (diecisiete)
18 diez y ocho (dieciocho)
19 diez y nueve (diecinueve)
20 veinte
21 veinte y uno (veintiuno)
22 veinte y dos (veintidós)
23 veinte y tres (veintitrés)
24 veinte y cuatro (veinticuatro)
25 veinte y cinco (veinticinco)
26 veinte y seis (veintiséis)
27 veinte y siete (veintisiete)
28 veinte y ocho (ventiocho)
29 veinte y nueve (ventinueve)
30 treinta
31 treinta y uno
32 treinta y dos
33 treinta y tres
34 treinta y cuatro
35 treinta y cinco
36 treinta y seis
37 treinta y siete
38 treinta y ocho
39 treinta y nueve
40 cuarenta
41 cuarenta y uno
42 cuarenta y dos
43 cuarenta y tres
44 cuarenta y cuatro
45 cuarenta y cinco
46 cuarenta y seis
47 cuarenta y siete
48 cuarenta y ocho
49 cuarenta y nueve
50 cincuenta
51 cincuenta y uno
52 cincuenta y dos
53 cincuenta y tres
54 cincuenta y cuatro
55 cincuenta y cinco
56 cincuenta y seis
57 cincuenta y siete
58 cincuenta y ocho
59 cincuenta y nueve
60 sesenta
61 sesenta y uno
62 sesenta y dos
63 sesenta y tres
64 sesenta y cuatro
65 sesenta y cinco
66 sesenta y seis
67 sesenta y siete
68 sesenta y ocho
69 sesenta y nueve
70 setenta
71 setenta y uno
72 setenta y dos
73 setenta y tres
74 setenta y cuatro
75 setenta y cinco
76 setenta y seis
77 setenta y siete
78 setenta y ocho
79 setenta y nueve
80 ochenta
81 ochenta y uno
82 ochenta y dos
83 ochenta y tres
84 ochenta y cuatro
85 ochenta y cinco
86 ochenta y seis
87 ochenta y siete
88 ochenta y ocho
89 ochenta y nueve
90 noventa
91 noventa y uno
92 noventa y dos
93 noventa y tres
94 noventa y cuatro
95 noventa y cinco
96 noventa y seis
97 noventa y siete
98 noventa y ocho
99 noventa y nueve
100 cien
101 ciento uno

EXTRA VOCABULARY FOR LESSON 2

Number Song 1–100:

One way to remember the numbers to 100 is to the tune of " I'm a little teapot."
Use sign language for each word. Any movement will help you remember the words better.
Note: For exact pronunciation see the chart on page 30.

10 = diez *(D-ACE)* Action: playing cards
20 = veinte *(Vein-teh)* Action: touch veins
30 = treinta *(Train-tah)* Pull train horn
40 = cuarenta *(Car-rent-tah)* Drive a car
50 = cincuenta *(SING-qwehn-tah)* Sing
60 = sesenta *(Seh-Sent-tah)* Send a letter
70 = setenta *(Seh-tent-tah)* Make a tent with fingertips
80 = ochenta *(Ocean-tah)* Swim
90 = noventa *(No-vent-ah)* Fan yourself
100 = cien *(See-N)* Point to an N

Meat = la carne:

bacon = el tocino
BBQ = la barbacoa, la parrillada, el churrasco
beef = la carne de res
bones = los huesos
chicken = el pollo
chicken breast = la pechuga de pollo
deer = el venado
eggs = los huevos
eggs (hardboiled) = los huevos duros
eggs (fried) = los huevos fritos
eggs (scrambled) = los huevos revueltos
grease = la grasa
ham = el jamón
hamburger = la hamburguesa
hot dog = la salchicha, el perro caliente
lamb = el cordero
loin = el lomo
meatballs = las albóndigas
pork = el cerdo, el puerco
pork chop = la chuleta de puerco
rabbit = el conejo
ribs = las costillas, las costillitas
roast beef = la carne asada
sausage = la salchicha, el chorizo
steak = el bistec
turkey = el pavo, el guajolote
tripe = el mondongo, la tripa
veal = la ternera

From the ocean / Seafood = Del mar / Los Mariscos

bass = el róbalo
bones = los huesos
cod = el bacalao
clam = la almeja
crab = el cangrejo
fish = el pescado
lobster = la langosta
octopus = el pulpo
oysters = las ostras
perch = la perca
salmon = el salmón
sardine = la sardina
seafood = los mariscos
shrimp = los camarones, las gambas
skin = el cuero
snail = el caracol
squid = el calamar
trout = la trucha
tuna = el atún

EXTRA VOCABULARY FOR LESSON 2

Pastas = las Pastas, Side dishes = la comida para acompañar, Appetizers = los Entremeses, los Aperitivos:

baked beans = frijoles cocidos al horno
broth = el caldo
chips = las papitas
french fries = las papas fritas
fried cheese = el queso frito
gelatin = la gelatina
goat cheese = el queso de cabra
lentils = las lentejas
macaroni = los macarrones
noodles = los fideos
onion rings = los anillos de cebolla

olives = las aceitunas
omelett = la tortilla española
refried beans = los frijoles refritos
pizza = la pizza
popcorn = las palomitas
potatoes = las papas
salad = la ensalada
soup = la sopa
stock = el caldo
tofu = el tofu, el queso de soya
yogurt = el yogur

Condiments = Los condimentos

barbeque sauce = la salsa de barbacoa
blue cheese = el queso azul
catsup = la salsa de tomate
cream = la crema, la leche
dressing (salad) = el aderezo
hot sauce = la salsa picante
honey = la miel
horseradish = el rábano picante
ketchup = la salsa de tomate
marmalade = la mermelada
mayonnaise = la mayonesa
mustard = la mostaza
olive oil = el aceite de oliva
peanut butter = la mantequilla de
    cacahuate, maní

pepper (black) = la pimienta
pepper mill = el pimentero
ranch dressing = el aderezo ranchero
relish = el encurtido de pepino
salad dressing = el aderezo
salt = la sal
salt shaker = el salero
sauce = la salsa
sour cream = la crema agria
soy sauce = la salsa de soya
sweet-and-sour sauce = la salsa agridulce
syrup (maple) = el jarabe de arce
sugar container = el azucarero
tarter sauce = la salsa tártara
vinegar = el vinagre

EXTRA VOCABULARY FOR LESSON 3

Beverages = Las bebidas:

beer = la cerveza
bottle = la botella
bottled water = agua de botella
champagne = la champaña
coffee = el café
coffee (decaf) = café descafeinado
coffee (with milk) = café con leche
coffee (with cream and sugar) = café con leche y azúcar
diet soda = la soda lite, el refresco de dieta, gaseosa de dieta
gin = la ginebra
hot chocolate = el chocolate caliente
ice = el hielo
ice machine = la hielera
iced tea = el té helado
jar = la jarra
juice = el jugo
juice (orange) = el jugo de manzana
lemonade = la limonada
liquor = el licor
milk = la leche
milk (chocolate) = la leche con chocolate
pop = la soda, el refresco, la gaseosa
red wine = el vino tinto
rice milk = la leche de arroz
rum = el ron
shake = el batido
soft drink = el refresco, la soda, la gaseosa
soft drink (boxes) = las cajas de soda/refresco/gaseosa
soy milk = la leche de soya
straw = la pajita, el popote, el pitillo
tea = el té
tea (with lemon) = el té con limón
toothpicks = los palillos de dientes
water = el agua
water (tap) = el agua del grifo
water with carbonation = agua con gas
water without carbonation = agua sin gas
wine (red) = el vino tinto
wine (white) = el vino blanco

Front of the house restaurant tour = Recorrido del frente del restaurante

bakery = la panadería
building = el edificio
cash = el efectivo
cash register = la caja
CD = el disco compacto
delivery = la entrega
door = la puerta
downtown = el centro
entrance = la entrada
elevator = el ascensor
exit = la salida
expenses = los gastos
fan = el ventilador
first floor = la planta baja
floor = el piso
fountain = la fuente
hostess stand = el puesto de la anfitriona
lobby = el vestíbulo
patio = el patio
plants = las plantas
price = el precio
receipt = el recibo
repairs = los arreglos
roof/ ceiling = el techo
rug = la alfombra
shelf = el estante
sink = el fregadero
small change = el cambio
stairs = las escaleras
station = la estación
teller = el cajero
tip = la propina
to-go = para llevar
window = la ventana

EXTRA VOCABULARY FOR LESSON 3

Set the table / in the dining room = Prepara/ Pon la mesa / en el comedor:

- ash tray = el cenicero
- basket = la cesta
- bill = la cuenta
- booster seat = la silla para bebé
- bowl = el tazón, el plato hondo
- bowl (small) la taza pequeña
- bowl (soup) = la taza para sopa
- change = el cambio
- dish (square) = la olla cuadrada, el plato cuadrado
- fork = el tenedor
- glass = el vaso
- glass (beer) = el vaso para cerveza
- glass (wine) = el vaso de vino, la copa de vino
- glass (water) = el vaso de agua
- high chair = la silla para bebé
- knife = el cuchillo
- knives (butter)= los cuchillos para mantequilla
- knives (steak)= los cuchillos para bistec
- mug/cup = la taza
- napkin = la servilleta
- pitcher = la jarra
- pitcher (aluminum) = la jarra de aluminio
- pitcher (plastic) = la jarra de plástico
- placemats = los tapetes de mesa
- plastic bag = el saco plástico, la bolsa plástica
- plate = el plato
- plate (medium) = el plato mediano
- plate (small) = el plato pequeño
- saucer = el platillo
- silverware = los cubiertos
- spoon = la cuchara
- tablecloth = el mantel
- tray = la bandeja
- to go box= la caja para llevar
- tip = la propina

Family / Relatives = La Familia / Los Parientes:

My (relative's) name is _____. = Mi _____ se llama _____.

- mother = madre
- mother-in-law = suegra
- sister = hermana
- sister-in-law = cuñada
- daughter = hija
- daughter-in-law = nuera
- aunt = tía
- cousin (female) = prima
- godmother = madrina
- girlfriend (fiancé) = novia
- grandmother = abuela
- granddaughter = nieta
- niece = sobrina
- stepmother = madrastra
- stepsister = hermanastra
- father = padre
- father-in-law = suegro
- brother = hermano
- brother-in-law = cuñado
- son = hijo
- son-in-law=yerno
- uncle= tío
- cousin (male) = primo
- godfather = padrino
- boyfriend (fiancé) = novio
- grandfather = abuelo
- grandson = nieto
- nephew = sobrino
- stepfather = padrastro
- stepbrother = hermanastro

EXTRA VOCABULARY FOR LESSON 3

Professions = Trabajos: HR/Personnel = Los Recursos Humanos

I am a _____. = Soy un/una _____.
Remember un is for males and una is for females.
I want to be a _____. = Yo quiero ser un/una _____.

architect = arquitecto(a)
artist = el / la artista
assistant = el / la asistante, ayudante
baker = el / la panadero(a)
banker = el/la banquero(a)
barber/hairdresser = el barbero, la peluquera
bartender = el cantinero
bellboy = el/ la botones
boss = el / la jefe
buser = el / la ayudante de camarero, limpiador(a), corredor(a), asistente de mesero
butcher = el carnicero
carpenter = el carpintero(a)
chef = el / la chef
cleaning crew = el grupo de limpiadores
cook = el / la cocinero(a)
co-worker (female) = la compañera de trabajo
co-worker (male) = el compañero de trabajo
cashier = el cajero
delivery driver = el chofer de la entrega
dentist = el / la dentista
dishwasher = el / la lavaplatos
doctor = el / la doctor(a) or médico(a)
employee (female) = la empleada
employee (male) = el empleado
employer (male) = el patrón
employer (female) = la patrona
engineer = el / la ingeniero(a)

finance director = director(ora) de finanzas
full-time = tiempo completo
host (female) = la anfitriona
host (male) = el anfitrión
housekeeping = el / la hotelero(a)
insurance agent = agente de seguros
lawyer = el / la abogado(a)
manager = el / la gerente, manijer
manager (front house) = el / la gerente en frente
manager (back house) = el/la gerente atrás
nurse = el / la enfermero(a)
owner = el / la dueño/a
part-time = medio tiempo
president = el / la presidente
retired = el / la retirado(a)/jubilado(a)
salesperson = el / la vendedor(ora)
secretary = el / la secretario(a)
server (female) = la mesera, la garotera, la camarera(hotel)
server (male) = el mesero, el camarero, el garotero
staff = los empleados
teacher in grade school = el/ la maestro(a)
teacher in high school or university = el/la profesor(ora)
treasurer = el/ la tesorero(a)
waiter = el mesero, el camarero, el mozo
waitress = la mesera, la camarera, la moza

Work Places / I work at _____. = Lugares del Trabajo / Trabajo en _____.:

administration = administración
banking transactions = las transacciones bancarias
customer service = el servicio al cliente
finances = las finanzas
government = el gobierno
hospitality = la hospitalidad
human resources = los recursos humanos

kitchen = la cocina
legal department = el departamento legal
marketing = el mercadeo
production = la producción
restaurant = el restaurante
school = la escuela
sales = las ventas

EXTRA VOCABULARY FOR LESSON 3

I LIKE TO _____. = ME GUSTA _____:

do nothing = hacer nada
cook = cocinar
fish = pescar
go on vacation = ir de vacaciones
go shopping = ir de compras
go to a party = ir a la fiesta
go to the movies = ir al cine
play golf = jugar golf

play tennis = jugar tenis
play video games = jugar los videojuegos
read a book = leer un libro
ride a bike = montar una bicicleta
run = correr
swim = nadar
take a walk = dar un paseo
watch T. V. = mirar la televisión

EXTRA VOCABULARY FOR LESSON 4

CLEANING / MAINTENANCE SUPPLIES = LOS SUMINISTROS DE LIMPIEZA Y DE MANTENIMIENTO

bag = la bolsa
bag (garbage) = la bolsa de la basura
bag (linens) = la bolsa de la ropa, de trapos
batteries = las baterías, las pilas
bleach = el blanqueador
broom = la escoba
bucket = el balde, la cubeta
cleaner = el limpiador
detergent = el detergente
dishrag = el trapo
dish soap = el jabón de platos
disinfectant = el desinfectante
drain = desaguar
dumpster = el basurero
dust = el polvo
dustpan = el recogedor,
    pala de recoger la basura
electric plug = el enchufe
empty = vaciar
feather duster = el plumero
flyswatter = el matamoscas
lightbulb = el foco
linens = la ropa
gloves = los guantes
garbage can = el basurero
hand towel = toalla de mano
hand vacuum/dust buster =
    la aspiradora de mano

ladder = la escalera
maintenance = el mantenimiento
mop = el trapeador
mousetrap = la ratonera
paper towels = las toallas de papel
plunger = el émbolo, el destapador
replacer = reponer
scouring pads = el brillo
scrub = fregar
scrubber = el fregadero
slippery floor = el piso mojado
soap = el jabón
soap dispenser = el dispensador de jabón
sponge = la esponja
supplies = los suministros
tissue = el pañuelo desechable, klinex
toilet = el inodoro
toilet paper = el papel de baño, papel
    higiénico
towel = la toalla
towel (dirty) = la toalla sucia
towel (paper) = la toalla de papel
trash = la basura
trash bag = la bolsa de la basura
trash can = el basurero
vacuum = la aspiradora
wax = la cera

EXTRA VOCABULARY FOR LESSON 4

Parts of a Uniform / Clothing = Parte del Uniforme / La ropa:

apron = el delantal, el mandil
gloves = los guantes
hairnet = la redecilla
hat = la gorra
jewelry = las joyas
nametag = la identificadora
pants = los pantalones

proper work shoes = zapatos para trabajar, zapatos para cocina
shirt = la camisa
shoes = los zapatos
socks = los calcetines
tie = la corbata
towel = la toalla

EXTRA VOCABULARY FOR LESSON 6

Utensils / Containers / In the drawers = Los utensilios / los contenedores / En las gavetas

aluminum foil = el papel de aluminio
bag = la bolsa
bottle = la botella
basket = la canasta
box = la caja
can = la lata
can opener = el abrelatas
carving knife = el trinchante
coffee filters = los filtros para café
container = el envase, el recipiente, el contenedor, la vasija
dough hook = el gancho de la pasta
four sifter = el tamiz de la harina
grater = el rallador
ice cream scoop = la cuchara para helado
knife = el cuchillo
knife (block) = el bloque para cuchillos, el almacenamiento para cuchillos,
knife (bread) = el cuchillo para pan
knife (butcher's) el cuchillón
knife (steak) = el cuchillo para carne
ladle = el cucharón
lid = la tapa
measuring cup = la taza para medir
mixing bowls = los tazones para mezclar

non-stick cooking spray = el antiadherente, el aerosol de cocinar
oven mitt = el guante de cocina
paddle attachment = el accesorio de la paleta
parchment paper = el papel para hornear, el papel de pergamino
pastry bag = la bolsa para glaseado
pastry cutter = el cortapastas
peeler = el pelador
plastic wrap = el papel de plástico
ramekan = el recipiente, el "ramekan"
rolling pin = un rodillo (de cocina)
rubber spatula = la espátula de goma
scissors = las tijeras
spatula = la espátula
spoon (wooden) = la cuchara de madera
squeeze bottle = la botella para salsa
thermomenter = el termómetro
tongs = las tenazas, las pinzas
turners = los volteadores
whisk = el batidor de mano, la bata, la batidora
wooden spoon = la cuchara de madera

EXTRA VOCABULARY FOR LESSON 6

Kitchen equipment / Appliances = El equipo de cocina / Los aparatos/ electrodomésticos

baking sheet = la bandeja de horno, la chapa de horno, la charola, la media plancha, la cuarta plancha
basket (frying) = la canasta para freír
blender = la licuadora, la batidora
bowl (big) = el tazón grande, la olla
bowl (deep, square) = el plato hondo cuadrado
burners = los mecheros
bus tub = la bandeja
butcher block = el bloque de carnicero
bread pan = el molde para pan
bread slicer = la máquina rebanadora
broiler = la parrilla
cake pan = el molde para pastel
can = la lata
chopper = la picadora
coffeemaker= la cafetera
colander = el colador, el escurridor, la coladera
container = el envase, el recipiente, el contenedor, la vasija
cooler = el congelador, el cooler
cookie sheet = la bandeja para hornear galletas, la charola
cooling rack = el estante de enfriamiento
cupboard = la alacena
cutting board = la tabla de cortar
deep fryer = la freidora honda
dish racks = las rejillas
dish tray = la bandeja, la charola
dishwasher = el lavaplatos
drawer = el cajón, la gaveta
flat grill = la parilla plana, plancha
freezer = el congelador
fryer = la freidora
garbage disposal = el triturador de basura
griddle = el comal, la plancha

grill = la parrilla
half sheet = la media plancha
heat lamps =las lámparas de calor
ice maker = la hielera
kettle = la tetera
lid (aluminum) = la tapadera de aluminio
locker = el ropero, el casillero, el cajón
magnet = el imán
mat = mapete, tapeta
meat slicer = la rebanadora de la carne
microwave = el horno microondas
mixer= la batidora, la mezcladora
oven= el horno
oven (under stovetop) = el horno de la estufa
pan (big) = la cacerola grande, la cazuela
pan (cake) = el molde para pastel
pan (sauté) = el sartén
pan (hotel) = la cacerola, el contenedor
pan (muffin) = la cacerola del panecillo
pan (pie) = la tartera
pan (third) = contenedor tercio
pan (6 qt.) = contenedor de seis cuartos
pantry = la despensa
pantry room = el cuarto de la despensa
pots = las ollas
prep area= el área de preparación
prep table = la mesa para preparación
quarter sheet = la cuarta plancha
range = la estufa
refrigerator = el refrigerador
salad station = la estación de ensalada
salamander = la salamandra

sauce pan= la cacerola
sauté pans= los sartenes
scale = la váscula, pesadora, balanza
serving station = la estación para servir
serving trays= las charolas, las bandejas
sheet pan = la charola
shelves = los estantes
station = el estación
sifter = el tamiz
silverware bins = contenedores de cubiertos
sink = el fregadero
slicer = el rebanador
soda dispenser = el dispensador de soda, refrescos, gaseosas
soup pot = la olla para la sopa
steam jacket = la chaqueta del vapor
steam table = la mesa de vapor, la bandeja vaporera de aluminio
stock pots = la sopera, las ollas para caldo
stove = la estufa
strainer = el colador, el escurridor, la coladera
tilt skillet = el sartén grande
timer = el reloj de cocina
toaster = la tostadora
towel (kitchen) = la toalla de cocina
tray = la bandeja
tray jack = la tijera
vending machine = el distribuidor automático
walk-in cooler = la cámara refrigeradora, "cooler"
walk-in freezer = el congelador
walk-in fridge = refrigerador, la cámara refrigeradora, (fría), el refrigerador
warmers = los calentadores

EXTRA VOCABULARY FOR LESSON 7

THE ADJECTIVES AND OPPOSITES = LOS ADJECTIVOS Y OPUESTOS:

big = grande
short = bajo/a
strong = fuerte
smart = listo/a
old = viejo/a
thin = flaco/a
fast = rápido/a
rich = rico/a
happy = feliz
funny = cómico/a
good = bueno/a
friendly = amigable
cute = bonito/a
ugly = feo/a

small = pequeño/a (chiquito/a)
tall = alto/a
weak = débil
silly = tonto/a
young = joven
chubby = gordo/a
slow = lento/a
poor = pobre
sad = triste
serious = serio/a
bad = malo/a
shy = tímido/a
pretty = guapo/a
medium = mediano/a

THE COLORS = LOS COLORES:

blue = azul
red = rojo
orange = anaranjado
yellow = amarillo
white = blanco
green = verde

black = negro
brown = café or marrón
purple = morado
pink = rosa or rosado
gray = gris

GRAINS / BREADS = LOS GRANOS/ LOS PANES:

biscuit = el bizcocho
bread = el pan
bread basket = el cesto para el pan
bread crumbs = pan molido, migas
bread knives = cuchillos para pan
cake = el pastel
cereal = el cereal
cinnamon roll = el panecillo de canela
cookies = las galletas
cracker = la galleta salada
corn = el maíz, el elote
DohNut = el dónut, la rosquilla
flour = la harina
French toast = la tostada francesa
fritter = el buñuelo
gluten-free bread = pan sin gluten

grilled cheese = el sándwich de queso, el derretido
muffin = el muffin, la mantecada
oats = la avena
pancake = el panqueque
pizza = la pizza
popcorn = las palomitas
rice = el arroz
rice (brown) = el arroz integral
roll = el panecillo, el panecito, el bolillo
sandwich = el emparedado, el sándwich, la torta
sweet bread = el pan dulce
toast = el pan tostado
tortilla = la tortilla
waffle = el gofre
wheat = el trigo

EXTRA VOCABULARY FOR LESSON 7

Fruits = Las Frutas:

apple = la manzana
apricot = el albaricoque, el chabacano
banana = la banana, el banano, el guineo
blueberry = la mora azul, el arándano
cherry = la cereza
coconut = el coco
cranberry = la mora roja, el arándano agrio
date = el higo
grape = la uva
grapefruit = la toronja, el pomelo
lemon = el limón
lime = el limón verde, la lima
mango = el mango
melon = el melón
nectarine = la nectarina
orange = la naranja
papaya = la papaya
peach = el durazno, el melocotón
pear = la pera
pineapple = la piña
plantain = el plátano
plum = la ciruela
raisin = la pasa, las pasitas
raspberry = la frambuesa
seed = la semilla
stawberry = la fresa
tomato = el tomate
watermelon = la sandía

Vegetables = Los Vegetales, Las Verduras

artichoke = la alcachofa
asparagus = el espárrago
beans = frijoles
beans (black) = los frijoles negros
beans (garbanzo) = los garbanzos
beans (green) = los ejotes, las habichuelas
beans (pinto) = los frijoles pintos
broccoli = el brócoli
cabbage = el repollo
cactus = los nopales
carrot = la zanahoria
cauliflower = la coliflor
celery = el apio
chili pepper = el ají
corn = el maiz, el elote, el choclo
cucumber = el pepino
eggplant = la berenjena
fennel = el hinojo
garlic = el ajo
lettuce = la lechuga
mushrooms = los champiñones, los hongos
onion = las cebollas
onion (green) = cebolleta, cebollina
peas = los chícharos, los guisantes
pepper (green) = el pimiento verde
pickle = el encurtido
potato = la papa
potato (baked) = la papa al horno
potatoes (mashed) = el puré de papas
pumpkin = la calabaza
radish = el rábano
salad = la ensalada
scallions = la cebollina
spinach = la espinaca
squash = la calabaza
sweet potatoes = el camote
tomato = el tomate
vegetarian (female) = la vegetariana
vegetarian (male) = el vegetariano

EXTRA VOCABULARY FOR LESSON 7

Spices = Las Especias:

basil = la albahaca, el basílico
bay leaf = la hoja de laurel
bland = no tiene mucho sabor
black pepper (ground) = la pimienta negra molida
black pepper (whole) = la pimienta negra entera
caraway = la alcaravea
chamomile = la manzanilla
chili pepper-hot = el ají pimentón
chili powder = el chile en polvo
chives = los cebollinos
cilantro = el cilantro
cinnamon = la canela
cloves (ground) = los clavitos de olor (molidos)
cream of tartar = el crémor tártaro
cumin = el comino
dill = el eneldo
fennel = el hinojo
garlic = el ajo
garlic (powder) = el ajo en polvo
garlic (salt) = la sal de ajo
ginger = el jengibre
horseradish = el rábano picante
hot/spicy = picante
lemon grass = el limoncillo
marjoram = la mejorana
mint = la menta
needs more = necesita más
nutmeg = la nuez moscada
onion (powder) = la cebolla en polvo
oregano = el orégano
parsley = el perejil
pepper (black/white) = la pimienta (negra/blanca)
poppy seeds = las semillas de amapola
red chili = el chile rojo
rosemary = el rosmarino, el romero
saffron = el azafrán
sage = la salvia
salt (sea) = la sal de mar
salt (table) = la sal de mesa
sesame seeds = las semillas de sésamo
tamarind = el tamarindo
tarragon = el estragón
thyme = el tomillo
tumeric = la cúrcuma
watercress = el berro

Baking Ingredients / Nuts = Los ingredientes para hornear / las Nueces:

almond = la almendra
baking powder = el polvo para hornear, levadura en polvo
baking soda = el bicarbonato, el bicarbonato de sodio
butter (salted) = la mantequilla con sal
butter (unsalted) = la mantequilla sin sal
cashew = el anacardo, la nuez del marañón
cocoa = el cacao
corn syrup = el jarabe de maiz
dough = la masa, la pasta
egg = el huevo
egg (wash) = la colada del huevo, la lavada
egg (white) = la clara
egg (yolk) = la yema
evaporated milk = la leche evaporada
flour (all purpose) = la harina de uso múltiple
flour (bread) = la harina de pan
flour (cake) = la harina de la torta
food coloring = el colorante para alimentos
hazelnut = la avellana
honey = la miel
mint = la menta
non-stick cooking spray = el aerosol de cocinar, el aceite "espray," antiadherente
nut = la nuez
pecan = la pacana
peanut = el maní, el cacahuate
shortening/ lard = la manteca
sugar (brown) = el azúcar morena
sugar (granulated) = el azúcar granulada
sugar (confectioners') = el azúcar en polvo, pulverizado
sweetened condensed milk = la leche condensada
vanilla (pure extract) = el extracto de vainilla puro
vanilla (flavoring) = la esencia de vainilla
walnut = la nuez de Castilla
yeast (active dry) = la levadura seca activa

EXTRA VOCABULARY FOR LESSON 7

Desserts = Los postres:

brownies = los pastelitos de chocolate
cake = el pastel, la torta, el queque
candies = los caramelos, los confites
cheesecake = el pastel de queso
chocolate (dark) = el chocolate amargo
chocolate (white) = chocolate blanco
custard = la natilla, el flan
cookies = las galletas
DohNut = el dónut, la rosquilla
ice cream = el helado, la nieve
pie = el pastel, la tarta
pie filling (apple) = relleno de manzana
pudding = el pudín
sweets = los dulces
whipped cream = la crema batida, la crema dulce

EXTRA VOCABULARY FOR LESSON 8

First Aid, Health, Personal Hygiene = Primeros Auxilios, La salud, La Higiene Personal:

antibiotic = el antibiótico
anitiseptic = el antiséptico
ankle = tobillo
arm = brazo
aspirin = la aspirina
asthma attack = el ataque de asma
band-aid = la curita, la venda
blood = la sangre
burn = la quemadura
cold = Tengo catarro. Estoy resfriado.
contagious = contagioso
cough = la tos
CPR = respiración cardiopulmonar
dandruff = la caspa
deodorant = el desodorante
doctor = el médico, la doctora
diarrhea = la diarrea
dizzy = mareado
eye = ojo
fever = la fiebre, la calentura
finger = dedo
food poisoning = el envenenamiento
foot = pie
hand = mano
headache = dolor de cabeza
Help me. = Ayúdame.
hurt = el dolor

I have a problem with my … = Tengo un problema con mi…
ice bag = la bolsa de hielo
illness = la enfermedad
indigestion = indigestión
injury = el herido, la lesión
itch = picar
knee = rodilla
leg = pierna
mouth = boca
nose = nariz
poisonous = venenoso
shave = afeitarse
shower = bañarse, ducharse
something in my eye = algo en mi ojo
sore throat = inflamación de la garganta
stomach = estómago
stress = estrés
temperature = la temperatura
tooth = diente/ muela
workman's compensation = compensación de obrero
wound = la herida
Where does it hurt? = ¿Dónde le duele?
Where is the hospital? = ¿Dónde está el hospital?

EXTRA VOCABULARY FOR LESSON 8

Medical = El médico

Where do you have pain? = ¿Dónde tiene dolor? *(DohN-deh Tee/eh-neh Doh-lore?)* Do you have pain here? In _____ = ¿Tiene dolor aquí? en _____? *(Tee/eh-neh Doh-lore Ah-kee? Ehn _____?)*	I have pain in _____. = Tengo dolor en _____. *(Tehn-goh doh-lore Ehn _____.)*
Is he/she allergic to any medication? = ¿Es alérgico/alérgica a alguna medicina?) *(S All-lehr-hee-koh Ah- Ahl-goo-nah Meh-dee-see-nah?)*	What medicines is he/she taking? = ¿Cuáles medicinas está tomando? *(Qwahl-ehs Med-dee-scene-ahs Ehs-tah Toh-mahn-doh?)*
What is your reason for your consultation? = ¿Cuál es el motivo de su consulta? *(Qwahl Ehs Ehl Moh-tee-voh Deh Soo Con-sool-tah?)*	What are his/her/your symptoms? = ¿Cuáles son sus síntomas? *(Qwahl-ehs Sohn Soos Sin-toh-mahs?)*
Does he/she/you have a fever? = ¿Tiene fiebre? *(Tee/eh-neh Fee-eh-breh?)* ¿Does he/she/you have a cough? = Tiene tos? *(Tee/eh-neh Toss?)*	For how many days? = ¿Por cuántos días? *(Pohr Qwahn-tohs Dee-ahs?)* How many times? =¿Cuántas veces? *(Qwahn-tahs Veh-sehs?)*
Has he/she been vomiting? = ¿Ha estado vomitando? *(Ah Ehs-tah-doh Voh-mee-tahn-doh?)* Does she/he/you have diarrhea? = ¿Tiene diarrea? *(Tee/eh-neh Dee-ah-ree-ah?)*	Wait here. = Espere aquí *(Ehs-peh-reh Ah-kee)* Don't worry. = No se preocupe. *(No Seh Preh-oh-koo-peh)*
Undress her or him and leave the diaper on. = Quite su ropa y deje el pañal puesto. *(Kee-teh Soo Roh-pah Ee Deh-heh Ehl Pahn-yahl Pwest-toh.)*	I am going to give you/her/him _____ an injection. = Voy a darle _____ una inyección. *(Voy Ah Dahr-leh _____ Oo-nah In-yeck-see/ohn)*

EXTRA VOCABULARY FOR LESSON 8

Safety = La Seguridad:

accident = el accidente
ambulance = la ambulancia
broken dishes (plates) = los trastes rotos (platos rotos)
broken glass = los vidrios rotos
dangerous = peligroso
emergency exit = salida de emergencia
Fire! = ¡Fuego!
fire extinguisher = el extintor
flashlight = la linterna

gas leak = escape de gas
heavy = pesado
Help! = ¡Socorro! ¡Auxilio! ¡Ayúdame!
police = el/ la policía
safety procedures= Las medidas de seguridad
sign (warning) = señal (de advertencia)
sharp = filoso, agudo
wet floor = piso mojado

Stores / Around the town = Las Tiendas / Por la ciudad

I am going to _____. = Yo voy a _____.
Remember to use "a la" in front of feminine words and "al" in front of the masculine words.

Examples: Yo voy a la farmacia. = I'm going to the pharmacy.
Yo voy al supermercado. = I'm going to the supermarket.

bakery = la panadería
butcher = la carnicería
cafeteria = la cafetería
company = la compañía
hairdresser = la peluquería
hardware store = la ferretería
jewelry store = la joyería

laundry = la lavendería
market = el mercado
pharmacy = la farmacia
restaurant = el restaurante
shoe store = la zapatería
store = la tienda
supermarket = el supermercado

EXTRA VOCABULARY FOR LESSON 9

TOURIST NEEDS= Las Necesidades de la turista:

I need _____ = Necesito _____

a bank = un banco
a bus = un autobus
a highway = una autopista
a map = un mapa
a plane = un avión
a train = un tren
a vacation = unas vacaciones
an airport = un aeropuerto

How much does it cost? = ¿Cuánto cuesta?
Is it close by? = ¿Está cerca?
Is it far away? = ¿Está lejos?
It is cheap. = Es barato.
It is expensive. = Es caro.
I am lost. = Estoy perdido/a.
I am a tourist. = Soy un/a turista.

HOTEL = El hotel

I need _____ = Necesito _____

a blanket = una cobija
a pillow = una almohada
a room = un cuarto
a taxi = un taxi
a towel = una toalla

more soap = más jabón
more toilet paper = más papel higiénico
It is clean. = Está limpio/a
It is dirty. = Está sucio/a

MEASUREMENTS = Las medidas

For more Spanish vocabulary and phrases regarding weights, volumes, length, temperature and measurements, see page 125.

Metric system conversions:

1 centímetro = .39 inches
1 metro = 3.28 feet
1 kilómetro = .621 mile

1 litro = 1.75 pints
1 gramo = .0352 oz.
1 kilo = 2.2 lbs.

TEMPERATURE = Temperatura:

100 F = 37.8 Celsius
75 F = 23.9 C
50 F = 10 C
32 F = O Celsius

20 F = -6.7 C
10 F = -12.2 C
0 F = -17 Celsius

EXTRA GRAMMAR

This section goes above and beyond for anyone who wants to know more grammar. Buying a basic grammar book will help you to practice even more in depth. This section will help you avoid some of the basic errors a computer translator will cause. The basic problem with most computer translators is they aren't concerned with context. They will just find you a word. For example, one student told the group she had four "cabritos." What she was trying to say was she had four kids, but the computer translated that she had four little goats also known as "kids." All the answers to the grammar exercises are also in the Answer Key.

EXTRA GRAMMAR
FOR LESSON 1 — ACCENT MARKS
WHEN TO USE AN ACCENT:

Ask a native speaker to pronounce these words for you and circle where the emphasis or stress is heard.

- **CHECK #1** If a word ends in a vowel a-e-i-o-u or -n-s, the natural stress should be on the next to the last syllable. You do not need an accent mark. Examen abuelos hijo Maestra luces

- **CHECK #2** If a word ends in any other consonant, then the natural stress should be on the last syllable. You do not need an accent mark. Universidad español cultural electricidad medidor

- **BINGO!** Any exception to #1 or #2 will have an accent mark on the stressed vowel. sábado miércoles José teléfono número adiós dirección

ON A MAC:

To type: à, è, ì, ò, ù, À, È, Ì, Ò, Ù
On a Mac, hold down these two keys at the same time; then the next letter you type will have an accent mark.
Note: If this does not work, use the help function for your computer.

[Option] [E]

To type: ¿
On a Mac, hold down all three of these keys at the same time.

[Option] [Shift] [?]

To type: ¡
On a Mac, hold down these two keys at the same time.

[Option] [1]

To type: ñ
On a Mac, hold down these two keys at the same time; then type "n" or "N" and it will have a tilde.

[Option] [N]

ON A PC:

To type: à, è, ì, ò, ù, À, È, Ì, Ò, Ù

On a PC, hold down these two keys at the same time; then the next letter you type will have an accent mark.
Note: If this does not work, use the help function for your computer.

To type: ¿

On a PC, hold down all four of these keys at the same time.

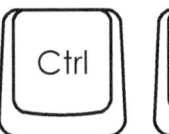   

To type: ¡

On a PC, hold down all four of these keys at the same time.

To type: ñ

On a PC, hold down all three of these keys at the same time; then type "n" or "N" and it will have a tilde.

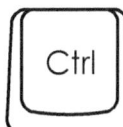  

La Práctica = The Practice

Find a native speaker and listen to them pronounce these words. Put an accent mark where you hear the stress. When you are finished, check your answers in the Answer Key.

1. Ingles
2. bibliografia
3. ficcion
4. dolares
5. puerta
6. periodico

EXTRA GRAMMAR FOR LESSON 3

Gustar The verb gustar is also helpful in basic Spanish phrases. It means to be pleasing to someone. It's mainly used in the third person either singular or plural. When you use this verb, you need an indirect object pronoun.

TO LIKE = GUSTAR:

I like. = Me gusta (n)	We like.= Nos gusta (n)
You like. (informal, singular) = Te gusta (n)	You like. (plural, Spain) = Os gusta (n)
He likes. = Le gusta (n) She likes = Le gusta (n) You like. (formal, singular) = Le gusta (n)	They like. = Les gusta (n) You like. (formal, plural) = Les gusta (n)

Here are some examples of correct usage of gustar:

I like to study. = Me gusta estudiar.
I like pizza. = Me gusta la pizza.
I like the books. = Me gustan los libros.
We like to work. = Nos gusta trabajar.
Do you like to study? = ¿Te gusta estudiar?
Renee, Chad, and Jude like to sleep. = A Reina, Carlos, y Judas les gustan dormir.
David likes the computer. = A David le gusta la computadora.

How would you translate these eight sentences?

1. She likes to swim. (to swim = nadar) _____

2. Do you like the book? _____

3. Mary and Bernard like to read. _____

4. He likes to fish. (to fish = pescar) _____

5. They like pizza. _____

6. I like the books. _____

7. You (plural) like to travel. (to travel = viajar) _____

8. We like to read Spanish. (to read= leer) _____

EXTRA GRAMMAR FOR LESSON 3 — INDIRECT AND DIRECT OBJECT PRONOUNS

A pronoun is a word that replaces a noun.
Here are the indirect and direct object pronouns in Spanish:

INDIRECT OBJECT PRONOUNS:

to me = me
to us = nos
to you (familiar) = te

to you (plural, Spain) = os
to him, to her, to you (formal) = le
to them, to you (plural, formal) = les

DIRECT OBJECT PRONOUNS:

me = me
us = nos
you (familiar) = te
you (plural, Spain) = os

him, it, you (masculine) = lo
her, it, you (feminine) = la
them, you (plural, masculine) = los
them, you (plural, feminine) = las

If you weren't paying attention in sixth-grade English class, it might be time for a little review. Let's start with a sentence in English. Example: Charlie throws the ball to Mary. Charlie is the subject of the sentence. Threw is the action word or verb. Ball would be the direct object. Mary is the indirect object.

Here is the same sentence in Spanish: Carlos tira la pelota a María. Carlos is the subject. Tira is the verb. Pelota is the direct object. María is the indirect object. Take this sentence and replace the direct and indirect objects with pronouns keeping in mind these three rules:

Rule #1: The pronouns have to agree with the word they're replacing.

Rule #2: When two pronouns are in one sentence, the indirect object comes before the direct object.

Rule #3: When le or les is followed by lo, la, los, or las, change the le or les to se.

Example #1: If you take the sentence (Carlos tira la pelota a María) and substitute the direct object for a pronoun, the new sentence would be the following: Carlos la tira a María. (Charlie threw it to Mary.) The direct object pronoun "la" replaces the word "pelota" and would be translated as it. (See Rule #1)

Example #2: If you substitute the indirect object with a pronoun, the new sentence would read: Carlos le tira la pelota. (Charlie threw the ball to her.) The indirect object pronoun "le" replaces the word "a María."

Example #3: Now if you replace both the direct and indirect objects with pronouns the new sentence would read: "Carlos se la tira." (Charlie threw it to her.) The "se" refers to Mary. The "la" refers to the ball. Originally it would be Carlos le la tira, but we have to change it to Carlos se la tira because of Rule #3.

For future reference, remember pronouns can be placed before any verb. Pronouns can go either before or after these three types of verbs:

1. an infinitive which is a verb that is not conjugated
2. a verb ending in –ando or –iendo This is the equivalent of –ing in Spanish. See Extra Grammar-Lesson 5.
3. affirmative commands

EXTRA GRAMMAR FOR LESSON 5 — REFLEXIVE VERBS

When people perform an action that reflects back onto them, in Spanish use reflexive verbs. In the dictionary you might see the reflexive pronoun –se attached to the verb. , you might see the verbs lavar and lavarse. Lavar means to wash. Lavarse means to wash oneself. Unless you are a baby, you have to wash yourself so use lavarse. Read this chart showing how to conjugate lavarse.

To wash oneself = Lavarse (present tense):

I wash myself. = Me lavo.	We wash ourselves. = Nos lavamos.
You wash yourself. (informal, singular) = Te lavas.	You wash yourself. (plural, Spain) = Os laváis.
He washes himself. = Se lava. She washes herself. = Se lava. You wash yourself. (formal, singular) = Se lava.	They wash themselves. = Se lavan. You wash yourself. (formal, plural) = Se lavan.

Other reflexive verbs:

To go to bed = Acostarse (o-ue)
To shave = Afeitarse
To bathe = Bañarse

To put on makeup = Maquillarse
To wake up = Despertarse (e-ie)
To put on clothes = Ponerse la ropa

PRESENT PROGRESSIVE

Here is how you say that something is in progress -ing

Example: I am trying to learn. = Estoy tratando de aprender.
Use this with an event actually in progress, not future intent.

-AR VERB:

estar + verbstem + ando= I am verb-ing
Estoy trabajando. = I am working

-ER/-IR VERB:

estar + verbstem + iendo
Estoy comiendo. = I am eating.

Here is how you conjugate the present progressive

Present progressive irregulars:

1. -er verbs ending in a,e,o replace i with y
2. -ir stem changing verbs use preterite form
3. some present irregulars like diciendo

EXTRA GRAMMAR FOR LESSON 7

Basic verb conjugation If you are allergic to grammar, you might want to skip this section all together. If you want a basic crash course in grammar because you are taking a Spanish course or have a child taking Spanish in high school, please continue reading. Understanding the subject pronouns is the key to verb conjugation. In lesson 6, you know conjugation is matching nouns with the verb. Here are the subject pronouns:

I = yo	we = nosotros
you (informal, singular) = tú	you (plural, Spain) = vosotros
he = él She = ella you (formal, singular) = usted Note: Ud. is the abbreviation for usted.	they (at least one male in the group) = ellos they (all female group) = ellas you (formal, plural) = ustedes Note: Uds. is the abbreviation for ustedes.

In this book, we focus on the more informal culinary communication. Therefore there isn't much reference to the usted or vosotros forms of the verb. Usted is more formal and is not used around close friends and family. Vosotros is used primarily in Spain. In the Americas most speakers substitute the vosotros form with the ustedes. Remember if you are unsure how to conjugate and the noun is singular, chances are it's the él, ella, usted form of the verb. If you are not sure how to conjugate the verb and the noun is plural, go with the ellos, ellas, ustedes form of the verb. A final note on the subject pronouns is nosotros can be used when it says nosotros or if it refers to two people as "we." For example, if the sentence says, "Carlos y yo," then the verb would be conjugated in the nosotros form.

Basic verb conjugation These are the regular present tense endings:

-AR PRESENT TENSE:

yo – o	nosotros - amos
tú - as	vosotros - áis
él - a ella - a usted - a	ellos - an ellas - an ustedes - an

EXTRA GRAMMAR FOR LESSON 7

-ER PRESENT TENSE:

yo - o	nosotros - emos
tú - es	vosotros - éis
él - e ella - e usted - e	ellos - en ellas - en ustedes - en

-IR PRESENT TENSE:

yo - o	nosotros - imos
tú - es	vosotros - ís
él - e ella - e usted - e	ellos - en ellas - en ustedes - en

La Práctica = The Practice: Conjugate the verb in the present tense.

Conjugate the verb to match the subject of each sentence.

1. **ACABAR:**
   Yo _____
   Usted _____
   Nosotros _____
   Ellos _____

2. **APRENDER:**
   Yo _____
   Luis _____
   Nosotros _____
   Franco y María _____

3. **VIVIR:**
   Yo _____
   Susana _____
   Zorro y yo _____
   Laura y Catarina _____

4. **TRAPEAR:**
   Yo _____ todo el día.
   Mi mamá _____ el piso.

5. **HABLAR:**
   Mi hijo, Juanito _____ mucho.
   Mi hija y mi esposo no _____ tanto como yo.

6. **CAMBIAR:**
   Mi hija, Elena _____ mucha.
   ¿Tú _____ las toallas de papel en el trabajo?

7. **LEER:**
   Yo _____ muchos libros.
   ¿Usted _____ mucho?
   Pancho _____ en la sala.

8. **LEER:**
   Las maestros _____ a sus clases.
   En la clase, nosotros _____ juntos.

9. **LEER:**
   Julia _____ a sus hijos cada noche.
   La biblioteca tiene muchos libros para _____.

10. **ASISTIR:**
    Yo _____ a la clase.
    Noe _____ a la clase.
    Lalo y Juana _____ a la fiesta.

11. **ASISTIR:**
    Nosotros _____ a la reunión.
    ¿Cristina, te gusta _____ a sus clases?

EXTRA GRAMMAR FOR LESSON 7

Boot Verbs = Stem Changing Verbs in the Present Tense:

Not all 10,000 verbs in Spanish follow the basic pattern of the regular verbs –ar, -er, and –ir. The rule-breakers must be memorized. Those irregularities are designed to make the verbs flow better when speaking. For example, some verbs are stem changing verbs and other verbs are irregular in the first person only. The purpose of this book is not to teach all the basics of Spanish grammar. Buying a basic grammar book would help with that. However, with a fundamental understanding of the rule-breakers, you will be able to eliminate some basic conversational errors and use a dictionary correctly.

For example, if you look up the verb poder in your dictionary, this verb means "to be able or can." Right after the word poder, you might see an abbreviation (v. irr.). This means the word is a verb and irregular in the present tense. The word poder n. mascl. is something different. This tells you poder is also used as a noun. El poder means the power. You should be familiar with all of the abbreviations in your dictionary to insure you are using the word correctly.

Here are a few of the basics of irregular verb conjugation. This isn't intended to be a complete list, but it's intended to jar a few flashbacks to Spanish 101. There are four basic types of stem changing verbs (e-ie, o-ue, e-i, and u-ue). We will conjugate an example of each. Enjoy!

Notice all the verb conjugations except the nosotros and vosotros forms have a spelling change in the stem. Some teachers call these types of verbs boot verbs. If you outline around all the verbs that have a spelling change in the stem, the outline shape will be a boot.

To Think = Pensar (ie) Present Tense Irregular:

I think. = Yo pienso.	We think. = Nosotros pensamos.
You think.= Tú piensas. (informal, singular)	You think. (plural, Spain) = Vosotros pensáis.
He thinks.= Él piensa. She thinks.= Ella piensa. You think. = Usted piensa. **(formal, singular)**	They think. = Ellos piensan. **(at least one male in the group)** They think. = Ellas piensan. **(all female group)** You think.= Ustedes piensan. **(formal, plural)**

Use the endings of the regular –ar, -er, and –ir endings. If you forgot, find the –ar endings in Lesson 6 and the –er/-ir endings in Lesson 7. The spell change in the stem makes this verb irregular. Here are some other common verbs with the e-ie stem changes.

to prefer = preferir   to want = querer   to close = cerrar
to begin = empezar   to understand = entender   to lose = perder

When you practice conjugating verbs, get in the habit of conjugating the singular pronouns on one side and the plural pronouns on the other side. This will help you to see the patterns and memorize the irregular verbs.

To be able to, can = Poder (ue) Present tense irregular:

I can. = Yo puedo.	We can. = Nosotros podemos.
You can. = Tú puedes. (informal, singular)	You can. = Vosotros podéis. (plural, Spain)
He can. = Él puede. She can. = Ella puede. You can. = Usted puede. (formal, singular)	They can. = Ellos pueden. (at least one male) They can. = Ellas pueden. (all females) You can. = Ustedes pueden. (formal, plural)

These are 6 other common verbs with the o-ue stem change:

to count, to tell = contar   to cost = costar   to return = volver
to sleep = dormir   to eat lunch = almorzar   to remember = recordar

To ask for = Pedir (ie) Present tense irregular:

I ask for = yo pido	we ask for = nosotros pedimos
you ask for = tú pides (informal, singular)	you ask for = vosotros pedís (plural, Spain)
he asks for = él pide she asks for = ella pide you ask for = usted pide (formal, singular)	they ask for = ellos piden (at least one male) they ask for = ellas piden (all females) you ask for = ustedes piden (formal, plural)

Another common verb with the e-i stem change is to repeat = repetir

EXTRA GRAMMAR FOR LESSON 7

To play a sport = Jugar (ue) present tense irregular:

I play. = Yo juego. =.	We play. = Nosotros jugamos.
You play. = Tú juegas. (informal, singular)	You play. = Vosotros jugáis. (plural, Spain)
He plays. = Él juega. She plays. = Ella juega. You play. Usted juega. (formal, singular)	They play. = Ellos juegan. (at least one male) They play. = Ellas juegan. (all females) You play. = Ustedes juegan. (formal, plural)

Present tense- first person irregular verbs:

There are some verbs in the present tense that are irregular in only the yo form of the verb. These are some of the most common irregular verbs in the present tense:

to know a fact = saber =. Yo sé.
to know a person or place. = conocer Yo conozco _____.

The verbs ending in the letters –go are known in some circles as Go-Go verbs. Go-Go verbs are like Go-Go dancers because they both take off items. The dancers shed clothes and the verbs shed the –go ending after the yo form. Now, aren't you glad you are reading the grammar section?

to do, make = hacer I make. = Yo hago.
to put = poner I put. = Yo pongo.
to bring = traer I bring. = Yo traigo.
to leave = salir I leave. Yo salgo.
to come = venir I come. = Yo vengo.
 (This is also an e--ie stem changing verb.)
to have = tener I have. Yo tengo. (This is an e--ie stem changing verb.)

EXTRA GRAMMAR FOR LESSON 8 — THIS/THAT, THESE, THOSE

To avoid repeating a noun, use éste, ése, aquél with an accent mark. Use the neutral forms, esto, eso, aquello to refer to an idea or to something that was said or done.

REGULAR PRETERITE ENDINGS

Preterite usually corresponds to the English –ed or did. Preterite is used to describe actions and events that happened once in the past as well as events that happened a specified number of times. These are the endings for the regular preterite tense:

TO BUY = COMPRAR (-AR PRETERITE):

I bought. = Yo compré.	We bought. = Nosotros compramos.
You bought. (informal, singular) = Tú compraste.	You bought. (plural, Spain) = Vosotros comprasteis.
He bought. = Él compró. She bought. = Ella compró. You bought. (formal, singular) = Usted compró.	They bought. (at least one male) = Ellos compraron. They bought. (all females) = Ellas compraron. You bought. (formal, plural) = Ustedes compraron.

TO SELL = VENDER (-ER PRETERITE):

I sold. = Yo vendí.	We sold. = Nosotros vendimos.
You sold. (informal, singular) = Tú vendiste.	You sold. (plural, Spain) = Vosotros vendisteis.
He sold. = Él vendió. She sold. = Ella vendió. You sold. (formal, singular) = Usted vendió.	They sold. = Ellos vendieron. They sold. = Ellas vendieron. You sold. (formal, plural) = Ustedes vendieron.

EXTRA GRAMMAR FOR LESSON 8 — REGULAR PRETERITE ENDINGS

To receive = Recibir (-ir preterite):

I received. = Yo recibí.	We received. = Nosotros recibimos.
You received. (informal, singular) = Tú recibiste.	You received. (plural, Spain) = Vosotros recibisteis.
He received. = Él recibió. She received. = Ella recibió. You received. (formal, singular) = Usted recibió.	They received. = Ellos recibieron. They received. = Ellas recibieron. You received. (formal, plural) = Ustedes recibieron.

Verbs ending in the letters –car, gar, and zar have a spelling change only in the yo form.

- buscar: Yo busqué. = I searched for.
- pagar: Yo pagué. = I paid.
- almorzar : Yo almorcé. = I ate lunch.

IRREGULAR PRETERITE

In Lesson 8 we have covered the basics of regular conjugation in the preterite past tense. However, do all 10,000 verbs have this regular conjugation? It would be wonderful if it did, but we are not that lucky. Some verbs are irregular in the preterite and must be memorized. Fortunately there are a few tricks to make this memorization come a little easier.

Many irregular preterite verbs end like this:

yo – e	nosotros - imos
tú – iste	vosotros - eis
él - o ella - o usted - o	ellos -ieron ellas -ieron ustedes -ieron

Here is an example of an irregular preterite:

TO WISH, TO WANT = QUERER (IRREGULAR PRETERITE):

I wanted. = Yo quise.	We wanted. = Nosotros quisimos.
You wanted. (informal, singular) = Tú quisiste.	You wanted. (plural, Spain) = Vosotros quisisteis.
He wanted. = Él quiso. She wanted. = Ella quiso. You wanted. (formal, singular) = Usted quiso.	They wanted. = Ellos quisieron. They wanted. = Ellas quisieron. You wanted. (formal, plural) = Ustedes quisieron.

Notice the preterite stem remains consistent throughout the conjugation and the endings come from the irregular preterite endings.

These are some of the irregular preterite verbs along with their preterite stems. The subject pronouns not listed will be conjugated in the regular form of preterite.:

- andar = to walk (Anduv) Yo anduve. Usted anduvo. Ellos anduvieron.
- caber = to fit into (Cup) Yo cupe. Usted cupo. Ellos cupieron.
- estar = to be (Estuv) Yo estuve. Usted estuvo. Ellos estuvieron.
- poder = to be able, can (Pud) Yo pude. Usted pudo. Ellos pudieron.
- poner = to put (Pus) Yo puse. Usted puso. Ellos pusieron.
- querer = to wish, want (Quis) Yo quise. Usted quiso. Ellos quisieron.
- saber = to know (Sup) Yo supe. Usted supo. Ellos supieron.
- tener = to have (Tuv) Yo tuve. Usted tuvo. Ellos tuvieron.
- venir = to come (Vin) Yo vine. Usted vino. Ellos vinieron.

EXTRA GRAMMAR FOR LESSON 8

Here are some of the irregular preterite verbs that you may have to memorize, since they don't exactly follow a pattern. These first four verbs will have a j in the stem and also drop the i in the ellos, ellas, and ustedes form. Here is an example;

TO BRING = TRAER (IRREGULAR PRETERITE):

I brought. = Yo traje.	We brought = Nosotros trajimos.
You brought. (informal, singular) = Tú trajiste.	You brought (plural, Spain) = Vosotros trajisteis.
He brought. = Él trajo. She brought. = Ella trajo. You brought (informal, singular) = Usted trajo.	They brought. = Ellos trajeron. They brought. = Ellas trajeron. You brought. (Fomal, plural) = Ustedes trajeron.

3 more verbs are similiar to traer in the preterite tense:

- 🌏 to say, to tell = decir(dij) Yo dije. Usted dijo. Ellos dijeron.

- 🌏 to conduct = conducir (Conduj) Yo conduje. Usted condujo. Ellos condujeron.

- 🌏 to translate = traducir (Traduj) Yo traduje. Usted tradujo. Ellos tradujeron.

Here is one of the few verbs with two preterite stems (hic and hiz). Here is an example;

TO DO OR TO MAKE = HACER (IRREGULAR PRETERITE):

I did. = Yo hice.	We did. = Nosotros hicimos.
You did. (informal, singular) = Tú hiciste.	You did. (plural, Spain) = Vosotros hicisteis.
He did. = Él hizo. She did. = Ella hizo. You did. (formal, singular) = Usted hizo.	They did. = Ellos hicieron. They did. = Ellas hicieron. You did. (formal, plural) = Ustedes hicieron.

Although they are classified as irregular preterites, the verbs ver = to see and dar = to give are very similar in the preterite. Here is the conjugation for dar; for ver just substitute the d with a v.

TO GIVE = DAR (IRREGULAR PRETERITE):

I gave. = Yo di.	We gave. = Nosotros dimos.
You gave. (informal, singular) = Tú diste.	You gave. (plural, Spain) = Vosotros disteis.
He gave. = Él dio. She gave. = Ella dio. You gave. (formal, singular) = Usted dio.	They gave. = Ellos dieron. They gave. = Ellas dieron. You gave. (formal, plural) = Ustedes dieron.

The final verbs that are irregular in the preterite are the verbs to go=ir and to be = ser. The good news is the conjugations are identical. This table is also found in 151 = ciento cincuenta y uno.

TO BE= SER + TO GO = IR (IRREGULAR PRETERITE):

I was. I went. = Yo fui.	We were. We went. = Nosotros fuimos.
You went. = Tú fuiste.	You went. (plural, Spain) = Vosotros fuisteis.
He was. He went. = Él fue. She was. She went. = Ella fue. You were. You went. (singular)= Usted fue. They were. They went. = Ellos fueron.	They were. They went. (all female) = Ellas fueron. You were. You went. (plural) = Ustedes fueron.

EXTRA GRAMMAR FOR LESSON 8

SKATEBOARD VERBS

Skateboard verbs are stem changing -ir verbs that only change in the third person preterite. Here is an example;

TO ASK FOR = PEDIR

I asked for = yo pedí

you asked for = Tú pediste

we asked for = nosotros pedimos

you asked for (plural, Spain) = vosotros pedisteis

> he asked for = él pidió.
> they asked for = ellos pidieron
> she asked for = ella pidió
> they asked for (all female) = ellas pidieron
> you asked for (singular) = usted pidió
> you asked for (plural) = ustedes pidieron

E CHANGES TO I

to obtain = conseguir
to have fun = divertirse
to ask for = pedir
to prefer = preferir
to follow = seguir

to feel = sentirse
to serve = servir
to dress yourself = vestirse
to wake yourself up = despedirse

O CHANGES TO U

morir = to die
dormir = to sleep

Note: The yo and ella form do have accent marks.

Verbs ending in –er and –ir and have a vowel at the end of the stem require a "y" in the preterite third person form. Here is an example;

TO READ = LEER:

I read. = Yo leí.	We read. = Nosotros leímos.
You read. (informal, singular) = Tú leíste.	You read. (plural, Spain) = Vosotros leísteis.
He reads. = Él leyó. She reads. = Ella leyó. You read. (formal, singular) = Usted leyó.	They read. = Ellos leyeron. They read. = Ellas leyeron. They read. (formal, plural) = Ustedes leyeron.

A few other examples are:

to hear = oir

to fall = caer

IMPERFECT PAST TENSE

Imperfect is used to talk about events or conditions in progress at a particular point in the past, often while something else was happening. In English this is translated as: was/were….ing. The imperfect past tense is used in these four situations:

1. To describe conditions ongoing in the past. Examples: physical characteristics, states of mind, weather, and emotions, as well as age.

2. To talk about events ongoing (in progress) in the past. Including simultaneous events expressed with mientras. Also look for the word cuando. The ongoing action will be in imperfect and the interrupting action will be in preterite.

3. The ir + a is almost always in the imperfect.

4. The imperfect is used to tell time in the past and talk about habitual events. Look for the Spanish words, siempre or generalmente or todos los días.

In the imperfect past tense there are no stem or spelling changes. The yo and ella forms are the same. This chart shows how to conjugate regular imperfect verbs:

-AR IMPERFECT PAST TENSE:

yo - aba	nosotros - ábamos
tú - abas	vosotros - abais
él - aba ella - aba usted - aba	ellos - aban ellas - aban ustedes - aban

-ER AND -IR IMPERFECT PAST TENSE:

yo - ía	nosotros - íamos
tú - ías	vosotros - íais
él - ía ella - ía usted - ía	ellos - ían ellas - ían ustedes - ían

THERE ARE ONLY THREE IRREGULAR IMPERFECT PAST TENSE VERBS:

to be = ser: Yo era. Tú eras. Alicia era. Nosotros èramos. Vosotros erais. Ellos eran.
to go = ir: Yo iba. Tú ibas. Timoteo iba. Nosotros íbamos. Vosotros ibais. Ellos iban.
to see = ver: Yo veía. Tú veías. Jaime veía. Nosotros veíamos. Vosotros veíais. Ellos veían.

LESSON 8 — PRETERITE VERSUS IMPERFECT

La Práctica = The Practice: Conjugate the verb in either the preterite or imperfect past depending on which is appropriate.

1. La clase de español _____ (ser) muy divertida en nuestra compañía.

2. Nosotros _____ (aprender) mucho.

3. En la primera clase, yo _____ (estudiar) frases importantes.

4. También en esta clase yo _____ (usar) un CD de frases.

5. ¿Usted _____ (escuchar) el CD?

6. María, Indira, Paca, y Cristina _____ (practicar) mucho.

7. Rosa y David _____ (hacer) comida buena.

8. Gracias a Miguel, él _____ (arreglar) las sillas cada semana.

9. Jorge y Juana y Vieva _____ (grabar) una película.

10. Gonzalo _____ (hablar) por teléfono en español con los clientes.

11. La maestra Julia _____ (estar) triste de decir, "¡Adiós!"

Note: All grammar answers are in the Answer Key

Don't worry if you struggled with this exercise. This takes some practice. Even if you use the wrong past tense, you will probably be understood and forgiven by the native speakers. With practice you will get better at this conjugation and the answers will start to sound right. Please keep this information handy. If you ever decide to take another Spanish class, you will find the information in this extra grammar section very useful. There are many great Spanish books containing more grammar exercises. If you would like more information and resources, check our Web site at www.SpanishChatCompany.com

ANSWER KEY

2 = DOS

1. hamburguesas = hamburgers
2. refrigerador = refrigerator
3. café = coffee, cafe-(a small cafeteria), the color brown
4. teléfono = telephone
5. restaurante = restaurant
6. coliflor = cauliflower

4 = CUATRO

1. C
2. B
3. B
4. A

12 = DOCE

CÓMO = how
ESTÁS = are
DÍA = day
NOCHE = night
AYÚDAME = help me
ENTIENDES = do you understand
BIEN = Fine
MÁS = more

TARDE = afternoon
MUCHO = much
GUSTO = pleasure
DESPACIO = slow
REPÍTELO = repeat it
POR FAVOR = please or for a favor
TÚ = you (informal)
TE LLAMAS = You are called (name)

		D	E	S	P	A	C	I	O				
						A	Y	Ú	D	A	M	E	S
	D	Í	A									Á	
										E	M		S
R	E	P	Í	T	E	L	O		S				E
			M					T		T			D
			U				Á			A			N
T	N		C	Ó	M	O	S		R	R			E
E	E		H					O		D			I
L	I		O				V			E	N		T
L	B					A					O		N
A					F						C		E
M				R							H		
A			O	T	S	U	G				E		
S		P		T	Ú								

13 = TRECE

1. G
2. E
3. B
4. L
5. N
6. M
7. C
8. K
9. D
10. H
11. F
12. I
13. O
14. A
15. J
16. Ñ

17 = DIECISIETE

1. Hello.
2. And you?
3. Good morning.
4. Goodbye!
5. I'm fine.
6. Do you understand?
7. Slow down.
8. Good night.
9. ¿Cómo te llamas?
10. Repítelo.
11. Buenas tardes.
12. Hasta luego.
13. Ayúdame, por favor.
14. Mucho gusto.
15. ¿Cómo estás?
16. Me llamo Julia.

20 = VEINTE

1. Buenos días.
2. ¿Y tú?
3. ¿Cómo estás?
4. Estoy bien.
5. Mucho gusto.
6. Ayúdame, por favor.
7. Hasta luego.

24 = VEINTICUATRO

```
        ¹M
²S  O  P  A
         Y
         O        ³F
      ⁴E  N  S  A  L  ⁵A  D  A
         N        S     P
⁶F  R  Í  A     T     ⁸P  L  A  T  ⁷O        ⁹T
         I     E        E         N           A
         S     R        T         I           B
         E              I         O           L      ¹¹H
                        Z            ¹⁰C  A  N  G  R  E  J  O
                        E                  S              T
            ¹²A  T  R  Á  S
```

25 = VEINTICINCO

1. C
2. C
3. D
4. A

33 = TREINTA Y TRES

Interesting things = Cosas interesantes:

1. Cierto.
2. Falso. Picasso had a blue period.
3. Cierto.

Food = Comida:

1. Falso. A tortilla in Spain would be an omelet with eggs, potatoes, onions, and cheese
2. Cierto.
3. Cierto.

35 = TREINTA Y CINCO

1. L
2. N
3. A
4. B
5. G
6. D
7. Ñ
8. I
9. M
10. H
11. J
12. C
13. F
14. K
15. E

36 = TREINTA Y SEIS

1. El apio
2. La hermana
3. Los hermanos
4. El limón
5. Las calabazas
6. Los cuchillos
7. La cuenta
8. Las uvas
9. La mitad
10. Las cucharas
11. Los tenedores
12. El atún

37 = TREINTA Y SIETE

1. Did you get the ticket for table 18?
2. Behind.
3. Put the mayonnaise on the side.
4. There is no crab.
5. Excuse me.
6. Hurry.
7. Remake it without onions.
8. Necesito la ensalada para la mesa quince.
9. La sopa está fría, caliéntala.
10. Cuánto tiempo más para el aperitivo?
11. Sin nueces, hay una alergia.
12. El plato está caliente.
13. No está correcto.
14. Faltan las papas fritas.
15. Más rápido.

41 = CUARENTA Y UNO

1. mother
2. father
3. son
4. daughter
5. husband
6. wife

46 = CUARENTA Y SEIS

1. Sí me gusta/No me gusta la comida.
2. Sí me gusta/No me gusta el café con leche.
3. Sí me gusta/No me gusta mi trabajo.
4. Sí me gustan/No me gustan los libros.

49 = CUARENTA Y NUEVE

Interesting things = Cosas interesantes:

1. Cierto.
2. Cierto.
3. Falso. The eagle was standing on a cactus with a snake in it's mouth.

Food = Comida:

1. Cierto.
2. Falso. Cacao beans were used as currency in Aztec times, but today it's pesos.
3. Cierto.

50 = CINCUENTA

1. Do you have family here?
   Yes or no, _____
   I have family here.

2. How many people are in your family?
   There are _____ people in my family.

3. What are your children's names?
   My children are named _____.

4. How old are your children?
   My children are _____ years old.

5. How is the family doing?
   My family is _____.

6. What do you like to do?
   I like to _____.

7. Where do you live?
   I live in _____.

8. Where are you from originally?
   I am from _____.

9. How long have you been here?
   I have been here for _____ years.

10. Do you like your job?
    Yes or no, _____
    I like my job.

52 = CINCUENTA Y DOS

1. D
2. C
3. A
4. C

55 = CINCUENTA Y CINCO

1. F
2. G
3. A
4. B
5. D
6. E
7. C

56 = CINCUENTA Y SEIS:

Puzzle phrase: Mírame. Pon la mesa así.

57 = CINCUENTA Y SIETE

1. Will you clean table seven for me?
2. Watch me.
3. Have you seen the manager?
4. Table 26 needs decaffeinated coffee.
5. Roll the silverware.
6. Set the table like this.
7. Put this in a "to-go" box.
8. Also, bring bread to them.
9. Traeme más hielo.
10. La mesa 13 necesita servicio.
11. Sígueme con esta bandeja
12. Allí te encargo mi área.
13. Quita los platos grandes.
14. Faltan dos sillas.
15. Voy al baño.
16. Caminando el plato principal de la mesa 12.
17. Dobla las servilletas.

64 = SESENTA Y CUATRO

1. C
2. A
3. D
4. B
5. C
6. A
7. B
8. D

67 = SESENTA Y SIETE

1. H
2. F
3. D
4. E
5. A
6. G
7. C
8. B

68 = SESENTA Y OCHO

1. tengo = I am 40 years old.
2. tienes = Do you have a dishrag or some paper towels?
3. tenemos = We have a lot of work.
4. tiene = Araceli (Arvaleen) is hungry.
5. tengo = I am cold.
6. tienen = They are not hot.
7. tiene = She is tired.
8. tiene = Franco (Frank) is in a hurry.
9. tienen = Melchor (Merle) y Carolina (Carolyn) are not thirsty.
10. tienes = You have to recycle the plastic bottles.

69 = SESENTA Y NUEVE

1. quiero = I want to cook.
2. quiere = She wants to water the plants.
3. quieres = Do you want to taste a stuffed chile pepper?
4. quiere = Catalina (Sharre Kate) wants to learn a little Spanish.
5. quieren = They want to have better service.
6. queremos = We don't want to smoke.

70 = SETENTA

1. voy = I am going to polish the spoons
2. va = Eliana goes to Guatemala.
3. van = The customers are going to pay their bills.
4. va = She is going to change the lightbulb.
5. vas = Are you going to work tomorrow?
6. vamos = We are going to have the meeting today.

72 = SETENTA Y DOS

NOTE: THE WORD SEARCH ANSWER KEY IS CONTINUED ON PAGE 254

1. limpia = clean
2. aspira = to vacuum Note: aspiradora = the vacuum
3. comedor = dining room
4. trapea = mop
5. cocina = (the) kitchen, he/she cooks
6. cuidado = (Be) careful
7. piso = floor
8. mojado = wet
9. barre = sweep
10. afuera = outside

72 = SETENTA Y DOS (ALSO-WORDS ON PAGE 253)

									O		
		L	I	M	P	I	A		S		
								I			C
	M	O	J	A	D	O		P			O
									.		M
			T								E
			R								D
			A								O
A	S	P	I	R	A	D	O	R	A		R
N		E									
I		A									
C				C	U	I	D	A	D	O	
O							E	R	R	A	B
C		A	R	E	U	F	A				

76 = SETENTA Y SEIS

INTERESTING THINGS = COSAS INTERESANTES:

1. Falso. It is freshwater, but there are sharks and tuna fish.
2. Cierto.
3. Cierto.

FOOD = COMIDA:

1. Cierto.
2. Cierto.
3. Falso. Tamales in Nicaragua are wrapped in banana leaves, not corn husks.

77 = SETENTA Y SIETE

1. Take out (empty) the trash.
2. The bathroom needs toilet paper.
3. Caution. (Careful./ Watch out.)
4. Where are the trash bags?
5. Mop the kitchen floor.
6. Clean the bathroom right away.
7. Use the disinfectant.
8. Barre afuera.
9. ¿Terminaste de limpiar?
10. Aspira el comedor.
11. Llena la jabonera.
12. Piso mojado.
13. Ponte los guantes.

80 = OCHENTA

Personal Information: Name (Last, First)
Phone number
Address
Social Security number
Interests and Special Abilities
Education: Name of School   Dates   Did you Graduate? Yes or No?
Last job: Name of Place   Position   Ending Salary
References: Name   Phone number   Number of years acquainted
Signature of Applicant   Date

82 = OCHENTA Y DOS

1. 1:00
2. 2:00
3. 3:00
4. 4:00
5. 5:05
6. 6:15
7. 7:30
8. 8:30
9. 8:40
10. 9:45
11. 10:50
12. 11:55
13. (Answers will vary. Here are some possible answers.) 6:00 A.M.
14. 6:30 A.M.
15. 11:15 A.M.
16. 2:00 P.M.
17. 5:30 P.M.
18. 9:00 P.M

85 = OCHENTA Y CINCO

1. D
2. C
3. A
4. D

88 = OCHENTA Y OCHO

1. Falso. Ayer fue lunes. Yesterday was Monday.
2. Cierto
3. Cierto
4. Falso. Ocho es más tarde que siete. 8:00 is later than 7:00. The person would have to come in earlier than 7:00.
5. Falso. El próximo mes será febrero. Next month would be February.

90 = NOVENTA

1. F
2. C
3. I
4. K
5. B
6. E
7. L
8. G
9. A
10. H
11. J
12. D

NOTE: 91 = NOVENTA Y UNO IS ON PAGE 257

94 = NOVENTA Y CUATRO

Interesting things = Cosas interesantes:

1. Cierto.
2. Cierto.
3. Falso. The best time is during the night.

Food = Comida:

1. Cierto.
2. Falso. The fish is actually cooked by soaking it in lemon. It is never put in an oven, microwave or cooked on a stove top.
3. Cierto.

91 = NOVENTA Y UNO

[Crossword puzzle with the following entries:]
- 1 Down: PAPELES
- 2 Across: HOUR
- 3 Down: CUÁL
- 4 Across: EVERYTHING
- 5 Down: JEFE
- 6 Down: S
- 7 Down: T
- 8 Across: EARLY
- 9 Down: LLEGA
- 10 Across: JOB
- 11 Down: SALIDA
- 13 Down: PREGUNTA

NOTE: 94 = NOVENTA Y CUATRO IS ON PAGE 256

96 = NOVENTA Y SEIS

1. estamos
2. estás
3. somos
4. es
5. son
6. están

97 = NOVENTA Y SIETE

1. Good job.
2. Your schedule is Thursday through Saturday from 3:00 to 10:00.
3. It's important to arrive on time.
4. Can you stay late?
5. Fill out these papers.
6. Did you already clock out?
7. What is your phone number?
8. Do you have questions?
9. ¿Cuáles días puedes trabajar?
10. El jefe quiere hablar contigo.
11. ¿A qué hora entraste?
12. ¿Puedes venir temprano?
13. ¿Está todo bien?
14. ¿Ya marcaste la entrada?
15. ¿Necesitas algo más?

103 = CIENTO TRES

1. Cierto. Elena has to work Monday.
2. Falso. Juan trabaja por treinta horas esta semana. Juan works for 30 hours this week, not 20.
3. Cierto. Juan can change (trade) with Julia on Tuesday.
4. Cierto. Francisco and Elena work 50 hours = 10 extra. (overtime.)
5. Falso. Francisco no trabaja muy tarde en la noche. Francisco does not work late at night, he only works until 5 p.m.
6. Falso. Julia trabaja tiempo completo = full time (40 hours). Julia works full time not part time = medio tiempo.

105 = CIENTO CINCO

1. J
2. G
3. F
4. B
5. C
6. A
7. K
8. D
9. E
10. H
11. I
12. L

106 = CIENTO SEIS

Puzzle phrase: Necesito uno nuevo, al vuelo.

109 = CIENTO NUEVE

INTERESTING THINGS = COSAS INTERESANTES:

1. Falso. The Salt Cathedral was carved underground in the salt deposits accessible by tunnels.
2. Cierto.
3. Cierto.

FOOD = COMIDA:

1. Cierto.
2. Falso. The first two are true but there is no pabellón expreso.
3. Cierto.

111 = CIENTO ONCE

Answers will vary.

114 = CIENTO CATORCE

1. D
2. C
3. B
4. A

115 = CIENTO QUINCE

1. cocino, cocinas, cocinan
2. trabaja, trabajamos, trabajan
3. limpio, limpia, limpian
4. corto, cortamos, cortan

116 = CIENTO DIECISÉIS

1. Yo lavo.
2. Tú llegas.
3. Ella mezcla.
4. Él prepara.
5. Nosotros miramos.
6. Ellos organizan.

117 = CIENTO DIECISIETE

1. Label it with the name and date.
2. Temp (prepare) the steak to medium.
3. I want the chicken breast ready by 11:30.
4. Have the chef taste it.
5. First In, First Out. FIFO
6. Steam the vegetables.
7. Train the new person.
8. Se está quemando.
9. Le falta sal.
10. Escurre las papas.
11. Necesito uno nuevo, al vuelo.
12. Fríe el pescado en el sartén.
13. ¿Qué es esto?

118 = CIENTO DIECIOCHO

"Bingo" game numbers to call out in the following order. Fill out the game board on page 126 before peeking at these numbers. To help pronounce these in Spanish see the number chart on page 30. Start with the left column and go down, and then proceed to the second column. Continue until someone yells "Bingo"!

81-90	801-925	34-40	31-33	101-150
11-15	75-80	302-400	201-250	47-50
21-26	41-46	91-100	712-750	71-74
251-301	401-501	751-800	51-54	1-10
650-711	601-649	151-200	926-1000	16-20
55-60	27-30	61-65	66-70	502-600

120 = CIENTO VEINTE

1. First, make the caramel. Put one cup of granulated sugar en a sauté pan. Melt it on medium heat. Stir it continuously until the sugar has liquefied. Put it quickly into the flan mold pan.

2. In a bowl, gently stir three large eggs. Add one can of evaporated milk, one can of sweetened condensed milk, and a Tablespoon of vanilla. Stir a little and put it in the caramelized mold.

3. Put the mold in a double boiler. Bake it for 45 minutes at 325 degrees.

4. Chill it in the refrigerator overnight or at least four hours.

5. Before serving, remove the flan from the mold. Simply, turn it over on a plate and let the caramel drop on top of the flan.

6. Eat it with a spoon. Invite your friends to enjoy it.

122 = CIENTO VEINTIDÓS

1. F
2. H
3. E
4. G
5. A
6. C
7. B
8. D

124 = CIENTO VEINTICUATRO

1. la menta verde = the green mint
   las cebollinas verdes = the green onions
   el espárrago verde = the green asparagus
   los nopales verdes = the green cactus

2. la salsa de tomate roja = the red ketchup
   las frambuesas rojas = the red raspberries
   el arándano rojo = the red cranberry
   los rábanos rojos = the red radishes

3. la leche blanca = the white milk
   las camisas blancas = the white shirts
   el bacalao blanco = the white cod
   los huesos blancos = the white bones

125 = CIENTO VEINTICINCO

1. el cliente rico
2. las jarras pequeñas
3. la cuenta cara
4. los servicios baratos
5. las ayudantes perezosas

128 = CIENTO VEINTIOCHO

1. C
2. A
3. D
4. B
5. A
6. B

129 = CIENTO VEINTINUEVE

1. Tupac told her to bake it for 55 min. at 550 and it should be 45 min. at 450.
2. Isabel is making bread.
3. There are no frozen vegetables, this restaurant uses fresh vegetables.

131 = CIENTO TREINTA Y UNO

					A	R	E	B	A	N	A		
				G				A	C	A	S		M
			A								A		
		P				A	C				S		
A					L			U		A			P
			E	A				B	D				I
		P		V			A		R				C
				A		D			A	E		H	A
					A				U			I	
				L					G			E	
			A			R	E	C	E	T	A	R	
		S										V	
	N				E	D	N	E	I	C	N	E	
E				R	E	C	I	P	I	E	N	T	E

REBANA = Slice
RECIPIENTE = Container
PELA = Peel
LAVA = Wash
SACA = Take out
ENSALADA = Salad
CUBRE = Cover

GUARDA = Put away/ Save
ENCIENDE = Turn on
PICA = Chop
RECETA = Recipe
MASA = Dough
APAGA = Turn off
HIERVE = Boil

133 = CIENTO TREINTA Y TRES

INTERESTING THINGS = COSAS INTERESANTES:

1. Cierto.
2. Cierto.
3. Falso. It is in the shape of a Condor. (See page 135)

FOOD = COMIDA:

1. Falso. The name comes from the former First Lady of Bolivia who invented Salteñas. She was from Salta, Argentina.
2. Cierto.
3. Cierto.

134 = CIENTO TREINTA Y CUATRO

1. comprendo, comprendes, compreden
2. barro, barre, barren
3. aprende, aprendemos, aprenden

135 = CIENTO TREINTA Y CINCO

1. añado, añades, añaden
2. recibo, recibe, reciben
3. abre, abrimos, abren

136 = CIENTO TREINTA Y SEIS

1. Take the meat out of the freezer.
2. Slice the watermelon.
3. Cut the dessert in eight portions.
4. Cover and put away the shrimp.
5. Turn off the oven.
6. Chop six big red apples.
7. Mix the dough.
8. Lava y pela las zanahorias.
9. Hornéalo por 45 minutos a 350 grados.
10. Usa esta receta.
11. Enciende la estufa.
12. Haz más ensalada con lechuga, pepinos y tomates.
13. Hierve el agua en la olla grande.
14. Ponla en un recipiente.

142 = CIENTO CUARENTA Y DOS

1. C
2. D
3. C
4. B
5. A
6. B
7. B
8. D

143 = CIENTO CUARENTA Y TRES

1. North
2. East
3. South
4. West

147 = CIENTO CUARENTA Y SIETE

Across:
- 2. JABÓN
- 4. TAZAS PEQUEÑAS
- 6. EMERGENCIA
- 8. MANOS
- 10. SECA
- 12. ENFERMO

Down:
- 1. INSOTWORKING
- 2. JABÓN
- 3. KNIFE
- 5. BROOK
- 7. WASH
- 9. ASPIRIN
- 11. FORKS

148 = CIENTO CUARENTA Y OCHO

1. C
2. F
3. I
4. L
5. K
6. J
7. H
8. G
9. E
10. D
11. B
12. A

149 = CIENTO CUARENTA Y NUEVE

1. Aquella mesera ayuda a ese lavaplatos con esos cuchillos filosos y estos platos calientes.
2. Estas ensaladas necesitan esas cebollas, pero haz esta ensalada sin esas cebollas.

152 = CIENTO CINCUENTA Y DOS

1. Nosotros estuvimos tarde ayer.
2. Yo fui a la clase de español el martes.
3. Tú estuviste (Usted estuvo) enfermo/a el lunes pasado.

153 = CIENTO CINCUENTA Y TRES

1. Ella vivió en Argentina.
2. Él habló español.
3. Nosotros comimos empanadas.
4. Ellos hablaron inglés.
5. Yo comí mucha carne.

155 = CIENTO CINCUENTA Y CINCO

Interesting things = Cosas interesantes:

1. Cierto.
2. Falso. Uruguay won the in 1930 and 1950 World Cups.
3. Cierto.

Food = Comida:

1. Falso. Herbs for Yerba Mate are placed in a gourd, then hot water is poured on the herbs. A "bombilla" metal straw strains the tea as you drink it. When the gourd is empty you usually pass it to the next family member.
2. Cierto.
3. Cierto.

157 = CIENTO CINCUENTA Y SIETE

1. Do you need a band-aid?
2. Dry the wine glasses.
3. Wash your hands with soap.
4. Is there something that is not working?
5. It's dirty.
6. The broken glass goes here.
7. Will you wash more forks?
8. No vengas al trabajo si estás enfermo/a.
9. Pon las tazas pequeñas en su lugar
10. En caso de emergencia, marca 911.
11. Dame un cuchillo filoso.
12. Lava esto otra vez.
13. Necesitas una aspirina?
14. Déjalo remojando.

160 = CIENTO SESENTA

During last summer, my family went to San Juan, Puerto Rico. There were many restaurants, churches, museum, buildings and people. There were almost 1.6 million inhabitants in the capital area. We liked The Moor and The Fort of St. Christopher We ate fried plantains, beans and chicken with rice and we drank "snow cone" iced drinks. Finally, my family loved to relax on the beach.

1. San Juan, Puerto Rico
2. 1.6 million
3. El Morro y El Yunque
4. Tostones, frijoles y arroz

162 = CIENTO SESENTA Y DOS

THE FOODS = LAS COMIDAS:

1. Answers will vary, here are a few examples; a cheeseburger = una hamburguesa con queso
2. a sausage = una salchicha/chorizo
3. some french fries = unas papas fritas
4. a fruit = una fruta
5. a salad = una ensalada

THE DRINKS = LAS BEBIDAS:

1. Answers will vary, here are a few examples;
a glass of water = un vaso de agua
2. a coffee with milk = un café con leche
3. a diet drink = un refresco lite
4. a bottle of red wine = una botella de vino tinto
5. a beer = una cerveza

165 = CIENTO SESENTA Y CINCO

1. B
2. D
3. D
4. A
5. B
6. C

168 = CIENTO SESENTA Y OCHO

1. I
2. F
3. D
4. J
5. A
6. C
7. E
8. G
9. H
10. B

169 = CIENTO SESENTA Y NUEVE

Puzzle phrase: Que le vaya bien.

171 = CIENTO SETENTA Y UNO

Answers will vary.
    Name of a restaurant, Name of a drink (twice), Your Favorite food, A Price

173 = CIENTO SETENTA Y TRES

Interesting things = Cosas interesantes:

1. Cierto.
2. Cierto.
3. Falso. Equatorial Guinea is located in West Africa.

Food = Comida:

1. Cierto.
2. Falso. Tostones are twice fried plantains that are usually fried in a skillet or deep fat fryer.
3. Cierto.

177 = CIENTO SETENTA Y SIETE

1. Where is the bathroom?
2. I will be the cashier whenever you're ready.
3. I recommend my favorite dish, the roast beef.
4. The bill, please.
5. Cheers! and/or Bless you!
6. How much does the plate of the day cost?
7. Thank you for coming.
8. What would you like to drink?
9. Bienvenidos a nuestro restaurante.
10. Aquí está la cuenta.
11. ¿Qué desea para comer?
12. Que le vaya bien.
13. Quiero pedir las tortillas de harina.
14. Cuesta 16 dólares.
15. Buen provecho.

178 = CIENTO SETENTA Y OCHO

Answers will vary.

181 = CIENTO OCHENTA Y UNO

1. C
2. E
3. A
4. F
5. J
6. H
7. M
8. I
9. N
10. L
11. G
12. B
13. D
14. K

ANSWER KEY TO EXTRA GRAMMAR

EXTRA GRAMMAR-LESSON 1 — ACCENTS

1. Inglés
2. bibliografía
3. ficción
4. dólares
5. puerta
6. periódico

EXTRA GRAMMAR-LESSON 3 — GUSTAR

1. A ella le gusta nadar.
2. Le gusta el libro.-formal
   (Te gusta el libro- informal)
3. A María y Bernardo les gusta leer.
4. A él le gusta pescar.
5. A ellos les gusta la pizza.
6. A mí me gustan los libros.
7. A mí me gusta viajar.
8. A nosotros nos gusta leer español.

EXTRA GRAMMAR LESSON 7 — PRESENT TENSE LA PRÁCTICA = THE PRACTICE

1. acabo, acaba, acabamos, acaban
2. aprendo, aprende, aprendemos, aprenden
3. vivo, vive, vivimos, viven
4. trapeo, trapea
5. habla, hablan
6. cambia, cambias
7. leo, lee, lee
8. leen, leemos
9. lee, leer
10. asisto, asiste, asisten
11. asistimos, asistir

EXTRA GRAMMAR LESSON 8 — PRETERITE AND IMPERFECT
LA PRÁCTICA = THE PRACTICE

1. fue
2. aprendimos
3. estudié
4. usé
5. escuchó
6. practicaban
7. hicieron
8. arreglaba
9. grabaron
10. hablaba
11. estuvo

Numbers 6, 8, and 10 are imperfect because they happened with regularity in the past. #8 is imperfect because it happened cada semana = each week. Numbers 1–5, 7 and 9 are completed past actions, and therefore are conjugated in the preterite.

IGUAZU FALLS = CATARATAS DEL IGUAZÚ IS THE WIDEST IN THE WORLD WITH 270 DISTINCT WATERFALLS. IGUAZU IS LOCATED ON THE BORDER BETWEEN BRAZIL AND ARGENTINA, NEAR PARAGUAY.

GLOSSARY

Spanish = English *(Pronunciation)*

A

¿A qué hora entraste? = What time did you come in? *(Ah Keh Oh-rah Ehn-trahs-teh?)* (Ch. 5)

¡Adiós! = Goodbye! *(Ah-dee/ohs!)* (Ch. 1)

Allí te encargo mi área. = You're in charge of my area.
(Ah-YEE Teh Ehn-kahr-goh Mee AH-ree-ah.) (Ch. 3)

Ándale. = Get going. *(AHN-dah-leh.)* (Ch. 2)

Apaga el horno. = Turn off the oven. *(Ah-pah-gah Ehl Or-noh.)* (Ch. 7)

Apúrate. = Hurry. *(Ah-POOH-rah-teh.)* (Ch. 2)

Aquí está la cuenta. Yo seré su cajera cuando usted esté listo. =
Here is the bill. I will be the cashier whenever you're ready.
(Ah-kee Ehs-tah Lah Qwehn-tah. Yoh Seh-reh Soo Cah-heh-rah Qwahn-doh Oos-tehd Ehs-teh Lees-toh.) (Ch. 9)

Aspira el comedor. = Vacuum the dining room. *(Ahs-pee-rah Ehl Koh-meh-dohr.)* (Ch. 4)

Atrás.= Behind. *(Ah-trahs.)* (Ch. 2)

Ayúdame, por favor. = Help me, please. *(Ah-YOU-dah-meh, Pohr Fah-vor.)* (Ch. 1)

B

Barre afuera. = Sweep outside. *(Bah-rreh Ah-fweh-rah.)* (Ch. 4)

Bienvenidos a nuestro restaurante. = Welcome to our restaurant.
(Bee/ehn-veh-nee-dohs Ah Noo/ehs-troh Rehs-tah/oo-rahn-teh.) (Ch. 8)

Buen provecho. = Enjoy your meal. / Bon Appétit. *(Bwhen Proh-veh-cho.)* (Ch. 9)

Buen trabajo. = Good job. *(Bwhen Trah-bah-hoh.)* (Ch. 5)

Buenas noches. = Good night. *(Bweh-nahs Noh-chehs.)* (Ch. 1)

Buenas tardes. = Good afternoon. / Good evening. Used from noon until dark.
(Bweh-nahs Tahr-dehs.) (Ch. 1)

Buenos días. = Good morning. *(Bweh-nohs Dee-ahs.)* (Ch. 1)

C

Caminando el plato principal de la mesa 12. = Walking the entrée to table 12.
(Cah-mee-nahn-doh Ehl Plah-toh Preen-see-pahl Deh Lah Meh-sah Doh-seh.) (Ch. 3)

Cocina los vegetales al vapor. = Steam the vegetables.
(Koh-see-nah Lohs Veh-heh-tah-lehs Ahl Vah-pohr.) (Ch. 6)

¿Cómo estás? = How are you? *(Koh-moh Ehs-tahs?)* (Ch. 1)

¿Cómo te llamas? = What is your name? *(Koh-moh Teh Yah-mahs?)* (Ch. 1)

Con permiso. = Excuse me. *(Kohn Pehr-mee-soh.)* (Ch. 2)

Corta el postre en ocho porciones. = Cut the dessert in eight portions.
(Kohr-tah Ehl Pohs-treh Ehn Oh-cho Pohr-see/ohn-nehs.) (Ch. 7)

¿Cuál es tu dirección? = What is your address?
(Qwahl Ehs Too Dee-rehk-see/ohn?) (Ch. 5)

¿Cuál es tu número de teléfono? = What is your phone number?
(Qwahl Ehs Too NOO-meh-roh Deh Teh-LEH-foh-noh?) (Ch. 5)

¿Cuáles días puedes trabajar? = What days can you work?
(Qwahl-ehs Dee-ahs Pweh-dehs Trah-bah-hahr?) (Ch. 5)

¿Cuánto cuesta el plato del día? (Prix fixe) = How much does the plate of the day cost?
(Qwahn-toh Qwehs-tah Ehl Plah-toh Dehl Dee-ah?) (Ch. 9)

¿Cuánto tiempo más para el aperitivo? = How much longer for the appetizer?
(Qwahn-toh Tee/ehm-poh Mahs Pah-rah Ehl Ah-peh-ree-tee-voh?) (Ch. 2)

Cubre y guarda los camarones. = Cover and put away the shrimp.?
(Koo-breh Ee Gwahr-dah Lohs Cah-mah-roh-nehs.) (Ch. 7)

Cuesta 16 dólares. = It costs 16 dollars.
(Qwehs-tah Dee/eh-see-seh/ace DOH-lah-rehs.) (Ch. 9)

Cuidado. Piso mojado. = Caution. Wet floor.
(Qwee-dah-doh. Pee-soh Moh-hah-doh.) (Ch. 4)

D

Dame un cuchillo filoso.= Give me a sharp knife.
(Dah-meh Oon Koo-chee-yoh Fee-loh-so?) (Ch. 8)

De nada. = You're welcome. *(Deh Nah-dah.)* (Ch. 9)

Deja que el chef lo pruebe. = Have the chef taste it.
(Deh-hah Keh Ehl Chehf Loh Proo/eh-beh.) (Ch. 3)

Déjalo remojando. = Let it soak. *(Deh-hah-loh Reh-moh-hahn-doh.)* (Ch. 8)

Dobla las servilletas. = Fold the napkins. *(Doh-blah Lahs Sehr-vee-yeh-tahs.)* (Ch. 3)

¿Dónde está el baño? = Where is the bathroom? *(DohN-deh Ehs-tah Ehl Bah-ñyoh?* (Ch. 9)

¿Dónde están las bolsas de basura? = Where are the trash bags?
(DohN-deh Ehs-tahn Lahs Bohl-sahs Deh Bah-soo-rah?) (Ch. 4)

E

El baño está allá. = The bathroom is over there. *(Ehl Bah-ñyoh Ehs-tah Ah-YAH.)* (Ch. 9)

El baño necesita papel higiénico. = The bathroom needs toilet paper.
(Ehl Bah-ñyoh Neh-seh-see-tah Pah-pehl Ee-hee/eh-nee-koh.) (Ch. 4)

El ingreso anual = The Annual Income *(Ehl Een-greh-soh Ah-noo/ahl)*
(Income of Spanish-speaking countries Lessons 2-9)

El jefe quiere hablar contigo. = The boss wants to talk to you.
(Ehl Heh-feh Kee/eh-reh Ah-blahr Kohn-Tee-goh.) (Ch. 5)

El plato está caliente. = The plate is hot. *(Ehl Plah-toh Ehs-tah Kah-lee/ehn-teh.)* (Ch. 2)

En caso de emergencia, marca 911. = In case of emergency, call 911.
(Ehn Kah-soh Deh Eh-mehr-hen-see/ah, Mahr-kah Noo/eh-veh Oo-no Oo-no.) (Ch. 8)

Enciende la estufa. = Turn on the stove. *(Ehn-see/ehn-deh Lah Ehs-too-fah.)* (Ch. 7)

¿Entiendes? = Do you understand? *(Ehn-tee/ehn-dehs?)* (Ch. 1)

Entrena a la persona nueva. = Train the new person.
(Ehn-treh-nah Ah Lah Pehr-soh-nah Noo/eh-vah.) (Ch. 6)

Envuelve los cubiertos. = Roll the silverware.
(Ehn-vwehl-veh Lohs Koo-bee/ehr-tohs.)(Ch. 3)

Es importante llegar a tiempo. = It's important to arrive on time.
(Ehs Eem-pohr-tahn-teh Yeh-gahr Ah Tee/ehm-poh.) (Ch. 5)

Escurre las papas. = Drain the potatoes. *(Ehs-koo-rreh Lahs Pah-pahs.)* (Ch. 6)

¿Está todo bien? = Is everything O.K.? *(Ehs-tah Toh-doh Bee/ehn?)* (Ch. 5)

Estoy bien. = I am fine. *(Ehs-toy Bee/ehn.)* (Ch. 1)

F

Faltan dos sillas. = Two chairs are missing. *(Fahl-tahn Dohs See-yahs.)* (Ch. 3)

Faltan las papas fritas. = I'm missing the fries.
(Fahl-tahn Lahs Pah-pahs Free-tahs.) (Ch. 2)

Fríe el pescado en el sartén. = Pan-fry the fish.
(FREE-eh Ehl Pehs-kah-doh Ehn Ehl Sahr-ten.) (Ch. 6)

G

Gracias por venir. = Thank you for coming. *(Grah-see/ahs Pohr Veh-neer.)* (Ch. 9)

H, I, J, K

¿Has visto al gerente? = Have you seen the manager?
(Ahs Vees-toh Ahl Heh-rehn-teh?) (Ch. 3)

Hasta luego. = See you later. *(Ahs-tah Loo/eh-goh.)* (Ch. 1)

¿Hay algo que no está funcionando? = Is there something that is not working?
(Eye Ahl-goh Keh No Ehs-tah Foon-see/oh-nahn-doh?) (Ch. 8)

Haz más ensalada con lechuga, pepinos y tomates.
Make more salad with lettuce, cucumbers and tomatoes.
(Ahs Mahs Ehn-sah-lah-dah Kohn Leh-choo-gah, Peh-pee-nohs Ee Toh-mah-tehs.) (Ch. 7)

Hazlo de nuevo sin cebollas. =Remake it without onions.
(Ahs-loh Deh Noo/eh-voh Seen Seh-boh-yahs.) (Ch. 2)

Hierve el agua en la olla grande. = Boil the water in the big pot.
(Ee/ehr-veh Ehl Ah-gwah Ehn Lah Oh/ee-yah Grahn-deh.) (Ch. 7)

Hola. = Hello. *(Oh-lah.)* (Ch. 1)

Hornéalo por 45 minutos a 350 grados. = Bake it for 45 minutes at 350 degrees.
(Or-NEH-ah-loh Pohr Qwah-rent-tah Ee Seen-koh Mee-noo-tohs Ah Treh-see/ehn-tohs Seen-qwehn-tah Grah-dohs.) (Ch. 7)

L

La comida = The food *(Lah Koh-mee-dah)*
(Food in Spanish-speaking countries Lessons 2-9)

La cuenta, por favor. = The bill, please. *(Lah Qwehn-tah, Pohr Fah-vor.)* (Ch. 9)

La gente famosa = The famous people *(Lah Hen-teh Fah-moh-sah)*
(Famous people in Spanish-speaking countries Lessons 2-9)

La mesa 13 necesita servicio. = Table 13 needs service.
(Lah Meh-sah Treh-seh Neh-seh-see-tah Sehr-vee-see/oh.) (Ch. 3)

La mesa 26 necesita café descafeinado. = Table 26 needs decaffeinated coffee.
(Lah Meh-sah Veh/een-teh-ee-seh/ace Neh-seh-see-tah Cah-feh Dehs-cah-feh/ee-nah-doh.) (Ch. 3)

La moneda nacional = The National currency *(Lah Moh-neh-dah Nah-see/oh-nahl)*
(Currency of Spanish-speaking countries Lessons 2-9)

La población = The population *(Lah Poh-blah-see/ohn)*
(Population of Spanish-speaking countries lessons 2-9)

La sopa está fría, caliéntala.= The soup is cold, warm it up.
(Lah Soh-pah Ehs-tah FREE-ah, Kah-lee/EHN-tah-lah.) (Ch. 2)

Lava esto otra vez. Está sucio. = Wash this again. It's dirty.
(Lah-vah Ehs-toh Oh-trah Vehs. Ehs-tah Soo-see/oh.) (Ch. 8)

Lava y pela las zanahorias. = Wash and peel the carrots.
(Lah-vah Ee Peh-lah Lahs Zah-nah-oh-ree/ahs.) (Ch. 7)

Lávate las manos con jabón. = Wash your hands with soap.
(LAH-vah-teh Lahs Mah-nohs Kohn Hah-bohN.) (Ch. 8)

Le falta sal. = It's missing salt. *(Leh Fahl-tah Sahl.)* (Ch. 6)

Limpia el baño ahora mismo. = Clean the bathroom right away.
(Leem-pee/yah Ehl Bah-ñyoh Ah-oh-rah Mees-moh.) (Ch. 4)

Llena la jabonera. = Fill up the soap dispenser. *(Yeh-nah Lah Hah-boh-neh-rah.)* (Ch. 4)

Llena estos papeles. = Fill out these papers. *(Yeh-nah Ehs-tohs Pah-peh-lehs.)* (Ch. 5)

Llévales pan. = Take bread to them. *(Yeh-vah-lehs Pahn.)* (Ch. 3)

Los lugares para visitar = The places to visit *(Lohs Loo-gah-rehs Pah-rah Vee-see-tahr)*
(Places to visit in Spanish-speaking countries Lessons 2-9)

Los vidrios rotos van aquí. = The broken glass goes here.
(Lohs Vee-dree-ohs Roh-tohs Vahn Ah-kee.) (Ch. 8)

M

Márcalo con nombre y fecha. = Label it with the name and date.
(Mahr-kah-loh Kohn Nohm-breh Ee Feh-cha.) (Ch. 6)

Más despacio. = Slow down. *(Mahs Dehs-pah-see/oh.)* (Ch. 1)

Más rápido. = Faster. *(Mahs RAH-pee-doh.)* (Ch. 2)

Me llamo Julia. = My name is Julie. *(Meh Yah-moh Who-lee/ah.)* (Ch. 1)

Mezcla la masa. = Mix the dough. *(Mehs-klah Lah Mah-sah.)* (Ch. 7)

Mírame. Pon la mesa así. = Watch me. Set the table like this.
(MEE-rah-meh. Pohn Lah Meh-sah Ah-SEE.) (Ch. 3)

Mucho gusto. = Nice to meet you. *(Moo-cho Goose-toh.)* (Ch. 1)

N, O

¿Necesitas algo más? = Do you need anything else?
(Neh-seh-see-tahs Ahl-goh Mahs?) (Ch. 5)

¿Necesitas una curita o una aspirina? = Do you need a band-aid or an aspirin?
(Neh-seh-see-tahs Oo-nah Koo-ree-tah Oh Oo-nah Ahs-pee-ree-nah?) (Ch. 8)

Necesito la ensalada para la mesa quince. = I need the salad for table 15.
(Neh-seh-see-toh Lah Ehn-sah-lah-dah Pah-rah Lah Meh-sah Keen-seh.) (Ch. 2)

Necesito uno nuevo, al vuelo. = I need a new one, on the fly.
(Neh-seh-see-toh Oo-no Noo/eh-voh, Ahl Vweh-loh.) (Ch. 6)

No está correcto. = This is wrong. *(No Ehs-tah Koh-rrehk-toh.)* (Ch. 2)

No hay cangrejo. (ochenta y seis) =There is no crab. (86)
(No Eye Kahn-greh-hoh. (Oh-chen-tah Ee Seh/ace) (Ch. 2)

No vengas al trabajo si estás enfermo/a. = Don't come to work if you are sick.
(No Vehn-gahs Ahl Trah-bah-hoh See Ehs-tahs Ehn-fehr-moh.) (Ch. 8)

P

Pica seis manzanas rojas grandes. = Chop six big red apples.
(Pee-kah Seh/ace Mahn-zah-nahs Roh-hahs Grahn-dehs.) (Ch. 7)

Piso mojado. = Wet floor. *(Pee-soh Moh-hah-doh.)* (Ch. 4)

Pon la mayonesa aparte. = Put the mayonnaise on the side.
(PohN Lah Mah-yoh-neh-sah Ah-pahr-teh.) (Ch. 2)

Pon las tazas pequeñas en su lugar. = Restock the small cups.
(PohN Lahs Tah-sahs Peh-keh-nyahs Ehn Soo Loo-gahr.) (Ch. 8)

Ponlo en una caja para llevar. = Put this in a "to-go" box.
(PohN-loh Ehn Oon-nah Cah-hah Pah-rah Yeh-vahr.) (Ch. 3)

Ponte los guantes y el mandil. = Put on the gloves and the apron.
(PohN-teh Lohs Gwahn-tehs Ee Ehl Mahn-deel.) (Ch. 4)

Prepara el bistec medio cocido. = Temp the steak to medium.
(Preh-pah-rah Ehl Bees-tehk Meh-dee/oh Koh-see-doh.) (Ch. 6)

Primero en Entrar, Primero en Salir. PEPS = First In, First Out. FIFO
(Pree-meh-roh Ehn Ehn-trah, Pree-meh-roh Ehn Sah-leer.) (Ch. 6)

¿Puedes lavar más tenedores? = Will you wash more forks?
(Pweh-dehs Lah-vahr Mahs Teh-neh-doh-rehs?) (Ch. 8)

¿Puedes limpiarme la mesa siete? = Will you clean table seven for me?
(Pweh-dehs Leem-pee/ahr-meh Lah Meh-sah See/eh-teh?) (Ch. 3)

¿Puedes quedarte tarde? = Can you stay late?
(Pweh-dehs Keh-dahr-teh Tahr-deh?) (Ch. 5)

¿Puedes venir temprano? = Can you come in early?
(Pweh-dehs Veh-neer Tehm-prah-noh?) (Ch. 5)

Q

¿Qué desea para tomar y comer? = What would you like to drink and eat?
(Keh Deh-seh-ah Pah-rah Toh-mahr Ee Koh-mehr?) (Ch. 9)

¿Qué es esto? = What is this? *(Keh Ehs Ehs-toh?)* (Ch. 6)

Que le vaya bien. = Hope all goes well. *(Keh Leh Vah-yah Bee/ehn.)* (Ch. 9)

Quiero la pechuga de pollo lista a las 11:30. = I want the chicken breast ready by 11:30.
(Key/air-oh Lah Peh-choo-gah Deh Poh-yoh Lees-tah Ah Lahs Ohn-seh Ee Meh-dee-ah.) (Ch. 6)

Quiero pedir las tortillas de harina. = I would like to order the flour tortillas.
(Key/air-oh Peh-deer Lahs Tohr-tee-yahs Deh Ah-ree-nah.) (Ch. 9)

Quita los platos grandes. = Clear the big plates.
(Kee-tah Lohs Plah-tohs Grahn-dehs.) (Ch. 3)

R

Rebana la sandía y ponla en un recipiente. = Slice the watermelon and put it in a container.
(Reh-bah-nah Lah Sahn-dee-ah Ee PohN-lah Ehn Oon Reh-see/pee-ehn-teh.) (Ch. 7)

¿Recibiste la orden para la mesa diez y ocho? = Did you get the ticket for table 18?
(Reh-see-bees-teh Lah Ohr-dehn Pah-rah Lah Meh-sah Dee/eh-see/oh-cho?) (Ch. 2)

Repítelo, por favor. = Repeat that, please. *(Reh-PEE-teh-loh, Pohr Fah-vohr.)* (Ch. 1)

S

Saca la basura. = Take out (empty) the trash. *(Sah-cah Lah Bah-soo-rah.)* (Ch. 4)

Saca la carne del congelador. = Take the meat out of the freezer.
(Sah-kah Lah Kahr-neh Dehl Kohn-heh-lah-dohr.) (Ch. 7)

¡Salud! = Cheers! and/or Bless you! *(Sah-lood!)* (Ch. 9)

Se está quemando. = It's burning. *(Seh Ehs-tah Keh-mahn-doh.)* (Ch. 6)

Seca las copas de vino. = Dry the wine glasses. =
(Seh-kah Lahs Koh-pahs Deh Vee-noh.) (Ch. 8)

Sígueme con esta bandeja. = Follow me with this tray.
(See-geh-meh Kohn Ehs-tah Bahn-deh-hah.) (Ch. 3)

Sin nueces, hay una alergia. = Without nuts, there is an allergy.
(Seen Noo/eh-sehs, Eye Oo-nah Ah-lehr-hee/ah.) (Ch. 2)

T

También, llévales pan. = Also, take bread to them.
(Tahm-bee/ehn Yeh-vah-lehs Pahn.) (Ch. 3)

¿Terminaste de limpiar? = Did you finish cleaning?
(Tehr-mee-nahs-teh Deh Leem-pee-ahr?) (Ch. 4)

¿Tienes preguntas? = Do you have questions? *(Tee-ehn-ehs Preh-goon-tahs?)* (Ch. 5)

Traeme más hielo. = Bring me more ice. *(Trah/eh-meh Mahs Ee/eh-loh.)* (Ch. 3)

Trapea el piso de la cocina. = Mop the kitchen floor.
(Trah-peh-ah Ehl Pee-soh Deh Lah Koh-see-nah.) (Ch. 4)

Tu horario es de jueves a sábado de 3:00 a 10:00. =
Your schedule is Thursday through Saturday from 3:00 to 10:00.
(Too Oh-rah-ree/oh Ehs Deh Who/eh-vehs Ah SAH-bah-doh Deh Trehs Ah Dee/ehs.) (Ch. 5)

U

Usa el desinfectante. = Use the disinfectant. *(Oo-sah Ehl Dehs-een-fehk-tahn-teh.)* (Ch. 4)

Usa esta receta. = Use this recipe. *(Oo-sah Ehs-tah Reh-seh-tah.)* (Ch. 7)

V, W, X

Voy al baño. = I am going to the bathroom. *(Voy Ahl Bah-ñyoh.)* (Ch. 3)

Y, Z

¿Y tú? = And you? *(Ee Too?)* (Ch. 1)

¿Ya marcaste la entrada? = Did you already clock in?
(Yah Mahr-kahs-teh Lah Ehn-trah-dah?) (Ch. 5)

¿Ya marcaste la salida? = Did you already clock out?
(Yah Mahr-kahs-teh Lah Sal-lee-dah?) (Ch. 5)

Yo le recomiendo mi plato preferido, la carne asada. =
I recommend my favorite dish, the roast beef.
(Yoh Leh Reh-koh-mee/ehn-doh Mee Plah-toh Preh-feh-ree-doh, Lah Kahr-neh Ah-sah-dah.) (Ch. 9)

Yo seré su cajera cuando usted esté listo. = I will be the cashier whenever you're ready.
(Yoh Seh-reh Soo Cah-heh-rah Qwahn-doh Oos-tehd Ehs-teh Lees-toh.) (Ch. 9)

USE THIS PAGE TO WRITE EXTRA SPANISH PHRASES THAT YOU HEAR AT YOUR JOB.

GLOSSARY

English = Spanish *(Pronunciation)*

A

Also, take bread to them. = También, llévales pan.
 (Tahm-bee/ehn Yeh-vah-lehs Pahn.) (Ch. 3)

And you? = ¿Y tú? *(Ee Too?)* (Ch. 1)

B

Bake it for 45 minutes at 350 degrees. = Hornéalo por 45 minutos a 350 grados.
 (Or-NEH-ah-loh Pohr Qwah-rent-tah Ee Seen-koh Mee-noo-tohs Ah Treh-see/ehn-tohs Seen-qwehn-tah Grah-dohs.) (Ch. 7)

Behind. = Atrás. *(Ah-trahs.)* (Ch. 2)

Bless you! = ¡Salud! *(Sah-lood!)* (Ch. 9)

Boil the water in the big pot. = Hierve el agua en la olla grande.
 (Ee/ehr-veh Ehl Ah-gwah Ehn Lah Oh/ee-yah Grahn-deh.) (Ch. 7)

Bon Appétit. = Buen provecho. *(Bwhen Proh-veh-cho.)* (Ch. 9)

Bring me more ice. = Traeme más hielo. *(Trah/eh-meh Mahs Ee/eh-loh.)* (Ch. 3)

C

Can you come in early? = ¿Puedes venir temprano?
 (Pweh-dehs Veh-neer Tehm-prah-noh?) (Ch. 5)

Can you stay late? = ¿Puedes quedarte tarde?
 (Pweh-dehs Keh-dahr-teh Tahr-deh?) (Ch. 5)

Caution. Wet floor. = Cuidado. Piso mojado.
 (Qwee-dah-doh. Pee-soh Moh-hah-doh.) (Ch. 4)

Cheers! = ¡Salud! *(Sah-lood!)* (Ch. 9)

Chop six big red apples. = Pica seis manzanas rojas grandes.
 (Pee-kah Seh/ace Mahn-zah-nahs Roh-hahs Grahn-dehs.) (Ch. 7)

Clean the bathroom right away. = Limpia el baño ahora mismo.
 (Leem-pee/yah Ehl Bah-ñyoh Ah-oh-rah Mees-moh.) (Ch. 4)

Clear the big plates. = Quita los platos grandes.
 (Kee-tah Lohs Plah-tohs Grahn-dehs.) (Ch. 3)

Cover and put away the shrimp. = Cubre y guarda los camarones.
 (Koo-breh Ee Gwahr-dah Lohs Cah-mah-roh-nehs.) (Ch. 7)

Cut the dessert in eight portions. = Corta el postre en ocho porciones.
 (Kohr-tah Ehl Pohs-treh Ehn Oh-cho Pohr-see/ohn-nehs.) (Ch. 7)

D

Did you already clock in? = ¿Ya marcaste la entrada?
(Yah Mahr-kahs-teh Lah Ehn-trah-dah?) (Ch. 5)

Did you already clock out? = ¿Ya marcaste la salida?
(Yah Mahr-kahs-teh Lah Sal-lee-dah?) (Ch. 5)

Did you finish cleaning? = ¿Terminaste de limpiar?
(Tehr-mee-nahs-teh Deh Leem-pee-ahr?) (Ch. 4)

Did you get the ticket for table 18? = ¿Recibiste la orden para la mesa diez y ocho?
(Reh-see-bees-teh Lah Ohr-dehn Pah-rah Lah Meh-sah Dee/eh-see/oh-cho?) (Ch. 2)

Do you have questions? = ¿Tienes preguntas? *(Tee/eh-nehs Preh-goon-tahs?)* (Ch. 5)

Do you need a band-aid or an aspirin? = ¿Necesitas una curita o una aspirina?
(Neh-seh-see-tahs Oo-nah Koo-ree-tah Oh Oo-nah Ahs-pee-ree-nah?) (Ch. 8)

Do you need anything else? = ¿Necesitas algo más? *(Neh-seh-see-tahs Ahl-goh Mahs?)* (Ch. 5)

Do you understand? = ¿Entiendes? *(Ehn-tee/ehn-dehs?)* (Ch. 1)

Don't come to work if you are sick. = No vengas al trabajo si estás enfermo/a.
(No Vehn-gahs Ahl Trah-bah-hoh See Ehs-tahs Ehn-fehr-moh.) (Ch. 8)

Drain the potatoes. = Escurre las papas. *(Ehs-koo-rreh Lahs Pah-pahs.)* (Ch. 6)

Dry the wine glasses. = Seca las copas de vino. *(Seh-kah Lahs Koh-pahs Deh Vee-noh.)* (Ch. 8)

E

Empty (Take out) the trash. = Saca la basura. *(Sah-cah Lah Bah-soo-rah.)* (Ch. 4)

Enjoy your meal. /Bon Appétit. = Buen provecho. *(Bwhen Proh-veh-cho.)* (Ch. 9)

Excuse me. = Con permiso. *(Kohn Pehr-mee-soh.)* (Ch. 2)

F

Faster. = Más rápido. *(Mahs RAH-pee-doh.)* (Ch. 2)

Fill out these papers. = Llena estos papeles. *(Yeh-nah Ehs-tohs Pah-peh-lehs.)* (Ch. 5)

Fill up the soap dispenser. = Llena la jabonera. *(Yeh-nah Lah Hah-boh-neh-rah)* (Ch. 4)

First In, First Out. FIFO = Primero en Entrar, Primero en Salir. PEPS
(Pree-meh-roh Ehn Ehn-trah, Pree-meh-roh Ehn Sah-leer.) (Ch. 6)

Fold the napkins. = Dobla las servilletas. *(Doh-blah Lahs Sehr-vee-yeh-tahs.)* (Ch. 3)

Follow me with this tray. = Sígueme con esta bandeja.
(See-geh-meh Kohn Ehs-tah Bahn-deh-hah.) (Ch. 3)

G

Get going. = Ándale. *(AHN-dah-leh.)* (Ch. 2)

Give me a sharp knife. = Dame un cuchillo filoso.
  (Dah-meh Oon Koo-chee-yoh Fee-loh-so?) (Ch. 8)

Good afternoon. (evening) = Buenas tardes. *(Bweh-nahs Tahr-dehs.)* Use Noon-dark (Ch. 1)

Good job. = Buen trabajo. *(Bwhen Trah-bah-hoh.)* (Ch. 5)

Good morning. = Buenos días. *(Bweh-nohs Dee-ahs.)* (Ch. 1)

Good night. = Buenas noches. *(Bweh-nahs Noh-chehs.)* (Ch. 1)

Goodbye! = ¡Adiós! *(Ah-dee/ohs!)* (Ch. 1)

H

Have the chef taste it. = Deja que el chef lo pruebe.
  (Deh-hah Keh Ehl Chehf Loh Proo/eh-beh.) (Ch. 3)

Have you seen the manager? = ¿Has visto al gerente?
  (Ahs Vees-toh Ahl Heh-rehn-teh?) (Ch. 3)

Hello. = Hola. *(Oh-lah.)* (Ch. 1)

Help me, please. = Ayúdame, por favor. *(Ah-YOU-dah-meh, Pohr Fah-vohr?)* (Ch. 1)

Here is the bill. I will be the cashier whenever you're ready. =
  Aquí está la cuenta. Yo seré su cajera cuando usted esté listo.
  (Ah-kee Ehs-tah Lah Qwehn-tah. Yoh Seh-reh Soo Cah-heh-rah Qwahn-doh Oos-tehd Ehs-teh Lees-toh.) (Ch. 9)

Hope all goes well. = Que le vaya bien. *(Keh Leh Vah-yah Bee/ehn.)* (Ch. 9)

How are you? = ¿Cómo estás? *(Koh-moh Ehs-tahs?)* (Ch. 1)

How much does the plate of the day cost? = ¿Cuánto cuesta el plato del día? (prix fixe)
  (Qwahn-toh Qwehs-tah Ehl Plah-toh Dehl Dee-ah?) (Ch. 9)

How much longer for the appetizer? = ¿Cuánto tiempo más para el aperitivo?
  (Qwahn-toh Tee/ehm-poh Mahs Pah-rah Ehl Ah-peh-ree-tee-voh?) (Ch. 2)

Hurry. = Apúrate. *(Ah-POOH-rah-teh.)* (Ch. 2)

I, J

I am fine. = Estoy bien. *(Ehs-toy Bee/ehn.)* (Ch. 1)

I am going to the bathroom. = Voy al baño. *(Voy Ahl Bah-ñyoh.)* (Ch. 3)

I need a new one, on the fly. = Necesito uno nuevo, al vuelo.
(Neh-seh-see-toh Oo-no Noo/eh-voh, Ahl Vweh-loh.) (Ch. 6)

I need the salad for table 15. = Necesito la ensalada para la mesa quince.
(Neh-seh-see-toh Lah Ehn-sah-lah-dah Pah-rah Lah Meh-sah Keen-seh.) (Ch. 2)

I recommend my favorite dish, the roast beef. =
Yo le recomiendo mi plato preferido, la carne asada.
(Yoh Leh Reh-koh-mee/ehn-doh Mee Plah-toh Preh-feh-ree-doh, Lah Kahr-neh Ah-sah-dah.) (Ch. 9)

I want the chicken breast ready by 11:30. =
Quiero la pechuga de pollo lista a las 11:30.
(Key/air-oh Lah Peh-choo-gah Deh Poh-yoh Lees-tah Ah Lahs Ohn-seh Ee Meh-dee-ah.) (Ch. 6)

I will be the cashier whenever you're ready. = Yo seré su cajera cuando usted esté listo.
(Yoh Seh-reh Soo Cah-heh-rah Qwahn-doh Oos-tehd Ehs-teh Lees-toh.) (Ch. 9)

I would like to order the flour tortillas. = Quiero pedir las tortillas de harina.
(Key/air-oh Peh-deer Lahs Tohr-tee-yahs Deh Ah-ree-nah.) (Ch. 9)

I'm missing the fries. = Faltan las papas fritas.
(Fahl-tahn Lahs Pah-pahs FREE-tahs.) (Ch. 2)

In case of emergency, call 911. = En caso de emergencia, marca 911.
(Ehn Kah-soh Deh ehm-mehr-hen-see/ah, Mahr-kah Noo/eh-veh Oo-no Oo-no.) (Ch. 8)

Is everything O.K.? = ¿Está todo bien? *(Ehs-tah Toh-doh Bee/ehn?)* (Ch. 5)

Is there something that is not working? = ¿Hay algo que no está funcionando?
(Eye Ahl-goh Keh No Ehs-tah Foon-see/oh-nahn-doh?) (Ch. 8)

It costs 16 dollars. = Cuesta 16 dólares.
(Qwehs-tah Dee/eh-see-seh/ace DOH-lah-rehs.) (Ch. 9)

It's burning. = Se está quemando. *(Seh Ehs-tah Keh-mahn-doh.)* (Ch. 6)

It's important to arrive on time. = Es importante llegar a tiempo.
(Ehs Eem-pohr-tahn-teh Yeh-gahr Ah Tee/ehm-poh.) (Ch. 5)

It's missing salt. = Le falta sal. *(Leh Fahl-tah Sahl.)* (Ch. 6)

K, L

Label it with the name and date. = Márcalo con nombre y fecha.
(Mahr-kah-loh Kohn Nohm-breh Ee Feh-cha.) (Ch. 6)

Let it soak. = Déjalo remojando. *(Deh-hah-loh Reh-moh-hahn-doh.)* (Ch. 8)

M

Make more salad with lettuce, cucumbers and tomatoes. = Haz más ensalada con lechuga, pepinos y tomates. *(AhsMahs Ehn-sah-lah-dah Kohn Leh-choo-gah, Peh-pee-nohs Ee Toh-mah-tehs.* (Ch. 7)

Mix the dough. = Mezcla la masa. *(Mehs-klah Lah Mah-sah.)* (Ch. 7)

Mop the kitchen floor. = Trapea el piso de la cocina. *(Trah-peh-ah Ehl Pee-soh Deh Lah Koh-see-nah.)* (Ch. 4)

My name is Julie. = Me llamo Julia. *(Meh Yah-moh Who-lee/ah.)* (Ch. 1)

N, O

Nice to meet you. = Mucho gusto. *(Moo-cho Goose-toh.)* (Ch. 1)

P, Q

Pan-fry the fish. = Fríe el pescado en el sartén. *(FREE-eh Ehl Pehs-kah-doh Ehn Ehl Sahr-ten.)* (Ch. 6)

Put on the gloves and the apron. = Ponte los guantes y el mandil. *(PohN-teh Lohs Gwahn-tehs Ee Ehl Mahn-deel.)* (Ch. 4)

Put the mayonnaise on the side. = Pon la mayonesa aparte. *(PohN Lah Mah-yoh-neh-sah Ah-pahr-teh.)* (Ch. 2)

Put this in a "to-go" box. = Ponlo en una caja para llevar. *(PohN-loh Ehn Oon-nah Cah-hah Pah-rah Yeh-vahr.)* (Ch. 3)

R

Remake it without onions. = Hazlo de nuevo sin cebollas. *(Ahs-loh Deh Noo/eh-voh Seen Seh-boh-yahs.)* (Ch. 2)

Repeat that, please. = Repítalo, por favor. *(Reh-PEE-tah-loh, Pohr Fah-vohr.)* (Ch. 1)

Restock the small cups. = Pon las tazas pequeñas en su lugar. *(PohN Lahs Tah-sahs Peh-keh-nyahs Ehn Soo Loo-gahr.)* (Ch. 8)

Roll the silverware. = Envuelve los cubiertos. *(Ehn-vwehl-veh Lohs Koo-bee/ehr-tohs.)* (Ch. 3)

S

See you later. = Hasta luego. *(Ahs-tah Loo/eh-goh.)* (Ch. 1)

Slice the watermelon and put it in a container. =
Rebana la sandía y ponla en un recipiente.
(Reh-bah-nah Lah Sahn-dee-ah Ee PohN-lah Ehn Oon Reh-see/pee-ehn-teh.) (Ch. 7)

Slow down. = Más despacio. *(Mahs Dehs-pah-see/oh.)* (Ch. 1)

Steam the vegetables. = Cocina los vegetales al vapor.
(Koh-see-nah Lohs Veh-heh-tah-lehs Ahl Vah-pohr.) (Ch. 6)

Sweep outside. = Barre afuera. *(Bah-rreh Ah-fweh-rah.)* (Ch. 4)

T

Table 13 needs service. = La mesa 13 necesita servicio.
(Lah Meh-sah Treh-seh Neh-seh-see-tah Sehr-vee-see/oh.) (Ch. 3)

Table 26 needs decaffeinated coffee. = La mesa 26 necesita café descafeinado.
(Lah Meh-sah Veh/een-teh-ee-seh/ace Neh-seh-see-tah Cah-feh Dehs-cah-feh/ee-nah-doh.) (Ch. 3)

Take out the trash. = Saca la basura. *(Sah-cah Lah Bah-soo-rah.)* (Ch. 4)

Take bread to them. = Llévales pan. *(Yeh-vah-lehs Pahn.)* (Ch. 3)

Take the meat out of the freezer. = Saca la carne del congelador.
(Sah-kah Lah Kahr-neh Dehl Kohn-heh-lah-dohr.) (Ch. 7)

Temp the steak to medium. = Prepara el bistec medio cocido.
(Preh-pah-rah Ehl Bees-tehk Meh-dee/oh Koh-see-doh.) (Ch. 6)

Thank you for coming. = Gracias por venir. *(Grah-see/ahs Pohr Veh-neer.)* (Ch. 9)

The Annual Income = El ingreso anual *(Ehl Een-greh-soh Ah-noo/ahl)*
(Income of Spanish-speaking countries Lessons 2-9)

The bathroom needs toilet paper. = El baño necesita papel higiénico.
(Ehl Bah-ñyoh Neh-seh-see-tah Pah-pehl Ee-hee/eh-nee-koh.) (Ch. 4)

The bathroom is over there. = El baño está allá. *(Ehl Bah-ñyoh Ehs-tah Ah-YAH.)* (Ch. 9)

The bill, please. = La cuenta, por favor. *(Lah Qwehn-tah, Pohr Fah-vohr.)* (Ch. 9)

The boss wants to talk to you. = El jefe quiere hablar contigo.
(Ehl Heh-feh Kee/eh-reh Ah-blahr Kohn-Tee-goh.) (Ch. 5)

The broken glass goes here. = Los vidrios rotos van aquí.
(Lohs Vee-dree-ohs Roh-tohs Vahn Ah-kee.) (Ch. 8)

The famous people = La gente famosa *(Lah Hen-teh Fah-moh-sah)*
(Famous people in Spanish-speaking countries Lessons 2-9)

The food = La comida *(Lah Koh-mee-dah)* (In Spanish-speaking countries Lessons 2-9)

The National currency = La moneda nacional *(Lah Moh-neh-dah Nah-see/oh-nahl)* (The currency of Spanish-speaking countries Lessons 2-9)

The places to visit = Los lugares para visitar *(Lohs Loo-gah-rehs Pah-rah Vee-see-tahr)* (The places to visit in Spanish-speaking countries Lessons 2-9)

The plate is hot. = El plato está caliente. *(Ehl Plah-toh Ehs-tah Kah-lee/ehn-teh.)* (Ch. 2)

The population = La población *(Lah Poh-blah-see/ohn)* (The population of Spanish-speaking countries Lessons 2-9)

The soup is cold, warm it up. = La sopa está fría, caliéntala. *(Lah Soh-pah Ehs-tah FREE-ah, Kah-lee/EHN-tah-lah.)* (Ch. 2)

There is no crab. (86) = No hay cangrejo. (ochenta y seis) *(No Eye Kahn-greh-hoh. (Oh-chen-tah Ee Seh/ace)* (Ch. 2)

This is wrong. = No está correcto. *(No Ehs-tah Koh-rrehk-toh.)* (Ch. 2)

Train the new person. = Entrena a la persona nueva. *(Ehn-treh-nah Ah Lah Pehr-soh-nah Noo/eh-vah.)* (Ch. 6)

Two chairs are missing. = Faltan dos sillas. *(Fahl-tahn Dohs See-yahs.)* (Ch. 3)

Turn off the oven. = Apaga el horno. *(Ah-pah-gah Ehl Or-noh.)* (Ch. 7)

Turn on the stove. = Enciende la estufa. *(Ehn-see/ehn-deh Lah Ehs-too-fah.)* (Ch. 7)

U

Use the disinfectant. = Usa el desinfectante. *(Oo-sah Ehl Dehs-een-fehk-tahn-teh.)* (Ch. 4)

Use this recipe. = Usa esta receta. *(Oo-sah Ehs-tah Reh-seh-tah.)* (Ch. 7)

V

Vacuum the dining room. = Aspira el comedor. *(Ahs-pee-rah Ehl Koh-meh-dohr.)* (Ch. 4)

W, X

Walking the entrée to table 12. = Caminando el plato principal de la mesa 12. *(Cah-mee-nahn-doh Ehl Plah-toh Preen-see-pahl Deh Lah Meh-sah Doh-seh.)* (Ch. 3)

Wash and peel the carrots. = Lava y pela las zanahorias. *(Lah-vah Ee Peh-lah Lahs Zah-nah-ohr-ree/ahs.)* (Ch. 7)

Wash this again. It's dirty. = Lava esto otra vez. Está sucio. *(Lah-vah Ehs-toh Oh-trah Vehs. Ehs-tah Soo-see/oh.)* (Ch. 8)

Wash your hands with soap. = Lávate las manos con jabón.
(LAH-vah-teh Lahs Mah-nohs Kohn Hah-bohN.) (Ch. 8)

Watch me. Set the table like this. = Mírame. Pon la mesa así.
(MEE-rah-meh. PohN Lah Meh-sah Ah-SEE) (Ch. 3)

Watch out! = ¡Cuidado! (Qwee-dah-doh!) (Ch. 4)

Welcome to our restaurant. = Bienvenidos a nuestro restaurante.
(Bee/ehn-veh-nee-dohs Ah Noo/ehs-troh Rehs-tah/oo-rahn-teh.) (Ch. 9)

Wet floor. = Piso mojado. (Pee-soh Moh-hah-doh.) (Ch. 4)

What days can you work? = ¿Cuáles días puedes trabajar?
(Qwahl-ehs Dee-ahs Pweh-dehs Trah-bah-hahr?) (Ch. 5)

What is this? = ¿Qué es esto? (Keh Ehs Ehs-toh?) (Ch. 6)

What is your address? = ¿Cuál es tu dirección?
(Qwahl Ehs Too Dee-rehk-see/ohn?) (Ch. 5)

What is your name? = ¿Cómo te llamas? (Koh-moh Teh Yah-mahs?) (Ch. 1)

What is your phone number? = ¿Cuál es tu número de teléfono?
(Qwahl Ehs Too NOO-meh-roh Deh Teh-LEH-foh-noh?) (Ch. 5)

What time did you come in? = ¿A qué hora entraste? (Ah Keh Oh-rah Ehn-trahs-teh?) (Ch. 5)

What would you like to drink and eat? = ¿Qué desea para tomar y comer?
(Keh Deh-seh-ah Pah-rah Toh-mahr Ee Koh-mehr?) (Ch. 9)

Where are the trash bags? = ¿Dónde están las bolsas de basura?
(DohN-deh Ehs-tahn Lahs Bohl-sahs Deh Bah-soo-rah?) (Ch. 4)

Where is the bathroom? = ¿Dónde está el baño? (DohN-deh Ehs-tah Ehl Bah-ñyoh?) (Ch. 9)

Will you clean table seven for me? = ¿Puedes limpiarme la mesa siete?
(Pweh-dehs Leem-pee/ahr-meh Lah Meh-sah See/eh-teh?) (Ch. 3)

Will you wash more forks? = ¿Puedes lavar más tenedores?
(Pweh-dehs Lah-vahr Mahs Teh-neh-doh-rehs?) (Ch. 8)

Without nuts, there is an allergy. = Sin nueces, hay una alergia.
(Seen Noo/eh-sehs, Eye Oo-nah Ah-lehr-hee/ah.) (Ch. 2)

Y, Z

Your schedule is Thursday through Saturday from 3:00 to 10:00. =
Tu horario es de jueves a sábado de 3:00 a 10:00.
(Too Oh-rah-ree/oh Ehs Deh Who/eh-vehs Ah SAH-bah-doh Deh Trehs Ah Dee/ehs.) (Ch. 5)

You're in charge of my area. = Allí te encargo mi área.
(Ah-YEE Teh Ehn-kahr-goh Mee AH-ree-ah.) (Ch. 3)

Need a native speaker to pronounce the phrases?
Wish you could practice in the car or while exercising?
Would you like to reinforce what you've learned?
Want to hear these Spanish words pronounced correctly?

Our *Culinary Spanish Chatbook* CD/Audio guide is now available. Enjoy listening to over 100 useful restaurant phrases and conversational role plays designed specifically for culinary professionals. To improve your pronunciation, purchase the *Culinary Spanish Chatbook* Audio tracks or CD. Each time you see the Audio symbol in the book, you will be able to follow along to improve your Spanish skills. Native speakers pronounce the Spanish phrases, allow time for you to repeat them, and act out each of the conversational role plays. Listen to these 125+ phrases and typical culinary conversations while driving, working, or exercising. Pair the book and audio together to maximize your learning experience! Order the CD/Audio from our website, www.SpanishChatCompany.com.

CULINARY SPANISH CHATBOOK AUDIO TRACKS

1. **Introduction to *Culinary Spanish Chatbook* CD/Audio**
2. Lesson 1 *p. 8* **Common greetings and goodbye phrases**
3. Lesson 1 *p. 13* **Helpful introductory phrases**
4. Lesson 1 *p. 16* **A conversational role play**
5. Lesson 2 *p. 26* **Useful restaurant lingo**
6. Lesson 2 *p. 27* **Phrases for connecting the front and the back of the house**
7. Lesson 2 *p. 31* **Servers talking with expo in the back**
8. Lesson 2 *p. 32* **A conversational role play**
9. Lesson 3 *p. 47* **A conversational role play**
10. Lesson 3 *p. 48* **Server communicates with buser**
11. Lesson 3 *p. 57* **Reset the dining room area**
12. Lesson 3 *p. 60* **Server requests a buser's help**
13. Lesson 4 *p. 69* **Communicating with the cleaning crew**
14. Lesson 4 *p. 72* **Cleaning the bathroom and/or kitchen areas**
15. Lesson 4 *p. 78* **Cleaning the floors**
16. Lesson 4 *p. 80* **A conversational role play**
17. Lesson 5 *p. 95* **Time for scheduling phrases**
18. Lesson 5 *p. 97* **Manager phrases to communicate with employees**
19. Lesson 5 *p. 103* **A conversational role play**
20. Lesson 6 *p. 114* **Kitchen/ Back of the house phrases**
21. Lesson 6 *p. 119* **Phrases for cooking on the line**
22. Lesson 6 *p. 120* **A conversational role play**
23. Lesson 7 *p. 131* **Back of the House- cooking on the line**
24. Lesson 7 *p. 136* **Baking phrases**
25. Lesson 7 *p. 138* **A conversational role play**
26. Lesson 8 *p. 152* **First Aid, safety and personal hygiene phrases**
27. Lesson 8 *p. 155* **Back of the house- Dishwasher**
28. Lesson 8 *p. 159* **A conversational role play**
29. Lesson 9 *p. 174* **Front of the House- Phrases for serving Hispanic customers**
30. Lesson 9 *p. 176* **Finishing restaurant service, Travel phrases to connect in Latin America,**
31. Lesson 9 *p. 178* **A conversational role play**
32. Lesson 10 *p. 194* **Tongue twisters – Pepe**
33. Lesson 10 *p. 194* **Tongue twisters – Guitarra**
34. Lesson 10 *p. 194* **Tongue twisters – Compadre**
35. Lesson 10 *p. 194* **Tongue twisters – Tristes tigres**
36. **Thank you and Final credits**

SUBJECT INDEX

A

Accent marks,
    Introduction to, 12
    Practice with, 224-225
Acquisition language, 160
Adjectives,
    Introduction to, 133-134
    List of, 216
AEIOU/vowels, 6
Age, 51-53, 75
Aid, First, Health, list of vocabulary, 219
Alphabet, 58-59
Answer key, 245-270
America,
    Central, 80, 101-102, 132, 173, 182, 196
    North, 17-18, 29.35, 47. 49. 59, 80, 91,
        100, 105, 112, 116, 156, 173, 175, 181
    South, 112, 117-118, 132-133, 135, 141-142,
        163-164
    Speaking Spanish throughout, 112
-ar verb conjugation,
    Imperfect past tense, 241-243
    Present tense, 122, 228-229, 232-234
    Preterite past tense, 160-162, 235, 243
Appetizers, list of, 209
Appliances, list of, 215
Argentina, 112, 118, 133, 163-164
Around the town, 221
Around the world game, 108
Audio/ CD track listing, 290
Aztec calendar, 54, 100

B

Back of house,
    Baking, 136
    Cooking on the line, 114, 119
    Connects with front of the house, 27, 31
    Dishwasher phrases, 155
    First Aid, 152
    Management, 95, 97
    Personal hygiene, 152
    Prep area phrases, 131, 136
    Safety, 152
Baking ingredients, list of 218
Baking phrases, 136
Bathroom cleaning, 69, 72
Beverages, list of, 210
Bilingual employees, 156
Bingo, game directions, 63-64, 126, 188, 260
Body parts, 221
Bolivia, 118, 141
Breads, list of, 216
Buser communicating with Server, 48, 57, 60
Business,
    Bilingual employees, 156
    Customers,
        Greeting, 8
        Introductions, 8
    Directions, giving and receiving, 154-156
    Direct deposit form, 96

Employees,
    Bilingual, 156
    Latino, supervision, 49, 156
    Personal descriptions, 51
    Tardiness, 91
Greetings, 8
Introductions, 8
Latin American schedules, 173
Personal descriptions, 51

C

Calendar,
    Aztec, 54, 100
    Days of the week, 93, 100
    Weather, 94
Categorizing, Hispanics and Latinos, 17-18
CD/Audio track list, 290
Central American countries,
    Costa Rica, 80, 101-102, 132, 173, 182, 196
    El Salvador, 80-82
    Guatemala, 17, 80-82
    Honduras, 80-82, 182
    Nicaragua, 80-82, 182
    Panamá, 80, 101-102
Chicanos, 17, 160
Chile, 118, 141-142
Choosing, Spanish name, 9, 206
Cleaning,
    Bathroom, 69, 72, 78
    Communicating with staff, 69, 72, 78
    Kitchen, 69, 72, 78
    Floors, 78
    Supplies, list of, 213
    Vocabulary, 213
Colombia, 117-118, 132
Colors,
    Introduction to, 133-134
    List of, 216
Communication,
    Buser and Server, 48
    Styles, 116
Condiments, list of, 209
Connecting, front and back of house, 27
Conquistadors, 112
Containers, list of 214
Contents of drawers, list of, 214
Continue learning in the future, 10 ideas, 195-196
Conversation starters, 188

Conversations, role plays, 16, 32-33, 47, 80, 103, 120, 138, 159, 178
Cooking on the line phrases, 114, 119
Costa Rica, 80, 101-102, 132, 173, 182, 196
Countries,
    Central America,
        Costa Rica, 80, 101-102, 132, 173, 182, 196
        El Salvador, 80-82
        Guatemala, 17, 80-82
        Honduras, 80-82, 182
        Nicaragua, 80-82, 182
        Panamá, 80, 101-102
    Equatorial Guinea, 179-180
    Island nations,
        Cuba, 179-180, 183, 185
        Dominican Republic, 179-180
        Puerto Rico, 91, 172, 179-180, 185, 267
    México, 17-18, 29, 38, 54-55, 80, 91, 100, 132, 183-186
    South America,
        Argentina, 112, 118, 133, 163-164
        Bolivia, 118, 141-142
        Chile, 118, 141-142
        Colombia, 117-118, 132
        Ecuador, 117-118
        Paraguay, 118, 163-164
        Perú, 118, 135, 141-142, 183
        Uruguay, 118, 163-164
        Venezuela, 117-118, 132
    Spain, 12, 17-18, 36-38, 47, 91, 112, 132, 173, 182, 184-186, 229
Crossword puzzle, 28, 99, 157
Cuba, 179-180, 183, 185
Customers,
    Greetings and introductions, 8
    Phrases for server, 174, 176

D

Daily routine, 90
Days of the week, 93, 96, 100
Deposits, Direct and paychecks, 96
Descriptions,
    Age, 51-53, 75
    Body parts, 221
    Colors,
        Introduction of, 133-134
        List of, 216
    Days of the week, 93, 96, 100
    Dislikes, 50-53, 213, 226

Family,
    Descriptions, 51
    Extended, 208
    Hispanic, 49
    Members, 46
    Presentation, 67
    Project, 51-53
    Tree, 10
    Job, 51-53, 212
    Likes, 49-53, 213, 226
Desktop phrase guide, 23
Desserts, list of, 219
Differences, gender, 47
Dining room,
    Phrases, 57
    Reset, 57
    Vocabulary, list of, 210, 211
Direct deposit form, 96
Directions, giving and receiving, 69, 154-156
Dishes,
    Sides and Appetizers, list of, 209
Dishwasher phrases, 155
Dislikes, likes,
    Extra practice, 218
    Introduction to, 49-53
    List of, 213
Diversity in the Spanish language, 38
Dominican Republic, 179-180
Drawers, list of contents, 214

E

Eating times, 173
Ecuador, 117-118
El Salvador, 80-82
Employees,
    Bilingual, 156
    Direct deposit form, 96
    Latino, supervision, 49
    Manager phrases, 95, 97
English vs. Spanish,
    Acquisition of language, 160
    Glossary of phrases, 271-290
Equatorial Guinea, 179-180
Equipment, kitchen, list of, 215
-er verb conjugation,
    Imperfect past tense, 241-243
    Present tense 143-144, 228, 230-234
    Preterite past tense, 162, 235

Estar vs. Ser, the verb to be,
    Present tense 104-106
    Preterite past tense, 160-162, 237, 239
Etiquette,
    Greetings, 8
    Helpful introductory phrases 13
    Restaurant, 175
    Table settings, 181
    Tardiness, 91
    Tú vs. Usted, 12
    Travel, 173-175
Exam, translation exercise, 19, 41, 62, 83, 107, 124-125, 146, 167, 187
Exclamations, 132
Expo connect with servers, 31
Expressing likes and dislikes,
    Extra practice, 213, 226
    Introduction to, 50
    List of, 213
Extra grammar, 224-243
Extra vocabulary, 206-222

F

Facts,
    Spanish-Speaking countries, 36, 54, 81, 101, 117, 141, 163, 179
    Historical, 112, 135
    Interesting 37, 55, 82, 102, 118, 142, 164, 180
Family,
    Descriptions, 51
    Extended, 211
    Hispanic, 49
    List of, 211
    Members, 46
    Presentation, 68
    Project, 51-53
    Tree, 10
Famous people, 36, 54, 81, 101, 117, 141, 163, 179
Feedback form, 201
Female, name list 206
Field trip, 197-200
Fiesta,
    For the class, 181, 192, 195
    In Latin America, 91
Final project,
    Ideas, 165-166
    Presentation, 192

First Aid,
    Phrases, 152
    List of, 219, 220
First person irregular verbs, present tense, 234
Flashcards, 21-22, 43-44, 65-66, 85-86,
    109-110, 127-128, 149-150, 169-170, 189-190
Floors, cleaning 78
Food,
    Grocery store scavenger hunt, 197-200
    Information, Countries 36, 54, 81, 101,
        117, 141, 163, 179
    Introduction to, 173
    List of, 208-219
    Menu, 173
    Phrases, 173
    Recipes, 182-186
    Trivia about countries, 37, 55, 82, 102, 118,
        142, 164, 180
Front of house
    Cleaning, 69, 72, 78
    Connects with back, 27, 31
    First Aid, 152
    List of vocabulary, 210
    Management, 95, 97
    Personal hygiene, 152
    Restaurant tour, list of, 210
    Safety, 152
    Server to Buser, 48, 57, 60
Fruit, list of, 217
Future ideas- to continue learning, 195-196

G

Games,
    Bingo, 63-64, 126, 188, 260
    Tic-Tac-Toe, 20, 108, 147
    Toma Todo, 42, 84, 168
Gender differences, 47
Giving and receiving directions, 154-156
Glossary of phrases, 271-290
Goals, survey needs, 3-4
Goodbye phrases, 8
Guatemala, 17, 80-82
Grains, list of, 216
Grammar,
    Adjectives, 133-134, 216
    English vs. Spanish, 38
    Extra activities, 223-244

Pronouns,
    Direct object, 227
    Indirect object, 227
    This/That/Those/These, 159, 235
    Tú vs. Usted, 12
    Usted vs. Tú, 12
    Verbs, *see also*
Greetings, introduction to, 8
Gringos, 17
Grocery store scavenger hunt, 197-200
Gustar, likes, dislikes,
    Extra practice, 226
    Introduction to, 49-53
    List of, 213

H

Health words,
    Extra medical phrases, 219-221
    List of, 219 - 221
    Hygiene,
        List of, 219
        Phrases, 152
Help, Server requests buser's, 48, 57, 60
Helpful introductory phrases, 13
Hispanic,
    Americans, 18
    Families, 49, 91
    Latino, categorizing, 17-18
    Restaurant customer service, 174, 176
Historical
    Perspectives, 100, 112, 135
    Figures, 36, 54, 81, 101, 117, 141, 163, 179
History of Spanish-speaking countries, 35, 100,
    112, 135
Holidays, 91, 165
Honduras, 80-82, 182
Hotel vocabulary, 222
Human resources,
    List of vocabulary, 212
    Phrases, 95, 97
House, (see Front of house / Back of house)
How to learn to read Spanish in five minutes,
    6-7
Hygiene, personal, 152

I

Ideas to continue learning in the future, 195-196
Imperfect past tense, 241-242
Important phrases, 8, 13, 26, 27, 31, 48, 57, 60, 69, 72, 78, 95, 97, 114, 119, 131, 136, 152, 155, 174, 176
Inca Empire, 54, 112, 135, 141-142, 182
Indirect object pronouns, 227
Information, personal, 56
Introductions, 1-2, 8
Introductory phrases, helpful, 13
Ir, 77, 161, 239
-ir verb conjugation,
    Imperfect past tense, 241-243
    Present tense, 145, 228, 230-234
    Preterite past tense, 162, 236, 240-241
Irregular verbs
    Imperfect tense, 242
    Present tense, 232-234
    Preterite tense, 236-241
Islands, 101, 117-118, 141-142, 179-181

J

Job,
    Application, 88
    Descriptions, 51-53
    List of, 212

K

Kitchen
    Baking phrases, 136
    Cleaning, 69, 72, 78
    Dishwasher phrases, 155
    Equipment, list of, 215
    First Aid, 152, 219, 220
    Line cook phrases, 114, 119
    Personal hygiene, 152
    Prep cook phrases, 131, 136
    Safety, 152

L

La Llorona, 68
Language acquisition, English vs. Spanish, 160
Latin American schedules, 173
Latino and Hispanic categorizing, 17-18
Latino employees' supervision, 49, 156
Legends and myths, 68, 100
Lesson plans,
    Continuing education ideas, 195-196
    Family project, 51-53
    Field trip, 197-200
    Fiesta,
        For the class, 181-186
        In Latin America, 91
    Final project,
        Ideas, 165-166
        Presentation, 192
    Grocery store scavenger hunt, 197-200
    Presentations,
        Family, 67
        Final presentation guidelines, 165-166
        Final presentation performance, 192
Likes/dislikes,
    Extra practice, 226
    Introduction to, 49-53
    List of, 213
Line cook phrases, 114, 119
Lingo, useful restaurant 26
Locating Central American countries, 80

M

Machismo, 49
Maintenance, list of supplies, 213
Manager phrases, 95, 97
Mañana, 91, 96
Matching activities, 15, 39, 61, 73, 98, 115, 132, 158, 177, 193
Mayan number system, 71
Medical phrases, 152, 219-221
Measurements, 125, 222
Meat, list of, 208
Menu, 173
Metric system conversion, 222
Mexican, 17, 54-55, 91, 184, 186, 197-200
Mexican-Americans, 17
México, 17-18, 29, 38, 54-55, 80, 91, 100, 132, 183-186
Months of the year, 92, 96
Multiple choice exercises, 9, 29, 57, 70, 93, 121, 137, 153, 175
Myths and Legends, 68, 100

N

Names,
- Choosing, Spanish name, 9
- Introductions, 9-11
- Famous people, 36, 54, 81, 101, 117, 141, 163, 179
- Last names, 10-11,
- List in Spanish, 206

Nicaragua, 80-82, 182
North America, 17-18, 29.35, 47. 49. 59, 80, 91, 100, 105, 112, 116, 156, 173, 175, 181
Numbers,
- Introduction to 1-9,000, 30
- Mayan system, 71
- Song, 208
- Spelled out 1-100, 207

Nuts, list of, 218

O

Oceanic food, list of, 208
Opposites, 216
Order form, 299

P

Panamá, 80, 101-102
Paraguay, 118, 163-164
Pastas, list of, 209
Paychecks, direct deposit, 96
Personal descriptions, 51,56
Personal questions, 56
Personal Hygiene, 152, 219
Perú, 118, 135, 141-142, 183
Phrases, important, 8, 13, 26, 27, 31, 48, 57, 60, 69, 72, 78, 95, 97, 114, 119, 131, 136, 152, 155, 174, 176
Phrases, introductory, helpful, 13
Places to work, list of, 212
Prep area phrases, 131, 136
Present progressive verbs, 228

Present tense verbs,
- -ar Introduction to, regular 122-123, 229, 231
- -ar Irregulars, 232-234
- -er Introduction to, regular, 143-144, 230-231
- -er Irregulars, 232-234
- -ir Introduction to, regular, 145, 230-231
- -ir Irregulars, 232-234

Presentations,
- Family, 51-53, 67
- Final Project ideas, 165-166
- Final project, 192

Preterite past tense,
- Introduction to, 160-162
- Further practice, 234-235
- Irregulars, 236-241

Professions/ jobs,
- Basic descriptions, 51-53
- Listing of, 212

Pronouns, 50, 74, 219, 229
Pronunciations of vowels and consonants, 6-7
Proverbs, 192-193
Puerto Rico, 91, 172, 179-189, 185, 267
Puzzle,
- Crossword, 28, 99, 157
- Secret phrase, 62, 116, 177
- Word search, 14, 79, 140

Q

Querer, 76, 224, 229
Question words, 34, 56

R

Receiving directions, 154-156
Recipes, 182-186
Reflexive verbs,
- Introduction to, 90
- Further practice, 228

Regular verbs,
- -ar present tense, 122-123, 229
- -er present tense, 143-144, 230-231
- Imperfect past tense, 241-243
- -ir present tense, 145, 230-231
- Present progressive, 228
- Present tense, 122-123, 144-145, 229-231
- Preterite past tense, 160-162, 235-236

Reset the dining room area, 57
Restaurant etiquette, 173-175
- Lingo, useful 26

Restaurant customer service, 174, 176
Role plays, conversations, 16, 32-33, 47, 80, 103, 120, 138, 159, 178

S

Safety, 152, 219
Scavenger hunt, 197-200
Schedules,
    Latin America, 173
    Management phrases, 95
Seafood, list of, 208
Secret phrase puzzle, 62, 116, 177
Ser vs. estar, the verb to be, 104-106, 161, 229
Servers
    To Buser, 48, 57, 60
    To Expo, 31
    To Hispanic customers, 174, 176
Set the table, dining room,
    Phrases, 57
    List of vocabulary, 211
Side dishes, list of, 209
South America,
    Argentina, 112, 118, 133, 163-164
    Bolivia, 118, 141-142
    Chile, 118, 141-142
    Colombia, 117-118, 132
    Ecuador, 117-118
    Paraguay, 118, 163-164
    Perú, 118, 135, 141-142, 183
    Uruguay, 118, 163-164
    Venezuela, 117-118, 132
Spain, 12, 17-18, 36-38, 47, 91, 112, 132, 173, 182, 184-186, 229
Spaniards, 17, 36-38
Spanish language,
    Accent marks,
        Introduction, 12
        Practice, 224-225
    Adjectives, 133-134
    AEIOU, 6
    Alphabet, 58-59
    American, speaking Spanish, 17-18
    Diversity, 38
    English vs. Spanish, 160
    Exclamations, 132
    Glossary, 271-290
    Grammar, *see also*
    Historical perspectives, 100, 112, 135
    Language acquisition, Spanish vs. English, 160

Pronouns,
    Direct object, 227
    Gustar, 49-53
    Indirect object, 227
    Subject, 74, 229
Question words, 34
Reading in Spanish in five minutes, 6-7
This/That/Those/These, 159, 235
Tú vs. Usted, 12
Using two last names, 10-11
Usted vs. Tú, 10-11
Verbs, *see also*
Vocabulary, Extra, 206-222
Vowels, 6
Spanish-speaking
    Countries,
        Facts, 36-37, 54-55, 81-82, 101-102, 117-118, 141-142, 163-164, 179-180
    History of, 33, 100, 112, 135
People throughout the Americas, 36, 54, 81, 101, 112, 117, 141, 163, 179
Spices, list of, 218
Stem changing verbs, 232-234
Stores,
    List of, 221
    Grocery scavenger hunt, 197-200
Styles, communication, 116
Subject pronouns, 74, 228
Supplies, cleaning, maintenance, list of, 213
Survey, welcome to Spanish, 3-4

T

Table settings, 57, 181, 211
Tardiness, 91
Ten ideas to continue learning in the future, 195-196
Tener = to have, 74-75, 234, 237
The, Four ways of saying, 40
Things you like to do, 49-53, 213, 226
This/That/These/Those, 159, 235
Throughout the Americas, speaking Spanish, 112
Tic-Tac-Toe, game 20, 108, 147
Time, 89-90, phrases 95
To be, the verbs, ser vs estar, 104-106, 161, 237

Toma Todo, game directions, 42, 84, 168
Tongue twisters, 194
Tour, book, 1-2
Tourist vocabulary, 222
Town, stores, 221
Translation exercise, exam, 19, 41, 62, 83, 107, 124, 146, 167, 187
Travel,
- Advice, 181
- Etiquette, 173-175
- Holidays, 91, 165
- Hotel vocabulary, 222
- Phrases, 174-176
- Schedules, Latin America, 173
- Tips, 181
- Tourist, 173-175, 222
- Weather, 94

True/False game, 84
Tú vs. Usted, 12

U

Uniform, list of, 214
Uruguay, 118, 163-164
Useful restaurant lingo, 26
Using two last names, 10-11
Usted vs. Tú, 12
Utensils, list of, 214

V

Variations in the Spanish language,
- Exclamations, 132
- Slang, regional dialects, 38, 112
- Cultural communication styles, 116

Vegetables, list of, 217
Venezuela, 117-118, 132
Verbs,
- Basic conjugation in past tense, 160-162, 235-243
- Basic conjugation in present tense, 122-123, 143-145, 229-234
  - -ar present tense, 122-123, 228-229, 231-234
  - er present tense, 143-144, 228, 230-234
- Estar = to be, 104, 106, 161, 237
- Gustar = to like, 49-53, 213, 226
- Imperfect past tense, 241-243
- Ir = to go, 77, 161, 239
- -ir present tense, 145, 228, 230-234
- Irregular
  - Imperfect tense, 242
  - Present tense, 232-234
  - Preterite tense, 236-241
- Present progressive, 228
- Present tense, 122-123, 143-145, 229-234
- Preterite past tense, 160-162, 235-243
- Querer = to want, 76, 229, 237
- Ser vs estar – to be, 104-106, 161, 237
- Stem changing verbs, 232-234
- Reflexive verbs, 90, 228
- Regular preterite, 160-162, 235-236
- Tener = to have, 74-75, 234, 237

Vocabulary, extra, 206-222
Vowels, 6

W, X, Y, Z

Weather, 94
Welcome to Spanish survey, 3-4
Why Spanish is spoken throughout the Americas, 112
Work, list of professions, 212

Want to order more books for coworkers, friends, or your entire company? Here is how: Order online at www.SpanishChatCompany.com or fill out this form and mail it to Spanish Chat Company, LLC.

Name _____

Address _____

City, State, Zip _____

Phone/email _____

Spanish Chat Company, LLC   Phone: (402) 398-1384   (7:00 a.m. to 7:00 p.m. CST)
PO Box 45934   Fax: (402) 398-1384
Omaha, NE 68145   E-mail: SpanishChatCompany@gmail.com
                                   Order online at www.SpanishChatCompany.com

Spanish Chatbook (Book) $19.95 x _____ = _____
ISBN 978-0-9824625-4-6   # of Books   Total

Spanish Chatbook (CD) $14.95 x _____ = _____
ISBN 978-0-9824625-7-7   # of CDs   Total

Culinary Spanish Chatbook (Book) $29.95 x _____ = _____
ISBN 978-0-9824625-2-2   # of Books   Total

Culinary Spanish Chatbook (CD) $14.95 x _____ = _____
ISBN 978-0-9824625-3-9   # of CDs   Total

Business Spanish Chatbook (Book) $29.95 x _____ = _____
ISBN 978-0-9824625-6-0   # of Books   Total

Business Spanish Chatbook (CD) $14.95 x _____ = _____
ISBN 978-0-9824625-5-3   # of CDs   Total

Sales Tax (Nebraska residents add 7% sales tax)   + $_____

Shipping & Handling ($6 per book or CD if within the United States)   + $_____

Total $_____

Credit Card and International orders:
Please order online at our Web site **www.SpanishChatCompany.com**
Make checks payable to Spanish Chat Company

www.ingramcontent.com/pod-product-compliance
Lightning Source LLC
Chambersburg PA
CBHW081210230426
43666CB00015B/2695